TURKISH CULTURE
IN GERMAN SOCIETY TODAY

Culture and Society in Germany
General Editors: Eva Kolinsky and David Horrocks
Department of Modern Languages, Keele University

Traditional German notions of cultural homogeneity and social conformism continue to inform social-policy makers and public opinion, but social and cultural diversity have begun to gain ground. The transformation of East Germany, since unification dismantled established cultural boundaries, has challenged writers and intellectuals to embrace new themes. Resident non-German minorities in German society have begun to generate their own culture and German-language literature against a backcloth of social exclusion. Persecuted minorities of yesteryear – Sinti and Roma, Jews – attempt to partake of Germany's social opportunities and also develop a distinctive cultural voice in a bid for identity without assimilation. The volumes in this series address the new links between culture and society in Germany, and its new complexity.

Each volume focuses on a German-language writer within the relevant social context. It normally includes a short work and an interview with the writer on 'culture and society in post-unification Germany', a critical study of his or her work and the literary context, a social-science based analysis of the relevant theme and of the social 'milieu' to which the writer belongs, as well as a brief biographical sketch, list of works and select bibliography.

Volume 1: *Turkish Culture in German Society Today*
Edited by David Horrocks and Eva Kolinsky

Volume 2: *Sinti and Roma in German-speaking Society and Literature*
Edited by Susan Tebbutt

Volume 3: *East German Intellectuals in the New German Society*
Edited by David Rock and Roger Jones

TURKISH CULTURE
IN GERMAN SOCIETY TODAY

Edited by David Horrocks and Eva Kolinsky

Berghahn Books
Providence • Oxford

First published in 1996 by

Berghahn Books

Editorial offices:
165, Taber Avenue, Providence, RI 02906, USA
Bush House, Merewood Avenue, Oxford, OX3 8EF, UK

Library of Congress Cataloging-in-Publication Data

Turkish culture in German society today / edited by David Horrocks and
    Eva Kolinsky.
        p.   cm. -- (Culture and society in Germany : v. 1)
    Includes bibliographical references and index.
    ISBN 1-57181-899-5 (alk. paper). -- ISBN 1-57181-047-1 (pbk. :
alk. paper)
      1. Turks--Germany--Social conditions.   2. Germany--Cultural
policy.   3. Turkish literature--German influences.   I. Horrocks,
David, 1943-   .   II. Kolinsky, Eva.   III. Series.
DD78.T87T87   1996   96-12385
305.894'35043--dc20   CIP

British Library Cataloguing in Publication Data

A catalogue record for this book is available from the British Library.

Printed in the USA on acid-free paper.

Table of Contents

Preface and Acknowledgments

In October 1994, the German Section of the Modern Languages Department at Keele University welcomed Emine Sevgi Özdamar as Visiting Writer. During her stay, she read from her works, discussed literary and non-literary themes, immersed herself in communication and made everyone feel thoughtful and inspired. To conclude her stay, the Centre for the Study of German Culture and Society held a one-day symposium entitled Schreiben und Leben – Writing and Living – on minorities in Germany, their literature, their culture and their place in contemporary society. Emine read from her novel *Karawanserei*, the editors of this volume presented papers on her work (David Horrocks) and on the Turkish minority (Eva Kolinsky). Ulrike Bran evaluated the plight of asylum seekers from Romania in the new Länder while Susan Tebbutt looked at the troubled history of gypsies – Sinti and Roma – in Germany and at their culture today.

Chaired by Moray McGowan, the symposium confirmed what Emine Sevgi Özdamar's stay as Visiting Writer had already revealed: little is known about the lifestyles and expectations of minorities in Germany and even less about their culture. Here *Turkish Culture in German Society* Today hopes to make a contribution by breaking stereotypes and presenting a differentiated picture of what it means to be Turkish in German society today as a writer, as an individual and as a group.

Many colleagues, friends and family members have commented on draft chapters and helped to shape this project by their enthusiasm and constructive criticism. Special thanks are due to Richard Schneider for his active co-operation and generous Goethe-Institut sponsorship. Val Elks provided masterly organisational support for the Visiting Writers programme and the symposium. Joe Andrew assisted with funds, Roger Jones with planning, all colleagues in the German Section with preparations and discussions. *Turkish Culture in German Society Today* would, however, not have been written without the keen interest of the students of German at Keele in Emine Sevgi Özdamar and her work, without Frank Krause's inspirational idea to invite her, and without her wonderful gift of radiating acceptance and bringing people together.

David Horrocks and Eva Kolinsky

List of Tables

List of Figures

INTRODUCTION

Migrants or Citizens?

Turks in Germany between Exclusion and Acceptance

David Horrocks and Eva Kolinsky

Terminology and Definitions

When the Conference on Security and Co-operation in Europe, CSCE, reflected on the nature of modern society, it envisaged mobility between countries, including from poorer regions of the world to more affluent ones, as the shape of things to come. In the era of global migration, European societies would no longer be homogenous (if they had ever been) but would include 'migrants'.[1] In a similar vein, the European Community referred to 'migrants' in the Schengen Agreement in order to draw attention to the increase in international mobility and argue the need to co-ordinate policies governing asylum seekers and their admission to member states.[2] Since then, the term 'migrant' has acquired political and academic respectability and has been applied liberally to cover a broad spectrum of non-nationals, from asylum seekers or political refugees to foreign workers and their families.[3]

In literature, the 'migrant' originating in one culture and writing in the language of another can be said to occupy a special role as a mediator between the two. Regardless of whether they themselves were migrants, or were born into families who settled in Germany, writers of Turkish, Italian, Greek or other origin have experienced both cultures and communicate between them. Their works may be called 'migrants' literature' and they 'migrant writers' since they bring the heritage of their fathers and forefathers into their present-day German environment and make it accessible to readers who would not normally encounter them personally. Migrant literature bridges social gaps which society leaves unbridged and allows insights into the personal experience of individual Turks, Italians, and Greeks living in Germany (or between Germany and their country of origin) and the problems of identity arising from that.

In Germany society, the term 'migrant' is less neutral and includes a hidden assumption about the destabilising and negative effect of migration. At its most descriptive, 'migrant' acknowledges the fact that the person or group in question has arrived at the present domicile through 'migration', i.e., leaving one place of residency and settling in another. A 'migrant', however, is also defined as a person who 'continues to move from place to place'.[4] Such a person either lives in nomadic fashion or alternates, not unlike migratory birds, between homes and countries. In either case, 'migrant' emphasises movement, not settlement, distance, not belonging. 'Migrants' in their new society seem under suspicion of detachment and divided loyalties.

The Turks whose culture and place in society are the subject matter of this book, opted to live in Germany for a variety of economic, social, personal and political reasons. They are not 'migrants' but residents. As residents they are 'social citizens', entitled to the personal protection and liberties as human beings which the Basic Law guarantees to all inhabitants of post-war Germany. Yet, neither long-term residents nor their children, even those born and raised in Germany, acquire a right of citizenship. They remain bearers of foreign passports and nationalities, non-Germans. In the sections on social development and cultural change in *Turkish Culture in German Society Today*, we will use the term 'resident non-Germans' to highlight the paradoxical status of Turks and other foreign nationals who find themselves between acceptance and exclusion.

In the choice of language, exclusion and acceptance have not been evenly balanced. A reference guide to political culture of 1981, for instance, headed the relevant entry plainly *Ausländer* – foreigners.[5] The author mused that assimilation and taking up German citizenship could overcome the handicap of a non-German nationality, if only foreigners (and Turks in particular) would seize their chance of acceptance into the German fold, rather than wanting to shirk national obligations such as military service, insisting on an identity of their own or even promoting some kind of *Mischkultur*, a melange of Turkish and German cultures between all stools.[6]

Sensitivities have since been sharpened. Only right-wing extremists and xenophobes refer to *Ausländer* without any linguistic gesture of acceptance. Recently, a negative portrayal of foreigners has become evident in so called 'Turkish jokes', a new brand of anti-Turkish computer games, and a disparate youth culture which includes neo-Nazi street gangs and skinheads, but is also evident in the everyday discourse and behaviour of many ordinary young Germans.[7]

German policy makers disapprove of the 'foreigners out' mentality around them and tend to opt for more functional terms and a milder form of exclusion: *ausländische Arbeitnehmer* – foreign members of the workforce or *ausländische Mitbürger* – foreigners next door. As in 'migrant', this use of language defines its subject in terms of national belonging or non-belonging. To be sure, expressions such as *ausländische Arbeitnehmer* and *ausländische Mitbürger* aim for acceptance, not exclusion. They were coined to indicate that living and working next to foreigners was normal and could not be reversed. In their plea for a multi-cultural democracy, Cohn-Bendit and Schmidt observe that migration has always taken place between economic regions or political havens, not between nations.[8] In Germany, the economic argument has been stressed since the 1950s to gain acceptance for foreigners as net contributors to the welfare state. Overtones of exclusion, however, came to prominence as unemployment among foreign nationals rose, as their families and children needed support and as asylum seekers activated their right to obtain accommodation and subsistence from public funds.

Since the late 1980s, Eastern European migration has swelled global migration. In this context, Germany is deemed to compare favourably with neighbouring states, as the country which admitted the largest number of asylum seekers and which has been home to millions of migrants since the 1950s. However, the comparative focus on world-wide migration obscures the significance of policy decisions against immigration, and even adds weight to persistent fears that too many foreigners may 'flood' Germany and dilute or destroy German heritage and culture. As long as German policy makers and large sectors of the German public believe in national and cultural homogeneity and refuse to develop an agenda for immigration, foreigners will remain migrants, migrants foreigners, and both outsiders in German society. Even the compassionate view of Germany's non-Germans as a kind of underclass assumes that their lifestyle lacks culture and value of its own. Due to their customs and Islamic orientations, Turks fare especially badly when measured against post-materialist and post-modernist yardsticks.

From the vantage point of the foreigners themselves, the issues are more clear cut, even if solutions prove elusive: they wish to be regarded as ethnic minorities, different in nationality, background and culture but recognised as a legitimate groupings in German society. Acceptance as a minority implies that residency, and not nationality, matters. It also implies that cultural diversity is not perceived as a danger but condoned as a social reality, if not welcomed as enrichment. That the would-be ethnic minorities in Germany have developed lifestyles, identities, cultural diversity and a voice or voices of their own, has yet to be acknowledged in the society and the country which has become their home. Here, contacts between people of German and non-German cultures, between Germans and Turks in Germany can create communication and bridge gaps. Migrants' literature itself creates contacts through its characters and stories, bridges gaps, and establishes communication.

For acceptance to displace exclusion, it has to be recognised that identity itself is not solely linked to national specificity, but can embrace cultural diversity. Emine Sevgi Özdamar, for example, the writer whose work inspired this book, collects words, as she puts it, to retrieve and bring to life the traditions, stories and customs of her own background. This turns out to be urban as well as rural, secular as well as religious, Turkish as well as Kurdish. Turkish culture, as she presents it, is modern and oppressive, liberating and cruel, attractive and repulsive in its manifestations and its people. She refuses to take sides. Neither an interested nor a disinterested party, Özdamar is involved and detached, insider and outsider, non-believer and believer, Turk and German in her identity and culture. This duality of identity and culture is the theme of this book.

Historical Perspectives

Long before the 'belated' unification as a nation state in 1871, migration was part of German history.[9] In the eighteenth and nineteenth centuries, industrial development was eased considerably by foreign experts, engineers, technicians, business men, and artisans who settled in Germany – often encouraged by a ruler keen to promote economic modernisation.[10] The emergence of the Ruhr as a key industrial region led many Germans to migrate there in pursuit of employment, but it also depended on Polish workers who settled in mining communities.[11] Similarly, East Prussia's development as the *Kornkammer*, the main grain producing region in Germany could not have occurred without migrant labour, *Wanderarbeiter* from Poland.

Labour migration occurred into and out of Germany. Certain regions were 'pull areas' attracting labour migrants, while others were 'push areas' with limited earning potential for their populations.[12] From these areas, a considerable number of Germans took to the road year after year, in search of seasonal employment in Holland, France, Spain, and Italy.[13] Others chose to leave Germany altogether in the hope of finding improved living conditions elsewhere.[14]

In the first decade of the twentieth century, when industrialisation and economic expansion began to raise living standards more widely, labour migration out of Germany slowed to a trickle, while the country continued to receive over one million migrant workers annually. From a 'push' country, Germany had changed into a 'pull' country – from a country where economic hardship and poverty drove people to work in foreign lands, it had turned into a country whose population was affluent enough to survive without labour migration. The parameters of acceptance and exclusion which determine the place of Turks in German society today date back to Imperial Germany and its position of relative affluence and economic strength.

Two policy principles in particular were formulated then and remain pertinent to this day: the principle of ensuring that recruitment and utilisation of labour matches employers' demand and market forces, and the principle of ensuring that migrants remain excluded from civic society, temporary in their status and without claims to citizenship or other forms of equality. This line of legal reasoning ensued from the German notion of citizenship as based on blood ties and origin – *jus sanguinis* – rather than residency, nativity or other circumstantial factors – *jus soli* – and it has lost none of its acuteness. Successive German governments have tended to stress: 'Germany is not a country of immigration'. In the Nazi era, non-acceptance of foreigners generally and in particular of allegedly inferior ethnic or religious groups such as Jews, Poles, and Gypsies resulted in a policy of systematic persecution and the Holocaust.[15] In the post-war era, immigration as a right of entry has been rejected repeatedly, although the commitment to a democratic political culture has extended human rights and social protection to foreigners. The spirit of exclusion extends to the refusal to link German citizenship to the place of birth. Children are deemed to have the nationality of their parents and remain non-Germans even if they have never set foot in their presumed home country and speak German as their main, native language.[16]

After Unification

In 1990, unification may have conjured up a brief moment in which it seemed that the new Germany might be large enough to sustain its place as one of Europe's economic giants without additional manpower through migration. Cultural homogeneity, which had been the stuff of nationalist dreams and proved elusive in social reality, seemed attainable as the excited masses streamed from East to West, from West to East through Berlin's Brandenburg Gate.

It was a fallacy from the outset. In the West, the slogan 'Germany for the Germans' has long featured as the battle cry of the extreme right, whereas society at large has grown culturally and nationally diverse enough to be hailed as 'multi-cultural' by some, while others feared for its fabric and future.[17] On the eve of unification, close to eight million foreigners lived in (West) Germany and more sought refuge and residency rights as political asylum seekers. In addition, studies of demographic change and labour-market development have demonstrated that postwar economic growth has depended, and will continue to depend, on population gain through migration. Estimates for the year 2010 suggest that a further eight million in-migrants will be required to sustain the German economy.[18] Germans in East and West appear ill prepared for it.

In the East, unification revealed the effectiveness of the exclusion which had obtained there. Socialist state policy had proclaimed internationalism, but did not allow migration of any kind. East Germans were to be kept inside their state behind its barbed-wire borders. The few foreigners who were admitted were separated from ordinary East Germans by over-privilege, if they happened to be foreign diplomats, or by rigid social exclusion (including locking hostels at seven o'clock at night) for contract labour.[19] From December 1990 onwards, acts of violence soared against individuals of foreign appearance, asylum seekers and former contract workers who were caught in East Germany between dismissal and deportation. East Germans had yet to create a culture of relating to non-Germans in their society, since no such culture had formed in the era of state-enforced segregation and Stasi harassment.

Unification also revealed that the established presence of foreigners in West German society did not amount to inclusion, but had produced its own web of social segregation. In the 1960s and 1970s, empirical surveys indicated that prejudice was more widespread among older, than among younger Germans with people of the pre-war generations least likely to accept foreigners.[20] Since prejudice and authoritarian attitudes appeared to be on the decline among the post-war generations, acceptance of foreigners and the end of exclusion seemed only a matter of time. In 1992, however, studies in the old and the new Länder found widespread non-acceptance of foreigners among the under twenty fives. Many were even prepared to use violence in support of their views. Forty percent in the West and fifty-one percent in the East agreed with the statement: 'I do not like so many foreigners in our country', while thirty percent and forty-one percent respectively wanted all foreigners to leave Germany.[21]

Of the various national groups in Germany, Turks remained where they had always been, in the forefront of hostility. One in three young West Germans and every second young East German proclaimed a strong or very strong dislike of Turks. At the time of the survey, the young East German xenophobes at least, would never have met a Turkish national in person, since virtually none lived in the new Länder.

After unification, a wave of xenophobic violence swept Germany. It flared up in 1991 and 1992 with pogrom-style attacks on hostels for asylum seekers in Hoyerswerda, Rostock-Lichtenhagen and elsewhere in the new Länder. When it spread to the West in 1992/1993, it was directed against asylum seekers and their hostels, Jews, disabled people, the homeless and especially against Turks. Many acts of violence, intimidation and assault went unrecorded and occurred amidst a ground swell of hostility towards asylum seekers and the apparent unwillingness of government and politicians to stem the flow.[22]

For a time, right-wing extremists even boasted that they dared to do in reality what most Germans wanted to be done. This dangerous liaison came to a sudden end in November 1992 when an arson attack on the homes of two Turkish families in the small town of Mölln in northern Germany claimed the lives of one woman and two children. Some newspapers spoke of murder, others of 'murder-attempts'.[23] Following the events in Mölln, hundreds of thousands of people staged candle-light demonstrations against right-wing extremism and xenophobic violence, and in support of democracy and the rule of law in Germany. Had the victims not lived quietly in Mölln for many years? Had their residency permits not been issued by German authorities? Were they not 'some of us', albeit of Turkish extraction? Had the victims lived in a hostel or shelter for asylum seekers, things would have looked different, but they lived in the centre of a small town.

The citizens of Mölln and countless other Germans demonstrated for the acceptable face and social climate of small-town Germany. Social peace is not automatically, however, to be equated with social acceptance. Mölln revealed how cut-off Turks had remained in their town and in Germany, unknown people in German lands. Intending to argue the case of acceptance, a feature in *Die Zeit* revealed the worlds separating them and us, Turks and Germans: 'only when their houses burn do we notice them'.[24]

A Voice of Their Own

More than thirty years after the first rail transports brought Turkish workers to be dispersed to their allocated hostels and employers, Turks constitute the largest national group in Germany. Initially, most had been labour migrants who resolved to escape economic hardship in their home country by working abroad. Initially also, employment was stipulated to be short term, involving different individuals every year. In the wake of its post-war economic miracle, West Germany had become a 'pull country', a country where labour market demand could not be met by its resident population and necessitated recruitment further afield. Sluggish economic development, paired with high population growth, had turned many Southern European and Mediterranean countries into 'push countries' unable to meet the employment needs and material expectations of all or part of their populations.[25] For Turks, adverse political circumstances also encouraged migration.

The 'pull country' Germany chose to call its labour recruits *Gastarbeiter*, guest workers, thus underlining their temporary status whilst also stressing that they should not be exploited as labour slaves after the Nazi fashion, but treated like guests.[26] In German everyday culture, the host is obliged to be polite, fair and courteous to a guest, while the guest is expected to follow the rules of conduct that prevail in the host's home. That guests should never outstay their welcome has been one of the key rules of German hospitality.

Social reality did not easily fit the host/guest model. Rather than creating a rotating workforce, employers soon preferred to renew contracts instead of needlessly replacing trained by untrained labour. German labour recruitment policy had envisaged that *Gastarbeiter* would remain at a distance from established society, neighbourhoods, schools, and social services. This degree of exclusion proved unsustainable after the recruitment ban in 1973. Forced to choose between an economically and often politically uncertain future in their country of origin, or settling in Germany for longer than originally intended, those who could obtain official permission opted to settle. Again depending on permission from the German authorities, wives and children joined their husbands and fathers from the mid-1970s onwards. At this point, Germany's foreign working population ceased being *Gastarbeiter* or migrant labour and became residents, citizens of Germany in all but their political rights and nationality.

Today, first generation *Gastarbeiter* are reaching pensionable age while a second and third generation of descendants who were born in Germany or have lived there most of their lives no longer share the personal history of labour migration. The younger generations are beginning to write their own history, create their own place, and voice their own expectations about what it means and what it should mean for Turks to live in Germany.

As labour migrants and during the early years of settlement, Turks in Germany did not appear to have their own voice. They had advocates, *Fürsprecher* among German policy makers, educators, journalists and academic elites. Since the 1970s, a large number of activities, initiatives, offices and action groups have emerged in Germany: programmes to improve the

German-language skills of Turks, to improve educational opportunities by setting up special classes for Turkish pupils, advisory centres to assist Turkish adults with tackling German bureaucracies, discussion groups for Turkish women that would allow them to meet others, learn German, and discover new interests outside their family situation.[27] All are liberal and supportive in their intention, committed against prejudice and determined to assist the social integration of their clientele. All are steeped in the assumption that foreigners – and especially Turks as the least liked and possibly the most disadvantaged – could be and should be helped to optimise their opportunities by learning how to adjust to the rules of the host, how to function in German society as effectively as a native German would. Were this notion of social integration ultimately to succeed, Turks would no longer be distinguished from Germans, would become German in their communicative skills, their appearance, their behaviour, manner and attitudes. Contrary to racists who assert that national and cultural difference are based on biological differences, liberal Germany believes in social conditioning and offers foreigners a chance of belonging. Yet, the price of belonging is to join German society on German terms. Taking up German citizenship has been propagated as the optimal path to assimilation. Barbara John, for instance, the Commissioner for Foreigners in Berlin, believes if all Turks were to surrender their Turkish passports and take out German citizenship, equal treatment would follow.[28] Others expect Turks to renounce Islam and its socio-cultural prescriptions, discard traditional dress or head coverings and become German in all but background.[29]

Over the years, some Turks have responded to the unspoken rules of exclusion and exchanged their Turkish for German citizenship in order to become doctors, lawyers, or journalists.[30] Yet the majority of Turks have remained Turkish. The German model of social integration may have been unattainable to first generation Turkish residents who lacked the language skills and social confidence to blend seamlessly into German society. To second and third-generation Turks integration may be attainable, but the model holds few attractions. Rather than shedding their identity and conforming to the host society, they do what their German peers do: voice their expectations about the lifestyles and opportunities they wish to enjoy, and adopt a critical stance towards a social and political environment which ignores their interests.

Speaking in 1990, Mehmed, a then twenty-year-old member of a Turkish youth gang, explained the distance between German and Turkish perceptions as follows:

> We young people, living in a country like the Federal Republic, are fully aware of the fact that there is no government that speaks for us and that we cannot identify with this state. Kohl and other people who fight election campaigns with slogans directed against foreigners can never be accepted as our government. I will never be able to support a government which is hostile to me. Instead, I just find my own people and try to make my own rules and follow laws that suit us.[31]

Many towns and cities today have Turkish youth gangs. Here, young Turks find acceptance rather than suffer anti-Turkish discrimination; here they also defy victimisation and confront neo-Nazi or skinhead gangs in defence of their Turkish identity and their neighbourhoods.

After the murders of Mölln and Solingen in 1992 and 1993, Turks organised their own demonstrations against the violence inflicted upon their community and also entered into their own negotiations with German authorities in search of remedies and protection. In the past, Turks may have accepted German advocates and condoned their goodwill; today, they are finding their own voice, their own advocates, and their own understanding of what it means and what is should mean to be of Turkish origin in German society. The German model of social integration continues to motivate German policy makers. For Turks in Germany, it has become increasingly obsolete as they confront the process of developing from migrant workers into an ethnic minority, from guests expected to comply with the domestic rules and behaviour code of their host into citizens with their own cultural traditions, their own values and their own voice.

Turkish Culture in German Society Today

A host society as intent as Germany on preserving its cultural and national homogeneity and as hesitant to embrace multi-culturalism tends to project a similarly homogeneous image onto all non-German minorities. Among the 'others' living in Germany, Turks seem to appear particularly monochrome, culturally backward, an underclass brainwashed by Islamic fundamentalism. Whether inspired by pity or contempt, observers from the outside tend to assume that Turk is like Turk, viewing the minority as a whole without internal differentiation and without its own history of social change.

The picture painted with the broad brush of generalisation is far from the truth. Not only did Turkish labour migrants differ in the educational background, vocational qualifications and regional traditions they brought from Turkey to Germany, the experiences of migration, settlement and adjustment themselves changed their socio-economic position and their cultural orientations. Moreover, members of the second and third generation did not experience the same history: many were born in Germany, many moved for visits or spells of residency between Germany and Turkey. All the *Nachgeborenen*, those born later, have their own personal history of dual identity and their own strategies for balancing Turkish traditions and German influences in their own lives. The story of a young Turkish woman touches on the complex nature of identity. As a pupil in Berlin, she expressed her own sense of belonging by wearing a head scarf. When her family went to live in Turkey, she found her head scarf regarded as a sign of cultural backwardness and banned by her school:

> I covered my head, and my clothes reached down to my ankles. But I did fol-low my own sense of fashion by choosing well matched colours, something pleasant to look at (...) Eventually, I went to Turkey wearing a head scarf but returned to Germany later on without one... I was the only pupil in my school [in Turkey] with a head scarf. Just imagine, I came from a European country and covered my head! The Deputy Head then ordered me to remove the head scarf.[32]

Structure and Themes

Turkish Culture in German Society Today aims to explore the meaning of identity between cultures, and the changing balance between Turkish and German experiences, reference points and traditions. One of its declared aims is to distinguish the Turkish minority from the broad church of 'foreigners' and *Gastarbeiter* and present a differentiated account of the cultural orientations and the socio-economic position of Turks in Germany today, and the changes that have transformed and reshaped them since the 1960s. No less central to the book is the aim of offering an analysis which is well founded in academic research, its data and traditions but which also evokes the personal perspective and experiences of Turks finding their identity and voice in Germany today.

One sphere in which the individual voice and personal perspective of Turks and members of other minorities might pre-eminently be expected to find expression is that of creative writing. Within the history of literature in post-war Germany there has, however, been a tendency to pigeon-hole all such writing by assigning it to the general category of *Betroffenheits-literatur* – literature produced in direct response to social victimisation – or even more narrowly to so-called *Gastarbeiter-literatur*. Whilst critical of these and other labels, Sabine Fischer and Moray McGowan (Chapter 1) recognise that, for obvious and understandable reasons, the earliest phase of 'migrant writing' was indeed characterised by a narrow range of shared, common themes and relatively simple, usually directly autobiographical forms. The picture that emerges from their broad survey of subsequent developments is, however, much more varied and complex. Not only do writers of the second and third generations reject the *Gastarbeiter* label; they also in many instances actively resist attempts to cast them in the role of spokesmen for particular ethnic groups or cultural traditions. Often focusing on the problems of personal identity, their writing is increasingly characterised by a complex interplay between individual and more culturally typical concerns. The resulting diversity is particularly evident in the contrasting and conflicting approaches of Turkish women writers in Germany to issues of cultural tradition on the one hand, and modernity and emancipation on the other.

One such writer is the novelist and dramatist Emine Sevgi Özdamar, whose work, whilst touching on many concerns common to the experience of Turks – and especially Turkish women – who have settled in Germany, is characterised by an independence of mind and breadth of imagination that defy easy categorisation. In a detailed reading of her long novel in German, *Das Leben ist eine Karawanserei*, David Horrocks (Chapter 2) first stresses the central importance of language, both Turkish and Arabic, to Özdamar's recollection and reconstruction of childhood and youth in Turkey. A subsequent analysis of the picture of Turkish history and society in the novel, culminating in a consideration of images of women, serves to emphasise the various ways in which Özdamar calls into question a great deal of received opinion in the West, not least by deploying a range of sophisticated narrative strategies extending far beyond that oral story-telling tradition of the 'Orient' for which she has been somewhat patronisingly praised by German critics.

In an interview with David Horrocks and Eva Kolinsky (Chapter 3), Özdamar sheds interesting light on the reasons for her writing in German, particularly when discussing the background to her first published work, the play *Karagöz in Alamania*. A view of language emerges that is highly sensuous, situational and flexible, not attached to any fixed cultural identity. Indeed, living simultaneously between languages, just like moving physically between different cultures and adjusting to changes in the pace of life, is seen as a potentially positive experience. Questioned about the negative aspects of life in contemporary Germany, especially recent violent manifestations of xenophobia, Özdamar is obviously reluctant to indulge in generalised condemnation of a whole people. Instead, she dwells on the damage caused by the events of Mölln and Solingen, and the reporting of them by the media, to everyday relations between Germans and non-Germans, generously sympathising with those of the host nation who now feel obliged to go to unnatural lengths to demonstrate their lack of hostility to the foreigners in their midst.

A similar reluctance to trot out ready-made answers to complex social problems is evident in the article Özdamar originally wrote in response to a request from the Hamburg weekly *Die Zeit*, to comment on the state of relations between Germans and non-Germans living together in the Federal Republic (Chapter 4). Here, contrary to the newspaper's expectations, she chose to write about the experience of directing a multi-national cast in rehearsals for the première of her play *Karagöz* in Frankfurt. The result, as David Horrocks and Frank Krause argue in their commentary, is a kind of Brechtian parable in which the interaction between actors of various nationalities – Germans, Greeks, Turks, Spaniards – casts an oblique light on relations in a multi-cultural society. The vision that emerges is far from utopian. Aggressions surface in the form of crude cultural and national stereotypes, but the very act of venting them is seen as a necessary, even healthy step towards establishing a viable working relationship. Özdamar's whole approach to the issue, combining humour and hard-headedness, is eminently practical, and her conclusion is cautiously optimistic.

In the post-war period, migration into Germany involved predominantly expellees, refugees and resettlers, all of them of German extraction and therefore with automatic claims to citizenship. The emergence of a non-German population in the wake of labour migration in the 1950s and 1960s was unintended, and not underpinned by a policy of immigration. As migrants settled, political exclusion from citizenship conflicted with social inclusion in terms of welfare provisions and institutional support. Eva Kolinsky (Chapter 5) shows that non-German minorities have enjoyed some occupational and educational mobility in the second and third generations compared with the original *Gastarbeiter*. Yet they continue to be locked into a cycle of disadvantage, a cycle that appears to be even more inescapable for Turks than for other national groups: the social modernisation from unskilled to skilled work, from blue to white-collar employment, from basic to advanced education, has transformed the lifestyles of Germans but largely eluded non-Germans. Despite a thirty-year history of social participation, non-Germans still inhabit separate worlds from Germans with little contact between them. On all counts, Turks appear to draw the short straw and are less likely than other minorities to benefit from avenues of acceptance and social opportunity.

For Elçin Kürsat-Ahlers the refusal of successive German governments to formulate an immigration policy, to grant rights of entry, residency, political participation and citizenship to non-Germans is the key to their unequal place in German society (Chapter 6). Segregation and disadvantage are endemic for the Turkish minorities with regard to housing, employment, income and education. In the early 1990s, close to forty percent of Turks in Germany lived in poverty. Moreover, Turks have been the target of hate campaigns and violence. They are both underclass and scapegoat.

A closer look at the day-to-day experience of Turks in Germany reveals a less depressing picture. Dursun Tan and Hans-Peter Waldhoff show that Turkish everyday culture has undergone significant change since the arrival of the first *Gastarbeiter* cohorts (Chapter 7). Traditional parent-child hierarchies have had to be modified as children outpaced their parents in their command of German and took on the role of interpreter *vis-à-vis* the outside world. Everyday culture was recast as the social history of migration and settlement took shape. When wives and children joined their husbands and fathers in Germany, religion, which had hardly mattered in Turkey, emerged as a hallmark of Turkish identity in Germany. Religious institutions took on a growing number of community and social welfare functions, particularly after labour contracts ran out and unemployment began to bite. Despite social segregation and disadvantages, Turks in Germany have become German-Turks. Their language draws on both cultures, although they are treated as strangers in both Turkey and Germany. Among the younger generations, some writers, journalists and academics have begun to communicate (in German) between the two cultures and contribute to a new sense of cross-cultural identity.

No aspect of Turkish everyday life and culture has been misunderstood more often, and given rise to a more mono-chrome and negative image of the Turkish minority than that of Islam. Although Islam has been, as Yasemin Karakasoglu shows in Chapter 8, central to Turkish culture and identity, it is itself divided into distinctive strands and has not remained unchal-lenged by secularisation. For the *Gastarbeiter* generation, Islam hardly mattered. Few requested that employers set up prayer rooms and few had been observant Muslims before they left Turkey. After labour migrants became a settled population, Islam assumed a more prominent role since the values and behaviour codes pertaining to everyday life and the family were derived from it. Karakasoglu shows that the German education system leaves religious instruction in Islam (the third largest religion in Germany) largely to Turkey and its religious establishment. Rather than linking Islam to the modern German environment in which young Turks live, the textbooks are produced in Turkey, the teachers are trained in Turkey, and the standards of this education are defined in Turkey, with the result that Islam appears segregated from and conflicting with life in Germany, not a regular facet of it.

Nevertheless, fundamentalism has gained very little ground among Turks of all ages. What has gained ground is a desire among the elderly to turn to religion and possibly re-migrate to Turkey before they die. In Germany itself, several interest groups have emerged with the declared aim of representing Turkish cultural and social concerns. All of these groups are rooted in Islam, each with its own focus and interpretation. The effect of this diversity has been that the Turkish minority lacks an effective voice to influence policy debates. Since the early 1990s, efforts have been made to agree on core demands such as the teaching of Islam to Muslim children within the school curriculum, i.e., equal status of Islam and Christianity, securing the agreement of local authorities to the construction of new mosques, and similar demands to consolidate institutional channels for the whole of Islam in Germany. As in Turkish culture generally, Islam itself is undergoing change as the second and third generations of Turks assume leadership roles in Islamic-Turkish organisations and bring their dual cultural identity to bear on traditions. By contributing to local decision making about religious and educational matters on advisory panels and committees, these generations involve themselves as fully as they are allowed to in the democratic process and are bringing the institutional world of Islam in Germany itself closer to democracy.

Notes

1. For a cogent summary see J. Krieger ed., *The Oxford Companion to the Politics of the World*, Oxford/New York, Oxford University Press, 1993, pp.177–178.

2. See Z. Layton-Henry, *The Politics of Immigration*, Oxford, Blackwell, 1992, pp.231–233.

3. See e.g., B. Marshall, 'German Migration Policies', in *Developments in German Politics*, ed. G. Smith et al., Basingstoke, Macmillan, 1992, pp.247–263; Z. Layton-Henry ed., *The Political Rights of Migrant Workers in Europe*, London, Sage, 1990; J. Fijalkowski ed., *Transnationale Migranten in der Arbeitswelt. Studien zur Ausländerbeschäftigung in der Bundesrepublik Deutschland und zum internationalen Vergleich*, Berlin, Colloquium, 1990; K. Schacht ed., *Politik der Migration. Eine Fachtagung im Hessischen Landtag zur Einwanderung*, Wiesbaden, Landeszentrale für politische Bildung, 1993.

4. Quotes from *Oxford Shorter Dictionary*.

5. M. Greiffenhagen et al. eds, *Handwörterbuch der politischen Kultur der Bundesrepublik Deutschland. Ein Lehr- und Nachschlagewerk*, Opladen, Westdeutscher Verlag, 1981, p.72ff.

6. A. von Heyl, 'Ausländer', in Greiffenhagen et al., *Handwörterbuch zur politischen Kultur*, p.74. Von Heyl's article is full of barely disguised disapproval, e.g.: 'What is wanted [by foreigners] is retention of identity as well as full equality of opportunities. In the long term, however, this is impossible if the dual strategy persists of leaving the choice between integration and re-migration open. The example of the USA shows that a partial integration of national minorities can take place in principle. Yet, the development of an unavoidable new identity does not appear to be feasible in a relatively stable society such as that in the Federal Republic. In either case, this would lead to the emergence of a national melange of cultures [*Mischkultur*] and the social segregation which is bound to arise from this.'

7. J.A. Helm, 'No Laughing Matter: Joking About Turks', *German Politics and Society*, vol.13, no.31, 1994, pp.47–62; W. Bergmann and R. Erb, eds,

Neo-nazismus und rechte Subkultur, Berlin, Metropol, 1994; H. Willems, *Fremdenfeindliche Gewalt. Einstellungen, Täter, Konflikteskalation,* Opladen, Leske & Budrich, 1993.

8. D. Cohn-Bendit and Th. Schmid, *Heimat Babylon. Das Wagnis der multikulturellen Demokratie,* Hamburg, Hoffmann & Campe, 1992, p.351, note 10.

9. The phrase 'belated nation' was coined by H. Plessner in his book of the same title, *Die verspätete Nation,* Stuttgart, Kohlhammer, 1959; for a history of migration in and out of Germany see K.J. Bade ed., *Deutsche im Ausland – Fremde in Deutschland. Migration in Geschichte und Gegenwart,* Munich, Beck, 1992.

10. Details in W.O. Henderson, *The Rise of German Industrial Power, 1834–1914,* London, Temple Smith, 1975.

11. W. Kröllmann et al., 'Bevölkerungsgeschichte', in *Das Ruhrgebiet im Industriezeitalter. Geschichte und Entwicklung,* vol.1, Düsseldorf, Schwann, 1990, pp.111–198.

12. This terminology is used to characterise labour migration flows by J. Lucassen, *Migrant Labour in Europe 1600–1900,* London, Croom Helm 1987.

13. Lucassen, *Migrant Labour in Europe,* p.111.

14. R. R. Doerries, 'German Transatlantic Migration from the Early 19th Century to the Outbreak of World War II', in *Population, Labour and Migration in 19th and 20th Century Germany,* ed. K. J. Bade, Oxford, Berg, 1987, pp.115–134.

15. See e.g., H. Krausnick et al., *Anatomy of the SS State,* London, Collins, 1968; M. Gilbert, *The Holocaust. The Jewish Tragedy,* London, Collins, 1986; D. Cesarani ed., *The Final Solution. Origins and Implementation,* London, Routledge, 1994.

16. R. Brubaker, *Citizenship and Nationhood in France and Germany,* Cambridge/Mass, Harvard University Press, 1992, pp.75–113.

17. A comprehensive discussion of the controversy in Cohn-Bendit and Schmidt, *Heimat Babylon.*

18. Based on calculations by the *Bundesanstalt für Landeskunde und Raumordnung* (1991) and quoted in *Arbeitsmappe Sozial- und Wirtschaftskunde,* Berlin, Erich Schmidt Verlag, no.5/21106, 1995.

19. Details in E. Kolinsky, 'Foreigners in the New Germany', *Keele German Papers Research Series,* no. 1, ed. T. Scharf, Keele University, 1995.

20. An overview in E. Kolinsky, 'A Future for Right-Extremism in Germany?', in *The Extreme Right in Europe and the USA,* ed. P. Hainsworth, London, Pinter, 1992; M. Minkenberg, 'Cultural Change and the Far Right in East and West Germany', *German Politics,* vol.3, no.3, 1994, pp.169–192.

21. Data from W. Metzler, *Jugend und Politik in Deutschland. Gesellschaftliche Einstellungen, Zukunftsorientierungen und Rechts-Potential Jugendlicher in Ost und West*, Opladen, Leske & Budrich, 1992, pp.121–141.

22. *Politbarometer*, ed. Forschungsgruppe Wahlen, showed that well over two-thirds of West Germans regarded the *Ausländerproblem*, the unresolved issue of foreigners in Germany, as the most pressing political topic. In the East, unemployment topped the list while other themes, including the *Ausländerproblem* seemed less urgent, although other surveys showed that East Germans were even less prepared than West Germans to include foreigners into their society as neighbours, colleagues or *de-facto* citizens.

23. *Frankfurter Allgemeine Zeitung*, 24 November 1992.

24. Quoted from E. Seidel-Pielen, 'Politik auf der Straße', in *Deutsche Türken. Das Ende der Geduld*, ed. C. Leggewie and Z. Senocak, Reinbek, Rowohlt, 1993, p.40.

25. See Lucassen, *Migrant Labour.*

26. *Der Große Duden. Herkunftswörterbuch. Die Etymologie der deutschen Sprache*, Mannheim, Dudenverlag, 1963, points out that 'Gast' is derived from the Latin 'hostis'= enemy; until the modern era, a 'Gast' was, above all, a stranger, a 'Fremdling'.

27. W. Benz ed., *Integration ist machbar. Ausländer in Deutschland*, Munich, Beck, 1993.

28. In her capacity as Commissioner for Foreigners' Affairs for Berlin, Barbara John has argued that in the absence of an immigration policy that would entail a right of citizenship, foreigners should make use of their right to apply for naturalisation and become German citizens.

29. For a detailed analysis of the German concept of social integration with reference to SPD and CDU policies, see P. O'Brien, *Germany's Migrant Problem*, London, Routledge, 1995.

30. H. Keskin, 'Wir bleiben hier. Plädoyer für eine offene Gesellschaft', in Leggewie and Senocak, eds, *Deutsche Türken*, p.73.

31. E. Seidel-Pielen, 'Politik auf der Straße', in Leggewie and Senocak eds, *Deutsche Türken*, pp.43–44.

32. ' "Immer einen Schritt weitergehen". Emine Demirbüken, Ausländerbeauftragte von Berlin-Schöneberg im Gespräch mit Gülay Durgut', in Leggewie and Senocak eds, *Deutsche Türken*, p.86.

CHAPTER 1

From *Pappkoffer* to Pluralism:
on the Development of Migrant Writing
in the German Federal Republic*

Sabine Fischer and Moray McGowan

Contemporary Germany has a diverse and diversifying population of *de facto* immigrants who form an integral part of German society as ethnic minorities. The term *Gastarbeiter* is clearly no longer – if it ever was – suitable to describe these social groups. However, the self-contradictory attitude of the German state towards its ethnic minorities means that the *de facto* immigrants remain German residents with a foreign passport. On the one hand the state, through its immigration laws, prevents foreign residents from integrating fully into German society, and on the other hand it demands their total assimilation to the 'legal, social and economic order of the Federal Republic, its cultural and political values' as specifically required of them by the *Ausländergesetz* (Foreigner Law) of 1991.[1] This paradox, which reveals the Eurocentric idea of a German nation with a homogeneous culture superior to, and to be protected from, foreign influence, shapes the acculturation of ethnic minorities, and their strategies in response to exclusion and the pressures of assimilation.

The example of the Turks, the largest ethnic minority in Germany and one of those subject to most prejudice and discrimination, shows the increasing diversity of these strategies between integration, ethnic isolationism and denial of ethnic identity, reflecting the diversity within the ethnic minorities themselves.[2] Though there are socio-economic and cultural determinants in

common, the acculturation process is an individual one, depending on each migrant's personal socialisation, opportunities, experiences, motives and perspectives. It can only be properly
understood if the conflicts inherent in multiculturalism are not
papered over by assertions of a false harmony,[3] and if minorities
are not treated as homogeneous groups, as may happen in the dis-
courses of traditional racism, of liberal tolerance and even of post-
structuralism.[4] 'A more careful, differentiated discourse is needed
to analyse patterns of cultural and gender identities within the
larger framework of Eurocentrism and German history',[5] a discourse, though, in which the texts themselves do not vanish below
the self-referential metadiscourse of post-colonial theory.[6]

Every act of migration reflects wider economic, political and
social developments, such as modernisation processes.[7] Thus, one
may wish to draw on migrant literature as social evidence.[8] On the
other hand, literature is individual, subjective and diverse. It may
reflect, but may also exaggerate, challenge or invert the social
experience that informs it. In finding a voice outside the established social discourse, and exploring the possible beyond the
given, it resists functionalisation as social evidence.[9] Interpretative
practice needs to take account of both the individual and the
social-historical significance of a text.

Like migration itself, its literary articulation is not new in
Germany, but the scale of demographic change through migration since the 1960s has generated literature of an entirely new
quantity and quality. By the 1990s, it had attained a diversity
contradicting all attempts to label it. *Gastarbeiterliteratur* (guest-
worker literature), *Migrantenliteratur* (migrant literature),
Ausländerliteratur (foreigner literature), *Literatur deutschschreibender
Ausländer* (the literature of foreigners writing in German): all are
either too narrow (the latter, for example, would exclude the work
of Aras Ören or Güney Dal, who write in Turkish, though they
live in Germany, write extensively about migrant experience, and
are also published in German), potentially patronising or indeed
racist (in implying that these texts are inferior appendages to
some culturally homogeneous 'real' German literature), or so
general that they erase crucial socio-economic, ethnic, cultural,
gender or generational differences between the authors, between
the patterns of experience their texts engage, and between the
aesthetic possibilities their texts manifest.[10] Thus, while we focus
here on literature which addresses migrant experience in those
ethnic groups from which most *Gastarbeiter* were recruited, it

should be remembered that there are many migrant writers in German with quite different origins, such as the Japanese Yoko Tawada (e.g., *Das Bad*, 1990; *Ein Gast*, 1993), the Iranian Torkan (e.g., *Tufan. Brief an einen islamischen Bruder*, 1983; *Kaltland. Wah'schate Ssard*, 1984), or the Mongolian Galsan Tschinag (*Eine tuwinische Geschichte*, 1992; *Das Ende des Liedes*, 1993).[11]

The development of this literature is linked to the phases of physical migration and psychological adjustment that characterise migrant experience in modern Germany, though the relationship is not crudely synchronous. On the one hand, several factors initially inhibited the production of this literature: the expectation of temporary sojourn, the lack of a written literary tradition in the social environments from which many *Gastarbeiter* were recruited, reinforced by the – usually more numbing than creatively stimulating – culture shock of transition to Western, urban-industrialised society. On the other hand, since its emergence in the 1960s much of the literature of *Gastarbeiter* experience has been by writers whose ethnic identity may have exposed them to comparable discrimination but who are not, socio-economically speaking, *Gastarbeiter* themselves, and whose spectrum of reactions to the German host culture's undifferentiating assumption that they are, contributes to the self-reflective, often ironical textures of this literature.

The 1970s, however, did see a wider movement to which workers without previous literary experience or education contributed, and within which preliterary forms – songs, diaries, letters, oral narrative – began to give way to poems, short stories and reportage, written and often published in the mother tongue (initially, predominantly Italian, since they were the first group of *Gastarbeiter*) in newspapers and magazines.[12] Mostly, they were written by men, reflecting both the demographic make up of the first phase of labour migration and the additional barriers between women from these cultures and access to the means and traditions of literary expression.

The texts generally focused on immediate *Gastarbeiter* experience: workplace, hostel, station, government office, the annual journey home; the themes were the dreams of Germany as the promised land of material wealth; the reality of heavy, dirty, unhealthy work in poor conditions and the experience of prejudice, indifference and rejection; homesickness and dreams of return; life between two worlds and two languages.[13] This binary view reflected both the *Gastarbeiter*'s internalisation of the host culture's simplistic polarisation, and his own undifferentiated projections and stereotypes acquired before, during and after the migration process. This literature was seen as, and to some extent was *Betroffenheitsliteratur*: therapeutic writing by victims of social processes, articulating, objectifying and establishing the commonality of experience by recording it in simple, conventional, usually autobiographical forms.

This literature developed in tandem with the growth of an infrastructure for its reception, which led in turn to its partial acceptance in the commercial literary market from the early 1980s.[14] German writing competitions for foreigners, sponsored by the Institute for German as a Foreign Language at Munich University, led to anthologies in a leading paperback imprint[15] and the founding of an annual Adalbert von Chamisso Prize for such literature in 1985,[16] and contributed to a widening awareness of this literature amongst German readers. However, the Institute also played a part in the stereotyping of this literature through a range of normative pronouncements.[17] This was still patronage by the dominant culture.

At the same time, a self-directed and more explicitly political trend was being instigated by writers themselves, some of whom had begun alongside German colleagues in the workers' literature group 'Werkkreis Literatur der Arbeitswelt'. The PoLi-Kunst-Verein and the publishing collective Südwind were established in 1980 as a bridge between the numerous migrant groups in Germany. The goal was a 'polynational culture', the political theme the material reality of the *Gastarbeiter* and the furtherance of change: 'From tears to civil rights' was how Franco Biondi, one of its leading members, summarised this move from *Betroffenheit* to political activism.[18] Südwind insisted on the terms *Gastarbeiter* and *Gastarbeiterliteratur* precisely because they name an exploitation process and an outsider status. The aim was to further a solidarity amongst the exploited which recognised the hierarchies *within* racial discrimination that help underpin socio-economic exploitation, but sought to counteract attempts to play one migrant group off against another as a means of social control. In Biondi's 'Aufstieg' ('Climbing the ladder'), a *Gastarbeiter* remarks: 'It's obvious, German: biggest fish. Italian, big fish. Turk, little fish. You [Pakistani], even smaller fish. African: all the worst jobs. Where there's rich and poor, always like that.'[19]

The affirmation of *Gastarbeiter* identity as a political act led, logically, to a policy of publishing in German as the potential common language of the migrant workers (later, seeing how little German some migrants understand even after years, Südwind experimented with parallel texts).[20] From 1980 on, a series of 'Südwind-gastarbeiterdeutsch' anthologies appeared, whose shaping ideas were solidarity and the examination of the material conditions of immigrant experience. *Im neuen Land* (In the New Land, 1980) focused on discrimination, lack of political rights, confrontation with an alien lifestyle, prejudices and fears, *Zwischen Fabrik und Bahnhof* (Between Factory and Railway Station, 1981) on images of the home country and longings to return. *Annäherungen* (Approaches, 1982) examined the contacts between *Gastarbeiter* and the German population and between the various *Gastarbeiter* communities, *Zwischen zwei Giganten* (Between Two Giants, 1983) the specific experiences of the second and third generations.[21]

The Südwind group saw their work in the tradition of socialist workers' literature. With *Das Unsichtbare sagen* (Speaking the Invisible, 1983) the subtitle of the anthologies changes from 'Südwind gastarbeiterdeutsch' to 'Südwind-Literatur'.[22] But this is not a depoliticisation: the goal is the articulation and dissemination of a '*zweite Kultur*', a cultural experience excluded from the mainstream and common not just to migrant labourers, but to the whole working class in Germany. In .1980, the Spaniard Antonio Hernando responded to the question of his access, as a *Gastarbeiter*, to German culture: 'Not even the German workers have any access to the so-called "German culture".That is in fact a culture of privileged Germans for privileged Germans.'[23]

It was these and other anthologies with programmatic titles such as *Sehnsucht im Koffer* (Longing in a Suitcase, 1981),[24] rather than work by individual authors, which established this literature in the awareness of the German reading public, but in doing so perpetuated a normative perception of a homogeneous *Gastarbeiterliteratur*.

However, there were other currents, represented particularly strongly within Turkish-German culture, partly because Turkey's own political and economic situation created more pressure than in other major sender countries for intellectuals, as well as traditional migrant workers, to emigrate. For example, Yüksel Pazarkaya and the publishers Ararat aimed to show German readers that Turkish culture was more than *Gastarbeiter* culture, by publishing both modern Turkish literary classics such as Nazim

Hikmet and Turkey's own *Deutschlandliteratur*, works on migrant experience in Germany published in Turkey itself.[25]Pazarkaya has written on *Gastarbeiter* experience since the 1960s, but rejects all categorisations, arguing that 'literature is literature'.[26] Highly educated, he views the German language not as a barrier to social participation, but as the path to the universal humanist tradition of Lessing and Heine, Schiller and Brecht, Leibniz and Feuerbach, Hegel and Marx.[27] The marked contrast to the position of Hernando demonstrates how class and educational factors may cut across the common experience of migration. Pazarkaya is an example of the pitfalls of viewing the culture and experience of Turkish migrants (let alone all migrants) *en bloc*, since he belongs to a very specific group: middle-class intellectuals of a generation profoundly influenced by Atatürk's Westernising and Europeanising reforms.[28]

Some *Gastarbeiterliteratur*, in the conventional sense of simple autobiographical accounts of prejudice, identity conflict and broken dreams, continues to be written. However, publication gave many authors confidence to reflect critically on the limitations of this approach. Moreover, the anthologies, while promoting a misleading image of homogeneity, also established this literature as a market factor, which in turn widened access to publication for a much broader range of authors, many of whom never acquired the *Gastarbeiter* label, explicitly reject it, or set out to deconstruct it. Authors of the second and third generations appeared, critical in new ways of the prejudice they encounter in Germany, but also of the self-pity, subservience, backwardness or greed of their parents' generation. Women writers became increasingly prominent. More single-author volumes were published, leading, in turn, to a recognition of the diversity and in some cases thematic, stylistic and linguistic sophistication of this literature, though its reception in the German media has remained dogged by stereotypes.[29]

In the following we examine a small selection of texts from the 1970s to the 1990s which are characteristic of the various phases of migrant literature in Germany, whilst having qualities which take them beyond the merely typical. In focusing largely on prose, we necessarily neglect whole areas of a diverse picture: the vast output of poetry, the satires and cabaret programmes of Sinasi Dikmen (*Wir werden das Knoblauchkind schon schaukeln*, 1983; *Der andere Türke*, 1985), the half-subversive, half-whimsical fairy tales of Rafik Schami (*Das letzte Wort der Wanderratte*, 1984; *Der erste*

Ritt durchs Nadelohr, 1985; *Erzähler der Nacht*, 1986), or the development of ethnic theatre (*Teatro Siciliano*, Frankfurt; Turkish groups in several cities).[30]

From First to Third Generation

Franco Biondi's story 'Die Rückkehr von Passavanti', first published in 1976 in the Italian emigrant newspaper *Corriere d'Italia*, has become a classic of the first phase of *Gastarbeiter* experience, showing the migrant labourer as disoriented, embittered, rootless, his dreams of return doomed to disillusion.[31] Passavanti is a bricklayer from a Southern Italian village. Recruited to Germany in 1960, he works as a labourer, in a fridge factory, in a tar works. In 1975 he returns to his village: for good, he says. He carries the same *Pappkoffer* (cardboard suitcase: an emblem of the first generation of *Gastarbeiter*) with which he set out, and little else to show for fifteen years in limbo. However, now he finds the village '*fremd*' ('alien'), and can only squabble with family and friends. Eventually shunned and mocked as '*der Deutsche*', he returns to Germany.

The text bitterly attacks the semi-feudal, subsidy-grubbing landlords who dominate the village. Thus, unlike many early migrant texts, it does not convert homesickness into an over-rosy portrayal of the homeland. However, it does not look beyond Passavanti's melancholy fatalism.

Güney Dal's novel *Wenn Ali die Glocken läuten hört* (When Ali Hears the Bells Ringing, 1979), is set amongst Turkish workers in Cologne during an unofficial strike at Ford, and also in Berlin. It too has many typical themes and milieus of *Gastarbeiterliteratur*, ironic memories of the dreams of wealth that had motivated migration, hostel life, isolation, puzzlement at the alien language and culture, experience of everyday prejudice and racism, stress-related illness, corruption of traditional values, a sometimes crude location of the roots of migrant misery in capitalism.

Even so, the intercut scenes and multiple focalisers (the sociology student Ali, the Ford workers Schevket and Hamdi, the laboratory assistant Kadir) permit a complex and differentiated portrayal of how experiences before, as well as after, migration condition the very disparate attitudes of Turks in contemporary Germany. There are the politically active, the apathetic and the ignorant; there are the strike-breakers – dreams of wealth having lured most *Gastarbeiter* in the first place, some could always be bought off; there are the Turkish government agents hand-in-glove with the German employers to undermine the strike; finally the religious fundamentalists, who despise the godless Germans, the Communists and their own government: anybody and anything associated with modernity, secularisation and Westernisation.

Thus, deep divisions run through the Turkish community itself. However, the novel also reflects the antagonism that the Turks, above all, were already encountering in late 1970s Germany: they are seen by disadvantaged Germans not as class comrades but as ugly, loud and garishly dressed, dragging swarms of children, 'a rapidly spreading epidemic'.[32] The novel also shows the mutual process whereby each culture encounters the other with surprise, distance, suspicion, alienation and a sense of its own superiority, so creating a double ethnographic Other. It subverts German stereotypes of 'the Turks' and of the cowed, culturally inferior *Gastarbeiter* in general, but also perpetuates Turkish stereotypes of 'the Germans' as godless, heartless, bureaucratic and materialistic, generalisations which undermine the text's call for trans-ethnic class solidarity.

However, with the Kadir figure, a parody of the ignorant, helpless, powerless, speechless Turkish migrant, Dal shows his literary self-awareness, even playfulness, traits more common in migrant literature than the stereotype would have it. Kadir is dependent on his elder son to interpret the German his younger son mumbles in his sleep, and trustingly takes the pills his employer (director of a laboratory where Kadir cares for the animals) thoughtlessly gives him for his stomach pains. They are hormone pills; Kadir acquires breasts, and, too ashamed to consult anyone, mutilates himself with a kitchen knife.[33] This is a grotesque metaphor for German treatment of *Gastarbeiter*, especially Turks, as subhuman beings, and for the helpless and self-destructive response of a man unprepared for the bewildering complexities of urban technological society.

Dal's *Europastraße 5* (1981) displays in its narrative form the multiple voices in the individual Turkish experience: the cultural and religious tradition, the family, the contemporary homeland, the dream of Germany and the reality, the nightmare experiences on the trans-Balkan route E5 that gives the novel its title. The consciousness of the central character, Salim, becomes the arena in which conflicting cultural forces fight their battles. The plot is gloriously grotesque, and, like the story of Kadir's breasts, just believable (it is found, with variants, in other migrant texts). Salim's father dies in Berlin while staying there illegally. Salim tries to smuggle the body back to Turkey crammed in a television carton on the roofrack. Border delays, accidents, breakdowns, and alternate heat and heavy rain cause his plans to disintegrate along with the carton and the body in a nightmare of comic complications. *Europastraße 5* is a complex novel, in which migrant experience is expressed not in autobiographical complaint, but in the broken consciousness mediated by the narrative structure.

Though less sophisticated in form than Dal's work, Franco Biondi's *Abschied der zerschellten Jahre* (Farewell to the Shattered Years, 1984), marks another historical stage of migrant experience; the third generation, those born in Germany who generally regard it as their home and often perceive their parents' country as no more than a holiday destination. Mamo, a young Italian, has received a deportation notice. He barricades himself in his flat with a Browning automatic, and reviews his life in a series of flashbacks.

Mamo cannot identify with the German society that oppresses him. Yet, born and brought up in Germany, he does not feel an *Ausländer*. He speaks a teenage working-class argot not specific to immigrants: 'He spoke like the natives. After all, he was one.'[34] Much of his bitterness is actually related to his generation and class as a whole, treated as 'broken dolls in a lumber room' (pp.24–25), trained for useless jobs which will soon be automated. Like Hernando, Biondi sees class, as well as ethnic identity, as being at the root of exclusion and oppression. He dedicates his novella to 'all native foreigners of German and non-German origins'.

Mamo scorns the *Pappkoffer* images of immigrants in his well-meaning schoolbooks: 'miserable, moaning figures with cardboard suitcases [...] people choking on their homesickness and their tears' (pp.40–41). This is his father's generation (that too of Biondi's own Passavanti). When the theme of *Gastarbeiter* is discussed at school, he angrily resists the stares of fellow pupils. Gradually however, the experience of prejudice turns him into a *Gastarbeiter* by forcing him to develop a consciousness of his identity as the deviant, disliked Other. It is – like 'Jewish-ness' in Nazi Germany – an identity created by the oppressor. A fellow pupil taunts him with a *Blutwurst* which he tells him is a 'Turk's penis', indifferent to Mamo's actual ethnic identity: foreign is foreign. Mamo never felt much in common with

Turks, but now begins to feel 'foreign'; he dreams of studying his face in a mirror: that is, he is forced to view his identity as an image of himself as transmitted to him in the gaze of the powerful, a theme which echoes women's writing of the period (p.46). His identity as a *Gastarbeiter* is part of a script written by the socio-economic forces which created the *Gastarbeiter* in the first place. This script now declares that he should be deported from the country of his birth; hence his act of rebellion.

This is a familiar topos of modern literature and film: the hero or heroine forced into an extreme decision, which is irrevocable, but also engenders clarity, relief and a sense of power. Mamo compares it with the video game 'Player': there are no conjunctives, it is shoot or be shot. The myths and icons of his mental world and that of his class and his generation, German or migrant – films, rock music, the disco, the bowling alley and especially the video game – shape the metaphoric structures of his narrative: he is 'not a flying saucer on the screen, not a clay pigeon flashing by […] not a skittle waiting for the ball, no, if I've got to topple over, if I'm going to be deported […] then with dignity.' (p.97) Thus even the potentially authentic, identity-giving act, as a radical 'no' to socio-economic determination, is expressed in inauthentic metaphors from a sham world.

Ideological and social criticism of this kind links Biondi as much with German writers like Heinrich Böll or Günter Wallraff as with Italian-German or *Gastarbeiter*-German literature, a reminder that 'migrant' themes are often universal ones. However, there is another crucial dimension: while the culture, values and language of his parents' south Italian world play no part in Mamo's discourse, it is intercut by narratives from Costas, Mamo's Greek neighbour. In marked contrast to Mamo's colloquial tone, Costas relates folk tales about human greed and folly, about the once independent fishermen now in thrall to money-lenders, and forced by tourist development to emigrate, and so invokes a rural idyll lost permanently through the migration process. By intercutting the present-day experiences of a young, urban, third-generation Italian, who rejects his forbears' rural past, with the reminiscences of a dying Greek ex-fisherman, Biondi points to the extreme diversity of migrant experience in Germany and the contrasting forms of its textual articulation, yet also asserts their common material causes.

Abschied der zerschellten Jahre is a first-generation writer's view of third-generation experience. Rather different is that generation's

perspective as offered by the poet Nevfel Cumart. Born in
Germany in 1964, of Turkish parents but brought up by a
German foster family, Cumart calls Turkey 'my homeland', but
first visited it at the age of nine. He writes formally and linguistically confident, economical lyric poetry in his *German* 'mother
tongue'.[35] It reveals a poetic subject troubled but enriched by its
complex identity: *Herz in der Schlinge* (Heart in a Noose, 1985); *Ein
Schmelztiegel im Flammenmeer* (A Crucible in a Sea of Flames, 1988);
Das ewige Wasser (The Eternal Water, 1990). Landing in Berlin from
a visit to Turkey, his body stretches 'painfully / but also reassur-
ingly / across Europe / across the bridge' (p. 42). Cumart offers his
voice to 'those who sit between two stools / at home neither here
nor there / who daily walk the narrow ridge / on the edge of two
worlds'(p. 61). However, this is not only an ethnic solidarity but
also an existential one, with the lonely, the melancholic and the
rebellious. His work is not free of kitsch, and sometimes encourages a vicarious and socially unspecific identification with feelings
of alienation. Other poems, though, provoke German readers to
look behind their perception of *Gastarbeiter* identity as a one-
dimensional set of economic problems and cultural peculiarities,
to see individuals with spiritual needs shaped by a complex
dynamic of social forces (pp. 67–68).

Cumart views Turkey with 'paralysing indecision / between
magnetic longing / and repelling horror' (p. 108). The poem
'anatolische frau' evokes the crushing effects of rural poverty in a
barren landscape: 'at sunrise / in the fields / with your hands /
you break open / the furrowed scars / of the exhausted earth'
(p. 105).His view of the dehumanisation of the migrant labourer
as a 'dark shameful chapter of German history' (p. 66) is made
more credible by his refusal to idealise his Turkish 'homeland':
other poems attack the corruption of Turkish bureaucracy and
the oppression of the military regime.[36]

Cumart's work demonstrates the complex interaction of the
individual and the culturally typical, characteristic of the third
generation. It does not ignore or repress his Turkish identity, but
it also reflects his concerns as an inhabitant of an advanced
industrial society, and explores poetic subjectivity and the travails
of love in ways entirely familiar to the Western tradition.

When one turns to a consideration of articulations of migrant
experience by women writers, the complexities and diversity in
particular of Turkish identity (on which we focus here), take on a
further dimension.

Turkish Migrant Women's Writing:
Between Tradition and Modernity

The increasing immigration of women after the *Ausländerstopp* in 1973, as well as long periods of political unrest in Turkey, supported the emergence of an autonomous differentiated literature by Turkish women in the Federal Republic. The gender conflicts that aggravate the search for a bi-cultural female identity give this writing its distinctive perspective.[37] The patriarchal structures that shape the authors' socialisation in Turkish culture can also be found, in modified form, in the society of the host country and compound the discrimination which the writers experience as foreigners.

In the mid 1970s when research on Turkish women began, a stereotype was created which combined *gender* (the oppressed woman), *tradition* (the socialisation in underdeveloped rural areas) and *cultural background* (Islam's oppressive backwardness), and defined Turkish women as silent victims unable to adapt to modern German society without help.[38] This image continues to serve as a model for Turkish femininity not only in dominant male, but also in feminist, scholarship in the West.[39] This stereotype however, disregards the complexity and diversity of Turkish women's origins and lives. Turkish female identity today is influenced by radical changes in society, including the abolition of the veil and of *sharia* law, as well as the introduction of the woman's right to vote and her right of access to higher education. It is also defined by enormous geographical, economic, social and cultural differences.[40]

The following comparison of the work of three authors seeks to exemplify the disparate and often contradictory ways in which Turkish women's writing tackles the issues of *tradition* and *emancipation* in the face of German prejudice.

Saliha Scheinhardt is well known as the first Turkish migrant woman to write directly in German. She is influenced – especially in her early work – by the Turkish Marxist Left and the *Literatur der Betroffenheit* initiated by members of PoLiKunst. Consequently she defines her work in functional terms, arguing that literature should be committed, address contemporary problems critically and stimulate discussion.[41] Her first works form a cycle of fictional autobiographies of underprivileged Turkish women: *Frauen, die sterben ohne daß sie gelebt hätten* (Women Who Die Before They Have Lived, 1983); *Drei Zypressen* (Three

Cypresses, 1984); *Und die Frauen weinten Blut* (And The Women Wept Blood, 1985). Her protagonists come from the under-developed regions of Turkey, from Anatolian villages or the slums of the big cities. Their destinies lie completely in the hands of their fathers, brothers and husbands, who either force them to emigrate, subject them to extreme brutality, or abandon them penniless at home when they themselves leave their country. Fear and dependency hinder many of the protagonists from developing constructive strategies for liberating themselves from this situation. Their suffering often expresses itself in desperate deeds. Thus Suna, the narrator of *Frauen, die sterben, ohne daß sie gelebt haben*, murders her husband, only to suffer such anxiety that even prison becomes a place of liberation. Schein-hardt's protagonists recognise, in retrospect, some of the determinants of their lives. They see the principal causes of female oppression in Turkey's economic and social structures, in the people's poverty, their lack of education and their fatal-ism, which make them an easy target for Islamic Fundamentalism. In Scheinhardt's narratives men are depicted as victims of circumstance and women are presented as victims of the victims. The author considers the modernisation (i.e., Westernisation) of society to be the most important prerequisite for the emancipation of Turkish women. However, only her daughter-figures can profit from the advantages of modernisa-tion. By moving to the big cities or a Western European country they gain access to education and develop a critical distance from the lives of their mothers. With the critical capacity Scheinhardt gives to her daughter-figures, comes an emancipa-tory duty. Zeynep Z., the second generation migrant narrator of *Drei Zypressen*, appeals to her contemporaries: 'we, the daugh-ters, bear the responsibility for the unfulfilled dreams of the women of the generations before us' and to ensure that 'those who follow us [...] will never have to go through what we have been through.'[42]

Scheinhardt offers a very differentiated picture of the reasons for the oppression of Turkish women, but she does not contra-dict the stereotype of Turkish women as victims. Indeed her narrative style helps to perpetuate it, since her narratives do not show individual strategies of female identity formation, but rather unite separate identities into one single pattern, thereby supporting generalisation. In her writing she mixes the styles of authentic documentation, emotional accusation, moral appeal and political programme to create solidarity among her German readers. However, descriptions such as that of a woman as 'a quiet being, like the embodiment of patience, who carries out the heaviest jobs and makes no demands [and] moves round the house, the barn, the field like a shadow', tend rather to provoke the reader's pity.[43]

In her critique of Günter Wallraff's *Ganz Unten*, Aysel Özakin describes pity as a means of stabilising cultural dominance. In some respects it is the most refined form of contempt. By approaching ethnic minorities with pity, members of the German Left (like Wallraff) categorise them as inferior, uniform groups and at the same time purify themselves from historical guilt.[44] Before she chose exile in Germany in 1981, Özakin was already a prize-winning author in Turkey for her novel *Die Preisvergabe* (German edition 1982), a complex critique of the phases and orientations of Turkish feminism. Özakin often emphasises that she has nothing in common with the victimised Anatolian peasants who form the German stereotype of the Turkish woman. Although she expresses a strong solidarity with the Turkish immigrant workers in some of her texts, for example in the anthology *Soll ich hier alt werden* (1988), she clearly points out the cultural differences between them and herself. She claims that she had to emancipate herself from tradition to develop an individual identity: 'Tradition provided a collective identity and security but it did not give me the possibility to overcome my limits'.[45] Confronted with German prejudices, Özakin sees herself deprived of all her emancipatory achievements and of her recognition as a writer, leading to a profound undermining of her self-esteem.[46] Her texts written in Germany articulate the anxieties of exile which heighten her experience of everyday discrimination, her awareness of social, cultural and gender-specific hierarchies, and her struggle for individuality and creative autonomy.

In the novel *Die Leidenschaft der Anderen* (The Passions of Others, 1983), the narrator, an exiled Turkish writer, undertakes a reading tour through the Federal Republic: a tour which becomes a symbol of her rootlessness as her contact with Turkey is inter-rupted, the Federal Republic denies her a residence permit, she loses her flat and her relationship with a German man breaks up. The protagonist uses the journey for an intensive self-assessment. Her own dichotomous way of thinking becomes evident in her esoteric language. She perceives herself as the permanent victim of Eurocentrism and sexism, and positions herself outside of static homogeneous groups like 'the official Germany', the German Alternative Movement and the Turkish Left in Exile, which threaten her individuality with their demands and expectations. Her refusal to conform and her paranoid fear of discrimination prevent her from making contact even with people who do not seem to fit into her fixed categories. Like her author, she finds a sense of homeland and of identity only in her texts. She calls them her 'protective rampart,'[47] a metaphor which suggests the need for comfort as well as for self-isolation.

Özakin's struggle for creative independence expresses itself in her choice of literary language. Most of her work produced in Germany was originally written in Turkish. The author claims that the use of the German language forces her to focus on the 'Turkish question' and thereby worsens the quality of her writing.[48] In 1990 she emigrated to Cornwall to escape the limitations she experienced in Germany.

Confronted with Western images of oriental femininity, many Turkish migrant women feel the need to explore their own past in order to rewrite the female cultural history of the Orient from the perspective of the victims of prejudice, and to rediscover the origin of their own personal development. In her study of Muslim women between tradition and emancipation, the Turkish journalist Naila Minai writes:

> My Turkish-tartar grandmother was educated at home, married a polyga-mous man and did not take off her veil even on journeys abroad [...] My mother never wore a veil, she went to local schools and eventually became a housewife in a monogamous marriage. I left my family to study in the United States and Europe [and] hitchhiked from country to country.[49]

The awareness of this transformation through three generations informs Minai's research and its differentiated picture of changing gender roles in Islamic culture.

In her novel *Das Leben ist eine Karawanserei* (Life is a Caravanserai, 1992) Emine Sevgi Özdamar, in pursuit of a similar goal, also portrays a family over three generations from the perspective of the daughter-figure. War, political unrest and poverty are the moti-vating forces behind this odyssey from the Caucasus through a variety of Turkish landscapes and cities, ending with the narrator's emigration to Germany. By re-telling her own and her family's history the protagonist reconstructs her personal historical identity, which at the novel's conclusion she takes to Germany as 'luggage'. That Turkey itself is a multicultural society is illustrated by the narrator's socialisation: constant changes of place, countless events, numerous encounters with people of different social and ethnic backgrounds, the stories and tales of her grandfather, the prayers and superstitious sayings of her grandmother, the American films and comics which became popular in Turkey during the 1950s and 1960s. The interweaving of these elements makes female identity appear like an ever changing kaleidoscope, rather than a static construction. Female identity as Özdamar depicts it is partly determined by historically given structures and partly based on choice. The women of the family described in her novel develop survival strategies in the face of various adversities and create freedom of action for themselves, though always within given limits. In addition women who are outside society, like the prostitutes or the mentally ill, are presented as positive role models for the narrator. Özdamar's novel describes the formation of female identity in a society where elements of tradition and modernity unite and stimulate each other. The narrator is given an enormous freedom of movement. Growing up in an urban environment at a time when traditional patriarchal structures start to crumble under the influences of Western capitalism, she is allowed to visit places where older women of her family would not dare to go. The narrator even contributes to her grandmother's belated and partial liberation by letting her participate in her experience.

Increasing alienation from their culture of origin heightens the need of Turkish migrant women writers to go back to their roots. Their preoccupation with tradition brings a long buried cultural conflict to the surface. The abrupt break with the Arabic-Islamic culture of the Ottoman Empire, which was instigated by Atatürk's revolutionary reforms, brought women many advantages; but it also prevented a full critical engagement with an important part of their history. 'I / The supporter / Of the reforms of the dress codes / And of the Latin script / Learned as a small girl / To despise / The six-hundred-year rule / Of the Ottomans / I am trained for a future without a past.'[50]

In Özdamar's story *Mutterzunge* (*Mother Tongue*, 1991) the protagonist has, with the loss of her native language in the foreign environment, also been alienated emotionally and physically from a part of herself. To regain it, she elects to learn the Arabic language which had once been forbidden by Atatürk. This is not the reactionary act it superficially appears, but one of refilling a space in her cultural-historical identity left vacant by the expulsion of Arabic and filled instead by Westernised values.

The narrator deliberately undergoes forty days of ritualistic dependence on her teacher. Paradoxically, this subordination is her path to liberation; having entered and traversed the full historical experience of her culture, and been brought back to full contact with herself, she is able to adopt an active critical attitude to her new environment.

Once she has restored her roots, the protagonist is able to develop a flexible identity without losing herself. Like the narrator in *Das Leben ist eine Karawanserei*, the protagonist of *Mutterzunge* constantly crosses boundaries. She moves between East and West Berlin, between Arabic Islam and Western-orientated Turkey. Languages and cultures intermingle. In her imagination even gender boundaries are dissolved: in her dreams both she and her Koran teacher appear as hermaphrodites.

However, this text, in which an emancipated Turkish intellectual voluntarily subordinates herself to an Islamic Koran teacher, has brought Özdamar repeated attacks from her German public. They are unable, it seems, to accept that a Turkish woman might choose a different path of self-discovery to the Western feminist one they, Eurocentrically, assume to be universally applicable.

Özdamar, who has trained and worked in theatre in Berlin, Bochum, Frankfurt and Paris since the late 1970s and is familiar with the Western as well as the Turkish cultural tradition, reportedly deals with such criticism by quoting *Hamlet*: 'There are more things in heaven and earth, Horatio, than are dreamt of in your philosophy'.[51]

The urbane confidence of this response is a reminder that 'migrant literature' in German has progressed from *Pappkoffer* to pluralism, and by now encompasses a huge range of writing from the naively autobiographical to highly self-conscious, sophisticated narratives by authors with an equally wide range of backgrounds and experience. Its analysis should always respect both specific factors of ethnic and cultural background, class, generation and gender, and the shaping force of the individual literary imagination. At the same time, the common, migration-related socio-economic and cultural experiences of exclusion and discrimination that inform it should never be forgotten or obscured.

Notes

*This chapter is a revised version of 'From "Pappkoffer" to Pluralism: migrant writing in the German Federal Republic', in R. King, J. Connell, P. White eds, *Writing Across Worlds: Literature and Migration*, London, Routledge, 1995, pp.39–56.

1. Quoted in H. H. Heldmann, 'Zum Ausländergesetz 1991', *Vorgänge*, no.1,1991, p.63.

2. E. Uzun, 'Gastarbeiter – Immigranten – Minderheit. Vom Identitätswandel der Türken in Deutschland', in *Deutsche Türken. Türk Almanar*, ed. C. Leggewie and Z. Senocak, Reinbek, Rowohlt, 1993, pp.49–66.

3. D. Cohn-Bendit and T. Schmid, *Heimat Babylon. Das Wagnis der multikulturellen Demokratie*, Hamburg, Hoffmann & Campe, 1992, p.12.

4. See T. Wägenbaur, 'Postmoderne und Multikulturalität: Der feine Unterschied', in *Multikulturalität. Tendenzen, Probleme, Perspektiven im europäischen und internationalen Horizont*, ed. M. Kessler and J. Wertheimer, Tübingen, Stauffenburg, 1995, p.131.

5. S. Weigel, 'Notes on the Constellation of Gender and Cultural Identity in Contemporary Germany', *New German Critique*, vol. 55, 1992, p.49.

6. A point acutely argued by Ülker Gökberg, 'Fremdheit verstehen. "Ausländerliteratur" zwischen Relativismus und Universalismus', *Sirene*, vol. 7, no. 13/14, 1994, pp.43–76.

7. S. Castles and M.J. Miller, *The Age of Migration. International Population Movements in the Modern World*, London, Macmillan, 1993, p.18.

8. P. White, 'On the use of creative literature in migration study', *Area*, vol.17, no.4, 1985, pp.277–283.

9. R. Dove, 'Writing in the margin. Social meaning in *Gastarbeiterliteratur*', *Quinquireme*, vol.9, 1986, pp.16–31, though a pioneering engagement in English with this literature, is weakened by this reductive functionalisation.

10. See L. Adelson, 'Migrantenliteratur oder deutsche Literatur? Torkans *Tufan: Brief an einen islamischen Bruder*', in *Spätmoderne und Postmoderne. Beiträge zur deutschsprachigen Gegenwartsliteratur*, ed. P.M.Lützeler, Frankfurt/Main, Fischer, 1991, pp.67–72; H. Kreuzer, 'Gastarbeiter-Literatur, Ausländer-Literatur, Migranten-Literatur? Zur Einführung', *Zeitschrift für Literatur und Linguistik*, vol.56, 1984, pp.7–11; H. Suhr, ' "Ausländerliteratur": Minority Literature in the FRG', *New German Critique*, vol.46, 1989, pp.71–103; A. Teraoka, '*Gastarbeiterliteratur*: the Other speaks back', *Cultural Critique*, no. 7, Fall 1987, pp.77–101.

11. See Adelson, 'Migrantenliteratur oder deutsche Literatur?', pp.67–72.

12. G. Chiellino, *Literatur und Identität in der Fremde*. *Zur Literatur italienischer Autoren in der Bundesrepublik*, Kiel, Neuer Malik Verlag, 1989 (first published Augsburg 1985), pp.19–27; U. Reeg, *Schreiben in der Fremde*. *Literatur nationaler Minderheiten in der Bundesrepublik Deutschland*, Essen, Klartext, 1988, pp.17–79.

13. See Dove, 'Writing in the Margin'; H. Hamm, *Fremdgegangen – Freigeschrieben*. *Eine Einführung in die deutschsprachige Gastarbeiterliteratur*, Würzburg, Königshausen & Neumann, 1988; H. Heinze, *Migrantenliteratur in der Bundesrepublik Deutschland*, Berlin, Express Edition, 1986; H. Schierloh, *Das alles für ein Stück Brot*. *Migrantenliteratur als Objektivierung des 'Gastarbeiterdaseins'*, Frankfurt, P. Lang, 1984.

14. M. Frederking, *Schreiben gegen Vorurteile*. *Literatur türkischer Migranten in der Bundesrepublik Deutschland*, Berlin, Express Edition, 1985.

15. I. Ackermann ed., *Als Fremder in Deutschland: Berichte, Erzählungen, Gedichte von Ausländern*, Munich, dtv, 1982; I. Ackermann ed., *In zwei Sprachen leben: Berichte, Erzählungen, Gedichte von Ausländern*, Munich, dtv, 1983; I. Ackermann ed., *Türken deutscher Sprache: Berichte, Erzählungen, Gedichte*, Munich, dtv, 1984; K. Esselborn, *Über Grenzen*, Munich, dtv, 1987.

16. H. Friedrich, *Chamissos Enkel: Zur Literatur von Ausländern in Deutschland*, Munich, dtv, 1986.

17. H. Weinrich, 'Um eine deutsche Literatur von außen bittend', *Merkur*, vol.37, 1983, pp.911–20; Idem, 'Gastarbeiterliteratur in der Bundesrepublik Deutschland',*Zeitschrift für Literaturwissenschaft und Linguistik*, vol.56, 1984, pp.12–22; this tendency is criticised especially acutely by Teraoka (note 10).

18. F. Biondi, 'Von den Tränen zu den Bürgerrechten: ein Einblick in die italienische Emigrantenliteratur', *Zeitschrift für Literaturwissenschaft und Linguistik*, vol.56, 1984, pp.75–100.

19. Quoted in C. Schaffernicht ed., *Zuhause in der Fremde. Ein bundesdeutsches Ausländer-Lesebuch*, Reinbek, Rowohlt, 1984, p.56 (first published 1981).

20. E.g., Giuseppe Giambusso, *Jenseits des Horizonts. Al di la dell'orrizonte*, Bremen, Edition CON, 1985.

21. F. Biondi et al., eds, *Im neuen Land*, Bremen, Edition CON, 1980; Idem, *Zwischen Fabrik und Bahnhof*, Bremen, Edition CON, 1981; Idem, *Annäherungen*, Bremen, Edition CON, 1982; Idem, *Zwischen zwei Giganten: Prosa, Lyrik und Grafik aus dem Gastarbeiteralltag*, Bremen, Edition CON, 1983.

22. H. Bektas et al., eds, *Das Unsichtbare sagen! Prosa und Lyrik aus dem Alltag des Gastarbeiters*, Kiel, Neuer Malik Verlag, 1983.

23. Quoted in Schaffernicht ed., *Zuhause in der Fremde*, p.136.

24. See also Schaffernicht ed., *Zuhause in der Fremde*; also Förderzentrum Jugend schreibt ed., *Täglich eine Reise von der Türkei nach Deutschland*, Fischerhude,

Atelier im Bauernhaus, 1980; Giuseppe Giambusso ed., *Wurzeln hier. Le radici qui. Gedichte italienischer Emigranten*, Bremen, Edition CON, 1982; E. Kroupi and W. Neumann eds, *Das Fremde und das Andere*. *Verständigungstexte*, Munich, Lauer & Richter, 1983; S. Taufiq ed., *Dies ist nicht die Welt, die wir suchen. Ausländer in Deutschland*, Essen, Klartext, 1983.

25. See W. Riemann, *Das Deutschlandbild in der modernen türkischen Literatur*, Wiesbaden, Harrasowitz 1983.

26. Y. Pazarkaya 'Literatur ist Literatur', in *Eine nicht nur deutsche Literatur. Zur Standortbestimmung der Ausländerliteratur*, ed. I. Ackermann and H. Weinrich, Munich, Piper, 1986.

27. See Schaffernicht ed., *Zuhause in der Fremde*, p.135.

28. See Teraoka, '*Gastarbeiterliteratur*: The Other Speaks Back', p.87; H. Scheuer, 'Das Eigene ist das Fremde', *Der Deutschunterricht*, vol.41, no.1, 1989, pp.96–104.

29. D. Göktürk, 'Muttikültürelle Zungenbrecher: Literatürken aus Deutschlands Nischen', *Sirene*, vol.7, no.12/13, 1994, pp.77–92, offers numerous examples.

30. G. Stenzaly, 'Ausländertheater in der Bundesrepublik Deutschland und West-Berlin am Beispiel der türkischen Theatergruppen', *Zeitschrift für Literatur und Linguistik*, vol.56, 1984, pp.125–141. Two of the Turkish-German plays that have played in the established theatre are Emine Sevgi Özdamar, *Karagöz in Alamania* (1986) and Nevihe Meriç, *Sevdican – Tor zur Hoffnung* (1985). The Sinti 'Theater Pralipe', based in the Theater an der Ruhr in Mülheim exemplifies the diversity of contemporary migrant culture beyond traditional *Gastarbeiter* communities.

31. F. Biondi, *Passavantis Rückkehr. Erzählungen*, Munich, dtv, 1985, pp.39–61.

32. G. Dal, *Wenn Ali die Glocken läuten hört*, Berlin, Edition der 2, 1979, p.84.

33. Ibid. pp.151–152.

34. F. Biondi, *Abschied der zerschellten Jahre*, Kiel, Neuer Malik Verlag, 1984, p.82; future references to this edition identified by page number in the text.

35. N. Cumart, *Ein Schmelztiegel im Flammenmeer*, Frankfurt/Main, Dagyeli, 1988, p.107. All subsequent page numbers after quotations refer to Cumart poems from this collection.

36. E.g., N. Cumart, *Das ewige Wasser*, Düsseldorf, Grupello Verlag, 1990, p.77.

37. See S. Weigel, 'Eine andere Migrantenliteratur oder eine andere Frauen literatur', in *Gegenwartsliteratur seit 1968*, ed. K. Briegleb and S. Weigel, Hansers Sozialgeschichte der deutschen Literatur, vol. 12, Munich, Hanser, 1992, pp.222–226.

38. H. Lutz, 'Orientalische Weiblichkeit. Das Bild der Türkin in der Literatur konfrontiert mit Selbstbildern', *Informationsdienst zur Ausländerarbeit*, vol.4, 1989, pp.32–38; U. Boos-Nünning, 'Frauen und Migration – Kultur im Wandel', *Informationsdienst zur Ausländerarbeit*, vol.4, 1989, pp.12–13.

39. C. Huth-Hildebrandt, 'Germanozentrismus oder interkulturelles Denken? Deutsche Frauen und ihre Bezieungen zu den Migrantinnen', in *Fremde Frauen. Von der Gastarbeiterin zur Bürgerin*, ed. M. Schulz, Frankfurt/Main, Verlag für interkulturelle Kommunikation, 1992, pp.6–25.

40. G. Wanner, 'Bericht aus der Arbeitsgruppe 5: Türkische Mädchen zwischen verschiedenen Erziehungsvorstellungen', in *Frauen zwischen zwei Kulturen. Frauen aus der Türkei in der Bundesrepublik Deutschland*, ed. H. Westmüller, Loccumer Protokolle, 34, Loccum, Evangelische Akademie, 1982, pp.63–72.

41. S. Scheinhardt, in J. Bohl, 'Wir müssen uns auf der Brücke begegnen. Interview mit der Offenbacher Turmschreiberin Saliha Scheinhardt', *Der Literat*, no. 9, 1987, pp.227–228.

42. S. Scheinhardt, *Drei Zypressen*, Frankfurt/Main, Dagyelei, 1990, p.139 (first published 1984).

43. Ibid., p.8.

44. A. Özakin, 'Ali hinter den Spiegeln', *Literatur konkret*, no.11,1986/87; quoted from *Kulturelles Wirken in einem anderen Land*, ed. O. Schwencke and B. Winkler-Pohler, Loccum, Kulturpolitisches Kolloquium der Evangelischen Akademie Loccum, 1987, pp.32–37. Another Turkish critic offers a much more positive view of *Ganz unten*: Sargut Sölçün, 'Ein Leben in der Republik – Ali-Woyzeck in Günter Wallraffs *Ganz unten*', in Sölçün, *Sein und Nichtsein. Zur Literatur in der multikulturellen Gesellschaft*, Bielefeld, Aisthesis, 1992, pp.125–142.This clash of opinion between the female, (self-)marginalised Özakin and the male employee of a German university Sölçün emphasises the need to differentiate positions within 'Turkish-German' culture.

45. A. Özakin, in A. Deuber-Mankowski, 'Tradition, Aufbruch, Selbständigkeit. Über die Schriftstellerin Aysel Özakin', *Frankfurter Rundschau*, 2 June 1990, p.3.

46. A. Özakin, 'Ali hinter den Spiegeln', p.32.

47. A. Özakin, *Die Leidenschaft der Anderen*, Hamburg, Luchterhand, 1992, p.18.

48. Quoted in *Literatur im interkulturellen Kontext*, ed. H. Rösch, Berlin, TUB-Dokumentation, 1989, p.65.

49. N. Minai, *Schwestern unterm Halbmond. Muslimische Frauen zwischen Tradition und Emanzipation*, Munich, dtv, 1991, pp.9–10.

50. A. Özakin, *Zart erhob sie sich bis sie flog*, Hamburg, Galgenberg, 1986, p.26.

51. Quoted in A. Burkhard, 'Vom Verlust der Zunge. Annäherung an das Fremde: Emine Sevgi Özdamar im Literaturhaus', *Frankfurter Rundschau*, 23 February 1991.

CHAPTER 2

In Search of a Lost Past:
A Reading of Emine Sevgi Özdamar's Novel
Das Leben ist eine Karawanserei, hat zwei Türen, aus einer kam ich rein aus der anderen ging ich raus

David Horrocks

Emine Sevgi Özdamar's novel *Das Leben ist eine Karawanserei* represents something of a new departure in the writing of Turks living in Germany, not only in its length, complexity and linguistic richness, but also in its subject matter. Barely touching on the confrontation with a new and strange culture, a central preoccupation of many earlier works by so-called migrant writers, it looks back at childhood and adolescence in Turkey from the perspective of a young female first-person narrator who has left her homeland in her late teens to start a job as a *Gastarbeiter* in Germany. The account of her train journey north, in the company of other female Turkish recruits to German industry, constitutes no more than a coda to the long novel, and even that breaks off in Yugoslavia before the destination is reached. Instead, the bulk of the almost four-hundred page long narrative is taken up by a migration of a different kind. Beginning with the narrator in her mother's womb, travelling by train from Istanbul to Malatya in Anatolia, the place of her birth, it retraces the steps of her and her extended family as they follow the father throughout Turkey in his often desperate search for work in the building trade.

Das Leben ist eine Karawanserei and the stories of Özdamar's collection *Mutterzunge* have already been briefly considered in Chapter 1 in the wider context of migrant writing in Germany in general, and more particularly as representing one trend within the diversity of contemporary German-Turkish women's writing. Some of the central themes highlighted there – the search for a lost identity, the key significance of language in this quest, and the situation of Turkish women between tradition and modernity – are expanded upon in the following more detailed analysis.

Language: Collecting Words to Recollect the Past

Towards the end of one of Emine Sevgi Özdamar's short prose pieces, entitled *Großvaterzunge* (Grandfather Tongue), the first-person narrator, a Turkish woman, gets into conversation with a German girl sitting on a park bench in Berlin. 'What are you doing in Germany?' she is asked, and her reply is: 'I'm a collector of words.'[1] It is tempting to see this as a description of the author herself, since above all else Özdamar is a writer fascinated by words, so concerned with language itself that it becomes a central theme of much of her work. In part, of course, this fascination must derive from her situation as a Turkish native speaker living in Germany and writing in German. Curiously, however, it is not primarily the German language that appears to whet her collector's appetite. After nearly twenty years residence in the country, she appears to be perfectly at home in German, writing it with great facility, fluency and invention. 'The tongue has no bones. Wherever you turn it, it turns,' she writes at the beginning of the title piece of her collection *Mutterzunge*.[2] Özdamar amply demonstrates this linguistic flexibility and adaptability in her long novel *Das Leben ist eine Karawanserei, hat zwei Türen, aus einer kam ich rein, aus der anderen ging ich raus*. (Life is a caravanserai; has two doors. I came in through one, went out through the other.)[3] When it first appeared in 1992, some German reviewers complained of odd grammatical errors and stylistic blemishes, but these are few and far-between, and may in any case have been deliberate.[4]

The words Özdamar is concerned to collect are not, then, German. Rather they are the words of her Turkish mother-tongue, which she is conscious of having lost. Beyond them, she is also searching for the tongue of her grandfather and grandmother, the Arabic familiar to them from the Koran, and which has also contributed a great deal in the way of vocabulary to modern Turkish itself. Here the sense of loss is even greater, because Turkey's abandonment of Arabic script in favour of the Roman alphabet in the course of Atatürk's modernisation policy in the 1920s has cut her off from the only language her grandfather is capable of reading. In *Großvaterzunge* the first-person narrator actively goes in search of this linguistic heritage, taking lessons in Arabic script from a learned teacher, Ibni Abdullah, in Berlin.

'In a foreign language words have no childhood,'[5] she maintains, and it is above all the world of her childhood that she seeks to recollect and regain by 'collecting' a basic vocabulary common to both Arabic and Turkish. Her response to these words and to the Arabic script she learns is not intellectual or analytical, but child-like in its sensuousness. As she voices them, the Arabic letters take on tangible physical shapes, come alive as animals, natural objects, even parts of the human body:

> The letters emerged from my mouth. Some looked like birds, some like a heart with an arrow in it, some like a caravan, some like sleeping camels, some like a river, some like trees scattered by the wind, some like snakes on the move ... some like angrily startled eyebrows ... some like the fat arse of a woman sitting on a hot stone in a Turkish bath.[6]

Özdamar re-uses this passage almost verbatim in her novel *Das Leben ist eine Karawanserei* when the young protagonist recalls hearing as a child her grandmother Ayse uttering the Arabic prayers for the dead in a cemetery.[7] Later, as she watches her father turn the pages of the Koran, the Arabic script of which he is unable to read, she again sees '... the picture-words that my grandmother had spoken to the dead in the cemetery', noting this time that: 'One letter stood on the page like the very beautiful eyes of a woman'.[8] Eventually she is to learn the Arabic prayers for the dead by heart from her grandmother, who recites them in the accent of her home village in Cappadocia. The young heroine may not understand them, but the grandmother's words, likened to a caravan of camels walking one behind the other, gather in her mouth and, as she puts it: 'her camels, which were bigger than mine, placed mine in front of their legs and taught my camels how to walk.'[9]

Özdamar includes these prayers for the dead in her text, transliterating the Arabic script into the Roman alphabet and thus giving the uninitiated reader some clue as to the sounds of the words.[10] However, since she offers no translation, readers without Arabic are initially forced to share the young girl's ignorance of their meaning. The prayers begin with the expression '*Bismillâhirahmanirrahim*', the formulaic invocation 'In the name of Allah, the compassionate and the merciful.' Whether in full or in the shortened form *Bismillâh*, this word then recurs throughout the novel as Özdamar illustrates its vital function within Turkish social life.

The first person narrator confesses that she never knew its meaning until looking it up at the age of eighteen when in Paris, but the formulation is nevertheless in constant use all around her during her childhood and teenage years, and she, like everyone else, once she learns it from her grandmother, employs it as is customary. It is uttered when entering a house, before washing, before eating the first bread of the day, when dressing or undressing, and on countless other occasions. As such it demonstrates clearly the power of language as a bonding force within the community. It also acts as a talisman for the protagonist on two occasions in her life, once in its written, once in its spoken form. In the first instance, when at grammar school, she writes *Bismillâhirahmanirrahim* at the head of her biology exam paper and, despite getting most of the answers hopelessly wrong, is rewarded with a good mark because her teacher is so moved by the gesture. The second instance occurs during a visit to Paris as an eighteen-year-old. Here, the caretaker of a student hostel, an Algerian, allows her to spend the night on the sofa of his and his wife's flat. She wakes more than once to find the man ogling her, but on each occasion she wards off the threat by uttering the formula *Bismillâhirahmanirrahim*. The Algerian caretaker repeats the word each time in ritual response until he eventually tires and returns to his own bed to sleep.

Other examples of Özdamar's awareness of particular words, and the vital function they have in oiling the wheels of social intercourse and serving in a quasi-ritualistic fashion to bind a community together, are two further Arabic expressions that her young protagonist hears all around her in her youth. The first is '*Ma-sallah*', literally 'whatever Allah wishes', which is used as a term of admiration, especially for children, but also to ward off the evil eye. The second is '*Insallah*', in practice not unlike German '*hoffentlich*' or the current English usage 'hopefully', but literally meaning 'God willing' or 'Allah willing' and thus retaining something of that submission to God's will that is central to the whole notion of Islam. Another, more secular expression may serve as a last example of the word collection

Özdamar assembles in her novel. This is a Turkish idiom used when one person suggests something and another responds in the affirmative. The suggestion takes the form '*tamam mi* ('OK?'), and the positive response is simply '*tamam*' ('OK' or 'agreed'). Frequently occurring in the conversations between the unnamed young protagonist and her elder brother Ali, it effectively captures the warmth, tenderness and understanding that characterise the relationship between the two children. On one occasion the word *tamam* also acts as a kind of magic talisman, though the grandmother has to pronounce it three times for it to take effect. The younger brother of the family goes missing after dark and other children claim to have seen him walking down to the stream in the company of a man. On his return home he is interrogated by the mother, Fatma, who threatens to bite into his flesh if he refuses to say where he has been:

> 'If you don't talk, I'll bite, *tamam mi*?' mother said. He said nothing. She sank her teeth into the flesh of my brother's hip. He still said nothing. Grandmother came and said: 'Fatma, *tamam, tamam, tamam.*' As if reacting to a magic word, mother let go of my brother's flesh.[11]

Passages such as the above, where specific words, whether Arabic or Turkish, are of the essence, serve to emphasise the crucial significance of language to Özdamar's whole project in the novel. The childhood and formative years she is intent on recapturing from oblivion are inextricably linked to the acquisition of a mother-tongue, that a foreign tongue, such as the German she writes in, can never entirely replace. Her young narrator's initiation into a particular culture and community consists to a large extent of such linguistic education. In this sense, *Das Leben ist eine Karawanserei* qualifies as a *Bildungsroman*. By virtue of its being written in German, and thus primarily for a German readership, it also – whether the author consciously intended it to or not – functions as a novel of education and initiation in a second sense. That is to say, it takes the reader into an unfamiliar world and affords him or her the vicarious experience of learning something of its language, its customs and its values just as the young central character herself learns them.

Images of Turkish Society and History

One thing the reader learns early on in Özdamar's novel is not to conceive of Turkey as a homogenous world. When the young

narrator-protagonist first goes to school in Istanbul she imme-
diately encounters a kind of internal Turkish racial prejudice,
just as crude and cruel as any Turk might encounter in Western
Europe. All the young children are asked to tell the teacher, a
woman, their names and where they were born. When the
narrator announces that she was born in Malatya in Eastern
Anatolia – Özdamar's own birthplace – the teacher responds
with the words: 'Then you are a Kurd with a tail growing out
of your arse.'[12] The teacher laughs at her own remark; all the
other children join in the laughter; and from then on the poor
girl is universally referred to as 'the Kurdish girl with the tail.'[13]
Later, when her maternal grandfather takes her off to Malatya
for two months during the school holidays, she herself feels that
the Eastern Anatolian town is '... another planet ... much
nearer to the sun than Istanbul.'[14] Özdamar has her encapsu-
late the vast gulf between the rural east and the developed,
Westernised Istanbul in an apt photographic image: 'The
people in Istanbul were the developed photos, the kind you like
to hang on your walls, and the people in Anatolia were the
negatives that you leave somewhere gathering dust and then
forget.'[15] The two months away also open up a linguistic gulf
between the young girl and her own mother. On her return she
is no longer able to speak pure Turkish because, as she puts it,
the Anatolian dialect has got stuck fast under her tongue. Now
she even pronounces the vital word 'mother' itself differently,
and can only be persuaded to revert to standard pronunciation
by means of financial penalties, 100 paras being deducted from
her savings tin whenever she transgresses.

Özdamar also exploits the trip to Eastern Anatolia with the
grandfather as an opportunity to give the young girl, and by
extension the reader, a lesson in Turkish history, albeit of a somewhat eccentric kind. The words 'Grandfather, tell a story' prompt
the old man to pass the long train journey east by spinning a yarn
or weaving a tale for his granddaughter and the soldiers who
share their compartment. The textile imagery is appropriate
because the tale becomes identified with, or objectivised as, the
beard that grows longer and longer on the grandfather's face,
producing a richly woven carpet, or perhaps tapestry: 'Grandfather spoke, and his unshaven beard began to weave a carpet.'[16]
The patterns that emerge are, however, hardly those of a conventional historical narrative. Instead, the reader is presented with
history as part fantasy, part farce; history distorted into a series of

grotesques that, whilst they bear some resemblance to the conventionally accepted facts and events, play fast and loose with chronology as well as with the characters involved. In what appears to be an oblique reference to the Russo-Turkish war of 1877, the tale begins with the Circassian grandfather's expulsion from the Caucasus. German-Turkish military co-operation, the building of the Baghdad railway, the archaeological excavation of the ancient city of Pergamon, and the exploitation of oil fields in the Near East are then all conflated, and seen as the work of one statesman – Bismarck:

> ... then a German flag was fluttering on the carpet next to a Turkish flag. Old Bismarck was building the Baghdad Railway on the carpet, through Turkey to the oil fields, and during the construction Bismarck saw the city of Pergamon ... Bismarck asked the Sultan politely whether he might take a few stones from Pergamon back with him to Germany as a souvenir. The Sultan said: 'There are so many stones in my empire, why not let the infidel have some of them too.' Bismarck trundled all the stones of Pergamon to Berlin, then he returned to the carpet, this time bringing German buckets in which to carry the oil of Baghdad back home.[17]

The grandfather then relates how the French, the Italians, and the British, joining the scramble for oil, also arrive on the scene with their buckets. Soon we find ourselves in the First World War, here dubbed the '*Öleimerkrieg*' or 'war of the oil-buckets', in which the grandfather joins the Turkish forces fighting on the side of Germany. Germany's eventual defeat means that after 1918 the British, French and Italians share the spoils, and Sultan Abdul Hamid II, sitting naked in his palace, daily washes his face in each of their national buckets in turn. The whole burlesque account reads as if Özdamar has chosen to take literally the German metaphor '*im Eimer sein*' – 'to be up the spout' – and that which is well and truly 'up the spout' is the once powerful Ottoman Empire.

The time is now ripe for the anti-imperialist campaign of Mustafa Kemal Pasha, later known as Atatürk. In the weave of the grandfather's narrative, Atatürk's army appears as a mobile forest, gradually advancing until it drives the occupying foreign buckets into the sea, together with the last Sultan. The campaign culminates in the triumphant declaration of the Turkish Republic in 1923, but the grandfather, who has fought with Atatürk, comes to feel betrayed when victory leads on to a secularisation and Westernisation of Turkish society, to government by what he contemptuously calls 'men in black bowler hats.'[18] One of the last images to appear on the carpet of his beard before the train reaches its destination and his narrative ends is that of a turkey. He ends up pursuing this embodiment of his nation, brandishing his sabre.

When the novel first appeared, most German reviewers of *Das Leben ist eine Karawanserei* seized with approval the grandfather's tale, as an example of Özdamar's consummate skill in handling the traditional oriental art of oral narrative. Many, indeed, likened her whole novel to the richly woven 'carpet' produced from the old man's beard. Such a response, whilst understandable, smacks of 'orientalism' in the negative sense as defined by Edward Said.[19] It threatens to stereotype her as an author working within a more primitive oral culture, which is attractive precisely because it is different from Western written culture with its supposedly rationalistic emphases. It is true that the act of oral story-telling figures prominently elsewhere in the novel, both grandmother and mother in particular recounting numerous fairy or folktales, many of them fascinating to the reader, and all of them obviously exerting a strong cultural influence on the young central character. However, the grandfather's fantastical historical survey belongs in a different category. It seems more akin to the quirky, grotesque visions of German history encountered in Günter Grass's novels or those of Indian history in Salman Rushdie's *Midnight's Children*. It shares with them a peculiarly modern blend of myth, fantasy and realism, together with a marked satirical and social critical edge. There is also a certain anarchical quality to such narratives, as if their authors are intent on blowing a great raspberry in the face of all official versions of history and all those who have wielded power in the past.

On two occasions in Özdamar's novel, this happens literally. One is when the grandfather, sitting in the sun, opens his legs to emit a series of farts. Each one is preceded by a dedication: 'This is for Sultan so-and-so; this is for the government official so-and-so; this is for general so-and-so; this is for mayor so-and-so; this is for the landed estate-owner so-and-so.'[20] The other instance occurs when Mehmet Ali Bey, an old supporter of the Republican People's Party, asks his son to bring him his school history textbook and proceeds to fart on its open pages before holding it under the nose of the narrator and other assembled children. This is the prelude to another irreverent oral account of Turkish history that mixes fantasy with strong political criticism.

Abdul Hamid II is caricatured as 'Sultan Nose', so sensitive to the size of this feature of his anatomy that he is said to have forbidden his subjects to utter the Turkish word for it (*burun*) throughout the thirty-two years of his despotic reign. The exploitation of Turkey, the 'sick man on the Bosporus', by Britain, France and Russia is again featured, as is Germany's involvement in the Baghdad Railway, the building of which is now seen to have entailed the devastation of Anatolia's forests, a point Mehmet Ali graphically illustrates by clambering up a pomegranate tree, breaking off some of its branches, and throwing them down at the listening children. The Young Turks fare no better in his account, the so-called freedom and progress they bring being denounced as alien imports that transform the country into one great gambling casino. In addition, the chief exponent of the new freedom, Enver Pasha, is deemed guilty of the most costly gamble of all, taking Turkey into the First World War on the side of Germany because, so Mehmet Ali argues, his vanity and his revulsion for all signs of weakness drove him to emulate the officers of the German High Command. The result was that Turkey, by the end of 1918, had lost four million lives. This stark statistic brings Mehmet Ali's alternative history lesson to a close, and this, above all else, is seen to impress itself on the mind of Özdamar's young narrator, as we shall see later.[21]

Such hard-hitting views of Turkey's past are matched in the novel by, at times, equally critical images of the country in the 1950s and 1960s, the period when Özdamar's narrator, just as she herself did, is growing up. The corruption of the Democratic Party; the abject poverty of the urban slums and shanty towns (the *gecekondus*, literally dwellings 'thrown up overnight'); the economic crisis and food shortages of 1959, leading to the military coup of 1960 with the fall of the Menderes government, and his eventual execution in 1961, are just some of the elements featured in what is anything but a portrait of an ideal world. These developments on the public stage are reflected in the fortunes of the young heroine's family in the private sphere.

Beginning in relative affluence in Istanbul, their story is one of constant house-moving as the father, employed in the building trade, wanders in search of employment, frequently sinking into debt and falling victim to the bailiffs. The fundamental insecurity of their existence – one day reasonably comfortable in Istanbul, the next banished to an inhospitable wasteland on the outskirts of Ankara – takes its toll. The narrator herself contracts tuberculosis in early youth, and both she and her mother later attempt suicide. The stress of life in such a society has, Özdamar makes clear, a great deal to do with the fact that extreme poverty and – by Western standards – backwardness coexist with an affluence largely based on the influx of foreign, especially American capital. The impact of the United States on post-war Turkey is testified to on a number of occasions in the novel. On a relatively trivial and harmless level it is there in the obvious attractions of the Hollywood dream-factory for the generation of the heroine's parents. In the early 1950s her father Mustafa, sporting dark glasses, drives around Istanbul in a flashy Chevrolet. At the same period Fatma, her mother, replaces her long straight hair with a perm and a kiss curl, appearing suddenly 'as if she had lots of thick macaroni on her head.'[22] Both parents regularly slip off to the cinema to see the favourite stars known to them variously as Erol Flayn, Humprey Pockart, Pürt Lankester and Ava Kartener. Whilst they play Frank Sinatra records on their newly acquired gramophone, the young heroine and her brother Ali are avid readers of Tom Mix comics.

A more sinister side to American influence is evident in Özdamar's critical references to the US military presence on Turkish soil, and the fact that as a member of the NATO alliance, Turkey is again sending its youth off to fight and die in foreign wars, such as that in Korea. More than once the view is expressed that the ruling party under Menderes is in fact little more than a stooge for the Americans. As one character, the widow Sidicka puts it: 'The Democratic Party, without asking our mothers' permission, has in one night made a whore of our country, serving her up to America on a plate.'[23] A staunch supporter of the opposition Republican People's Party, who regularly demonstrates her contempt for Menderes by sticking a finger through his photograph in the daily paper and twirling it above her head as she walks through the streets of Bursa, 'Auntie Sidicka', as the narrator calls her, can scarcely be regarded as an unbiased observer, but her views, one suspects, are not that remote from those of her author. At the end of the speech just quoted above, having accused the Democratic Party of burying everyone under a mountain of debts to the United States, she warns her listeners in even more crude and colourful terms of what lies in store for Turkey at the hands of the Western superpower: 'Arses at the ready, folks,' she says. 'America is about to screw the lot of us.'[24]

Images of Women

The political activism of a character like Mrs Sidicka, not to mention the forthright language her views are couched in, clearly runs counter to the stereotyped image often put about in the West of women and their role in Islamic countries. Nor is she alone in this. *Das Leben ist eine Karawanserei* abounds with female figures of strong-minded independence who have carved out lives of their own, often in the face of powerful social and religious pressures to conform. This is especially true of the 'crazy women' (*verrückte Frauen*), eccentrics living on the margins of society, to whom the heroine feels drawn and by whom she is influenced. However, these figures constitute only one element in the richly varied, finely nuanced picture of Turkish womanhood that emerges from the novel. To a large extent this is a reflection of complex realities: on the one hand the liberating influence of Atatürk's reforms, the introduction of a new family code based on that of Switzerland, the outlawing of polygamy, the granting of new rights to women in both the political and the educational sphere; on the other hand the persistence of patriarchal structures combined with the in practice, if not in theory, oppressive nature of many religious customs. All this is further complicated by regional, generational and class differences. However, if such realities in themselves resist easy generalisation, Özdamar's richly differentiated portrayal seems deliberately designed to thwart any lingering tendency on the part of the reader to view Turkish women in stereotypical ways.

Women as the victims of oppressive patriarchal attitudes and behaviour do form part of this portrayal. At its most extreme, this is evident in the actions and views of the protagonist's maternal grandfather Ahmet. Originating from the Caucasus, he is a throwback to an earlier, more violent age, as witnessed by the rusting silver swords, the knives and the whips that the young girl sees hanging on his walls when she visits him in Malatya during the school holidays. Then, too, she hears from his mouth the horrific story of her maternal grandmother's early death at his hands. One of his then several wives, she happened to be absent from home attending her sister's wedding celebrations up in the mountains on precisely the day that his son by another wife died. His response was to ride out for her on his horse, tie her by the hair to its tail, and drag her along home, where she died not long afterwards of tuberculosis. By the 1950s, Ahmet has long since repented of this act and made his peace with the protagonist's mother, daughter of the wife he had so brutally treated. Yet in the eyes of the other side of the family, the father Mustafa and the paternal grandmother from Cappadocia, he remains 'a merciless bandit'.[25]

On a rare visit to the family when they are living outside Ankara, he also serves as spokesman for the older generation's traditional view of gender roles, enjoining his granddaughter not to put her feet down too firmly when walking, lest her 'adornments' (*Schmuck*) should wobble and thus arouse the lust of men; then, to illustrate his point, he holds forth on the prophet Mohammed and what prompted him to prescribe particular dress codes for his wives. This is followed by detailed advice to the girl's two brothers as to how they should handle any disobedience from their future wives, including the extent to which beating is permissable. The whole culminates with the words: 'In one verse of the Koran it is written for the attention of men: "No house should be without a whip. You must hang it on the wall at a spot in your house where all the occupants have a good sight of it."'[26] During the same visit, Grandfather Ahmet also takes it upon himself to demonstrate to his granddaughter the role traditionally assigned to girls in life. As the family eats, he more than once takes the girl's fruit from her and slowly consumes it himself before her eyes before saying: 'A girl's lot is to be patient'.[27]

After this passage, as indeed throughout the novel, Özdamar refrains from direct authorial comment. The only word of criticism comes from Ayse, the grandmother, and that in a whispered aside to the victim, condemning the old Ahmet as 'merciless'. Yet, though the grandfather may be presented as something of an anachronism, his views are suffered in silence, one of a number of indications in the novel of the continuing inferior status of women in Turkish society. Many are clearly still required to live the life of drudges once they marry, however much they may be pampered and protected in youth.

A short verse recited by the grandmother illustrates succinctly the typical course a woman's life can be expected to take: 'When a girl, I was a Sultana, / when engaged, I was but a princess; / when a bride, I was a subject. / Now I'm just a sack at his feet.'[28] Women still go the rounds in search of potential brides for the sons of their family, as we see from a visit by two figures clad in head scarves to the home of the heroine. They first go to the toilet, as the mother later explains, to establish whether the daughter of the house is clean. Then they begin negotiations. In this instance the mother refuses their offer, arguing that her daughter is too young and still attending school, but the grandmother Ayse is of a different mind, saying: 'Why didn't you give the girl to them? They looked like good people. The girl's time has come.'[29] Many girls, when their time has come, also have to be trained to carry out their wifely duties as is illustrated by one Seher, the daughter of a building worker, who is sent to stay with the family for a period before her impending marriage so that she can learn the necessary domestic skills from the narrator's mother. These include making Turkish coffee with exactly the required amount of foam at the top of the cup, and ironing men's trousers with good sharp creases from the belt to the bottom of the legs. The narrator, who is of exactly the same age as Seher, performs the tasks with her, almost fainting with joy at her father's grateful reaction when she hands him his coffee or his freshly ironed trousers. Here patriarchal custom goes hand-in-hand with religious influence, as the father's gratitude is expressed in the form of prayer-like invocations to the effect that the hands of his 'lady-like daughter' may remain ever healthy or never be afflicted with grief, and she says she knows that 'if children get lots of prayers from their parents they are able to go to paradise.'[30]

In matters of sexuality girls, unlike boys, are portrayed as being kept on a very tight rein. Out walking with her father on one occasion, the narrator lingers too long to look at a boy and gets a slap across the face for her sins. The punishment is accepted without question by both her grandmother and her mother. 'Don't cry. Wherever your father strikes you in the face, a rose will bloom', says the one. And the other adds: 'Any man who doesn't slap his daughter ends up slapping himself on the knees.'[31] Later, when the narrator is nearing the age of puberty, she is told by her mother that she is unlikely ever to make a good wife because, rather than being content to sit around at home sewing and cooking, she is always drawn to the world outside. The ensuing dialogue, in which 'little box' is a standard euphemism for the vagina, makes clear the discrepancy between girls and boys in terms of the amount of freedom they are customarily granted: '"You are always taking your little box out for a walk," she said. She said: "A girl has to sit over her little box and work." "And the lads?" I asked. "The lads can promenade their wares."'[32]

However, as can be seen from the mother's reference to her young girl's frequent excursions into the outside world, practice frequently differs from that which custom demands. In fact, the narrator enjoys considerable freedom to roam the streets, especially when the family is living in the city of Bursa, where she goes playing with boys down by the river, often not returning home until after dark. True, she has to put up with the taunts of her father who asks whether she has changed into a boy, and her mother predicts that she 'will grow a willy',[33] but no attempt is made to discipline her. Most interesting of all is the reaction of her grandmother Ayse to this behaviour. Addressing the young girl as 'sister', and remarking that she has introduced quite new habits to the home, she proposes to follow suit by spending her days roaming the city streets in a similarly liberated fashion. These representatives of two very different generations then regularly meet up after dusk, by the fountain at the end of their street, and compare notes on the experiences of the day.

This is just one of a number of instances in the novel where Özdamar presents a culture in which, for all its male dominance, some women are able, through solidarity and close companionship, to establish independent niches in their lives. In doing so, she is implicitly questioning the notion, still prevalent in much feminist thinking, that the only way for Muslim women to improve their status is to abandon their native culture and adopt the ways of the West. It is significant, for instance, that the women who live the loneliest, most soul-destroying lives in the whole novel are those whose lifestyle is most Westernised. These are the bourgeois wives of the bakery owners, sugar manufacturers, proprietors of bus companies and silk-goods shops, who inhabit the stone houses of the street in Bursa where the narrator's family live briefly during a temporary spell of affluence. No smells of cooking emerge from the dwellings were the women remain cooped up all day, their complexions conspicuously pale. Even when their husbands return from work in the evening there is little sign of life in what the narrator dubs this 'soulless street' (*seelenlose Gasse*).

The poorer occupant of the street's one wooden house, the eccentric Mrs Saniye, aptly describes her female neighbours as 'women gone rusty, from their heads down to their little boxes, because they don't work.'[34] Perhaps over-schematically, Özdamar proceeds to contrast their existence with that of the lower-class women of the very next street, which consists wholly of wooden houses, and to which the narrator's family is soon forced to move.

Here doors are left open, and there is a lively sense of community amongst the women who meet in the street or congregate in each other's houses, their conversation a combination of formal, almost ritualistic enquiries as to the wellbeing of every last person connected with their families and gossip of an often earthily humorous nature. Far from having gone rusty, these are what Özdamar approvingly terms 'well-aired women'.[35]

They regularly find ways of escaping from their domestic confines, notably by going to the Turkish baths where they can confide in each other, offering mutual comfort and support, and also indulge in healthy ribaldry at the expense of their menfolk. At other times they 'shake out their worms', as they put it, by attending the matinée performance of their idol, the popular singer Zeki Müren, or spending the afternoon, when their husbands are away at work, watching the handsome young men of the officer-cadet school march through the main street to the accompaniment of a military band. The unabashed sensuality of the young womens' reaction to these parades is reminiscent of the drum-major scene in Georg Büchner's play *Woyzeck*. They stand there twitching in their tightly belted skirts, all 'flesh, material and eyes', and it is rumoured that on one occasion a woman even forgot to put her skirt on in the rush to join the rest of her street's female inhabitants at the parade. 'Auntie' Sidicka stands with the narrator and her mother in the second row, conducting the band and saying: 'The little boxes are flying, tantara, tantara; the little boxes are burning tantara; oh, if only the fire-brigade were near at hand, tantara.'[36]

The narrator's own gradual awakening to her sexuality as she goes through puberty is not without its torments – at times she is near suicidal – but at no stage does Özdamar attribute her problems solely to the specific culture in which she is growing up. If anything, the opposite is the case. She derives considerable benefit from the constant company of other women of different generations, whether they are members of her own extended family or the various 'mad women' she associates with. These relationships constitute just as valuable an education as that she gets in school. Learning may be one route to emancipation, as her grandmother points out with the words: 'Sister, study your books, so that you don't end up having to wash your husband's feet.'[37] However, it could be argued that the lessons she learns from Ayse and her like serve just as much, if not more, to liberate her.

The Omnipresence of Death

One thing the narrator certainly learns during the course of the novel, largely from her grandmother, is familiarity with death. Ayse, who herself has lost three husbands and eight children, instills in her granddaughter the awareness that death is not something alien, remote from everyday existence. 'Death is there between our eyebrows and our eyes. Is that far away?' she says.[38] It is she, as already mentioned, who first teaches the girl the Arabic prayers for the dead which, after her own recovery from tuberculosis, she takes to reciting nightly before going to sleep. Initially, she prays for a relatively small number of people from her close family circle or acquaintances, such as her maternal grandmother, or an old Armenian woman who had died in the same block of flats in Istanbul. Gradually, however, she adds to the list almost every deceased person she hears of, from famous figures such as Atatürk himself, or the dancer Isadora Duncan, to a pair of anonymous lovers who have thrown themselves to their death from the sacred mount in Bursa. Eventually she even includes the four million Turkish dead from the First World War, managing, on one occasion, to count up to the hundred and twenty-third before falling asleep. Özdamar makes her readers work at these litanies that sometimes extend for more than three pages, but by dint of repetition many of the figures mentioned remain in the memory, which is of course the point of the exercise. In addition, since the dead eventually far outnumber the cast of the 'living' in the novel, the lists also serve to underline a fundamental truth made explicit in her earlier story *Großvaterzunge* when the narrator says: 'This world is a world of dead people, if you compare the number of dead with the living.'[39]

The characters of *Das Leben ist eine Karawanserei* are shown to be highly conscious of this fact, particularly the women for whom cemeteries are frequent places of visit and communion with those who have passed on. Visiting Atatürk's mausoleum in Ankara, the narrator is struck by the unnaturalness of what she calls a 'garden of stone', for here death is walled off from life, made cold and remote:

… people walked around in the garden of stone. They were not like people in a cemetery. There people look at the other people who are walking among the graves or are sitting thinking how old the deceased were when they died, wondering whether they were younger or older than themselves. Everybody sees everybody else, and the shadows of the cemetery trees link the living to the dead.[40]

If Atatürk's mausoleum seems alien to a cultural tradition that honours death by assigning it a central position in life, so too do the effects of the Westernising policies he initiated. Women still go with candles to the graves of holy men in central Istanbul, but the gravestones now sit uneasily alongside a noisy and dusty modern road with its heavy traffic of cars and trams: 'The road covered with its dust the gravestones of the holy men, to which women came with candles in their misshapen hands. The gravestones standing on the edge of the road stared onto this now too noisy thoroughfare that had robbed them of their deadness.'[41]

A passage such as this prompts the thought that modernisation might lead to a marginalisation of death to the point where, as in many Western societies, it becomes something of an embarrassment, something to be hidden away. Perhaps conscious of this threat, Özdamar strongly emphasises the traditional cultural values of remembrance and of reverence for death in life. Here the old Circassian grandfather, Ahmet, serves as a positive spokesman in a long speech quoting the ancient poet Camud, which begins with the injunction: 'Do not forget death.'[42] Both his and the grandmother's influence are seen to live on in the long nightly prayers for the dead offered up by the young narrator, and the conspicuous effort she puts into mourning might well serve as an object lesson to Western readers, not least those Germans of the post-war era who have been criticised precisely for their '*Unfähigkeit zu trauern*' (inability to grieve).[43]

Conclusion

To read *Das Leben ist eine Karawanserei* largely with an eye to what the Western, and more specifically the German, reader can glean from the novel in terms of Turkish language, history, society and culture is of course to do less than justice to the novel as a work of creative imagination. Some insights into the work's stylistic variety and technical accomplishment will, it is hoped, have been afforded by the many examples quoted above. However, much more could have been said about Özdamar's literary strengths, such as the sheer verve of her story-telling, the descriptive power of her similes and metaphors, her amusing association of characters with specific leitmotifs, and above all her ability to evoke in words the sights, sounds and smells of the Turkey of her youth. Such powers of graphic representation are, to judge from a passage in *Mutterzunge*, probably more important to her as 'collector of words' than any ideas or messages. There, in what amounts to a rudimentary poetics, she draws on two expressions from her mother tongue in an attempt to distinguish superficial story-telling from narration that has real depth. Essential for the latter, she says, are firstly *Görmek*, the act of seeing, and secondly *Kaza gecirmek*, literally 'experiencing the accidents of life'. *Görmek* and *Kaza gecirmek*.[44] Both are richly in evidence in her novel *Das Leben ist eine Karawanserei*.

Notes

1. '"Was machen Sie in Deutschland?" … "Ich bin Wörtersammlerin."' *Großvater Zunge* is the second of four pieces in E.S. Özdamar, *Mutterzunge*, first published in 1990 by the Rotbuch Verlag, Berlin. This quotation is taken from the first paperback edition, Rotbuch Taschenbuch no.86, Berlin, 1993, p.46. All subsequent references are to this edition.

2. 'Zunge hat keine Knochen, wohin man sie dreht, dreht sie sich dorthin.' Özdamar *Mutterzunge*, p.7.

3. E.S. Özdamar, *Das Leben ist eine Karawanserei, hat zwei Türen, aus einer kam ich rein, aus der anderen ging ich raus*, first published in 1992 by Kiepenheuer & Witsch, Cologne. All subsequent page references are to the paperback edition, KiWi 334, Cologne, 1994.

4. See the interview in Chapter 3 for a statement by Özdamar herself to this effect.

5. 'In der Fremdsprache haben Wörter keine Kindheit.' *Mutterzunge*, p.42.

6. 'Es kamen aus meinem Mund die Buchstaben heraus. Manche sahen aus wie ein Vogel, manche wie ein Herz, auf dem ein Pfeil steckt, manche wie eine Karawane, manche wie schlafende Kamele, manche wie ein Fluß, manche wie im Wind auseinander fliegende Bäume, manche wie laufende Schlangen … manche wie böse geschreckte Augenbrauen … manche wie ein in einem türkischen Bad auf einem heißen Stein sitzender dicker Frauenarsch …' *Mutterzunge*, p.16.

7. *Karawanserei*, p.18.

8. '… die Bilderwörter, die meine Großmutter auf dem Friedhof zu den Toten gesagt hatte. Ein Buchstabe stand auf dem Blatt, wie die sehr schönen Augen einer Frau.' Ibid., p.29.

9. '... ihre Kamele, die größer waren als meine, nahmen meine vor ihre Beine und brachten meinen Kamelen das Laufen bei.' Ibid., p.55.

10. Ibid., p.17, then again p.57.

11. '"Wenn du nicht sprichst, beiße ich, tamam mi?" sagte Mutter. Er sagte nichts. Sie biß das Hüftfleisch meines Bruders. Er sagte weiter nichts. Die Großmutter kam und sagte: "Fatma, tamam, tamam, tamam." Wie durch ein Zauberwort ließ Mutter das Fleisch meines Bruders los.' Ibid., p.209.

12. 'Dann bist du Kurdin, du hast einen Schwanz am Arsch.' Ibid., p.37.

13. 'Kurdin mit Schwanz', Ibid., p.37.

14. '... ein anderer Planet ... viel näher an der Sonne als Istanbul.' Ibid., p.48.

15. 'Die Menschen in Istanbul waren die entwickelten Photos, die man gerne an die Wände hängt, und die Menschen in Anatolien waren die Negative, die man irgendwo im Staub liegen läßt und vergißt.' Ibid., p.48.

16. 'Großvater sprach, und sein unrasierter Bart fing an, einen Teppich zu weben.' Ibid., p.38.

17. '... dann flatterte auf dem Teppich eine deutsche Fahne neben einer türkischen Fahne. Auf dem Teppich baute der Bismarck die Bagdadbahn bis zu den Ölfeldern durch die Türkei, und beim Durchbauen sah Bismarck die Stadt Pergamon ... Bismarck fragte den Sultan höflich, ob er aus der Stadt Pergamon ein paar Steine als Andenken mit nach Deutschland nehmen dürfte. Der Sultan sagte: "In meinem Reich gibt es so viele Steine, der Ketzer soll auch was davon haben." Bismarck schleppte alle Steine aus Pergamon nach Berlin, dann kam Bismarck wieder zum Teppich und brachte deutsche Eimer, mit denen er das Öl von Bagdad mit nach Hause schleppen wollte.' Ibid., p.39. The 'stones' from Pergamon are of course the famous altar, the centrepiece of the museum of that name in Berlin.

18. 'Männer in schwarzen Melonenhüten', Ibid., p.42.

19. See Edward Said, *Orientalism*, London, Routledge & Kegan Paul, 1978.

20. 'Das ist für Sultan soundso, das ist für den regierenden Beamten soundso, das ist für den General soundso, das ist für den Bürgermeister soundso, das ist für den Großgrundbesitzer soundso.' *Karawanserei*, p.50.

21. See *Karawanserei*, pp.193–198 for the full text of Mehmet Ali's 'history lesson'.

22. '... als ob sie viele dicke Makkaronis auf dem Kopf trug.' Ibid., p.27.

23. 'Die Demokratische Partei hat das Land, ohne unsere Mütter zu fragen, Amerika in einer Nacht als Nutte serviert, auf dem Tablett.' Ibid., p.171.

24. 'Kinder, eure Ärsche bereithalten, es wird alles von Amerika gefickt.' Ibid., p.171.

25. '… ein unbarmherziger Bandit'. Ibid., p.307.

26. 'In einem Koranvers ist für die Männer geschrieben: "Die Peitsche darfst du nicht in einem Haus fehlen lassen. Du mußt sie in deinem Haus an eine Stelle an die Wand hängen, die alle Hausbewohner gut sehen können."' Ibid., p.310–311.

27. 'Mädchen sein, heißt Geduld haben.' Ibid., p.311.

28. 'Ich war Mädchen, war ich Sultanin, / ich war verlobt, wurde ich nur hanin (Prinzessin) / ich war Braut, wurde ich Untertanin. / Geworden bin ich ein Sack, vor den Füßen.' Ibid., p.121.

29. 'Warum hast du das Mädchen nicht gegeben. Sie haben wie gute Menschen ausgesehen. Die Zeit des Mädchens ist gekommen.' Ibid., p.272.

30. '… wenn Kinder sehr viele Gebete von ihren Eltern kriegten, konnten sie ins Paradies gehen.' Ibid., p.224.

31. 'Weine nicht, dort auf dem Gesicht, wohin der Vater schlägt, wird eine Rose blühen.' – 'Wer seine Tochter nicht schlägt, schlägt später seine eigenen Knie.' Ibid., p.82.

32. '"Du führst immer deine Schachtel spazieren", sagte sie. Sie sagte: "Ein Mädchen muß über ihrer Schachtel sitzen und arbeiten." "Und die Jungs?" fragte ich. "Die Jungs können ihre Waren spazieren führen."' Ibid., p.220.

33. 'Bei dir wird ein Pipi wachsen.' Ibid., p.147.

34. '… von Kopf bis zur Schachtel verrostete Frauen, weil sie nicht arbeiten.' Ibid., p.123.

35. '… gelüftete Frauen', Ibid., p.169.

36. '… die Schachteln fliegen tätärä tätärä, die Schachteln brennen tätärä, ach, wenn nur eine Feuerwehr in der Nähe wäre, tätärä.' Ibid., p.175.

37. 'Schwester, lerne deine Bücher, damit du nicht die Füße des Mannes waschen mußt.' Ibid., p.213.

38. 'Der Tod ist zwischen Augenbrauen und Augen, ist das weit weg?' Ibid., p.18.

39. 'Die Welt ist Welt von Toten, wenn man die Zahl von Toten mit den Lebenden vergleicht.' *Mutterzunge*, p.14.

40. '… die Menschen liefen in dem Garten aus Stein herum. Sie waren nicht wie die Menschen auf einem Friedhof. Dort schauen die Menschen auf die anderen Menschen, die zwischen den Gräbern gehen oder auf der Erde sitzen und sich überlegen, wie alt waren die Toten, als sie starben, waren sie jünger als sie selbst, waren sie älter als sie selbst. Jeder sieht jeden, und die Schatten von den Friedhofsbäumen verbinden die Lebenden mit den Toten.' *Karawanserei*, p.316.

41. 'Die Straße verstaubte die Grabsteine der heiligen Männer, zu denen die Frauen mit ihren buckligen Händen Kerzen brachten. Die am Rande der Straße stehenden Grabsteine guckten auf diese zu laut gewordene Straße, die ihnen das Totsein geraubt hatte.' Ibid., p.29.

42. 'Vergeßt den Tod nicht.' Ibid., p.308.

43. The reference is to the influential study of that title by Alexander and Margarete Mitscherlich, *Die Unfähigkeit zu trauern. Grundlagen kollektiven Verhaltens*, Munich, Piper, 1967.

44. For the passage in full, see *Mutterzunge*, pp.9–10.

CHAPTER 3

Living and Writing in Germany

Emine Sevgi Özdamar in Conversation with David Horrocks and Eva Kolinsky

Biographical Sketch

Born in Malatya, eastern Anatolia in 1946, Emine Sevgi Özdamar first went to Germany in 1965 at the age of nineteen. As part of the initial wave of so-called *Gastarbeiter* she stayed in Berlin for two years, living together with other Turkish women in a hostel and working in a factory. During this period she was first introduced to the plays of Brecht by the warden of her hostel, a Marxist who was involved with the work of the Berliner Ensemble. She also became politicised, taking part in many of the demonstrations that followed the killing of the student Benno Ohnesorg in June 1967 in Berlin.

Returning to Turkey later that year, Özdamar spent three years at drama school in Istanbul. As a twelve-year-old schoolgirl she had already acted in a production of Molière's *Le Bourgeois Gentilhomme* at the state theatre in Bursa and now, after completing her training as an actress, she took on her first professional roles, playing Charlotte Corday in Peter Weiss's *Marat-Sade* and widow Begbig in Brecht's *Mann ist Mann*. Still active in politics, she was briefly arrested and detained because of reports she had written after the military putsch of 1971.

Her career in Turkey at a standstill, Özdamar returned to Germany in 1976, this time to East Berlin, where she fulfilled a long cherished dream of working with a pupil of Brecht, the director Benno Besson, at the Volksbühne. After two years there as assistant director and actress, she moved to France for a spell, working with Besson in Paris and Avignon on a production of Brecht's *Kaukasischer Kreidekreis*. From 1979 to 1984 she had a long engagement at the Schauspielhaus in Bochum, under the general management of Claus Peymann, again working as both assistant director and actress.

It was now that she began to write. Her first play, *Karagöz in Alamania*, commissioned by Bochum, was completed in 1982, but did not reach the stage until 1986 when it was performed at the Schauspielhaus in Frankfurt with Özdamar herself directing. Since then she has published a collection of short prose pieces entitled *Mutterzunge* (1990) and the much-acclaimed novel *Das Leben ist eine Karawanserei* (1992), an excerpt from which won her the Ingeborg Bachmann prize at the annual literary competition in Klagenfurt, Austria in 1991. A second play, *Keloglan in Alamania*, published in 1991, has yet to be performed. Alongside her writing, Özdamar has continued to work as an actress, playing roles in Munich, Berlin and Frankfurt, as well as appearing in several films, amongst others *Yasemin*, directed by Hark Bohm and *Happy Birthday, Türke*, directed by Dorris Dörrie.

Now living in Düsseldorf, Emine Sevgi Özdamar was the guest of the German Section of the Modern Languages Department of Keele University in October 1994, when she gave readings to students, participated in a symposium on minorities in Germany organised by the Centre for the Study of German Culture and Society, and gave the following interview:

D.H.: Can you explain to us how it was that you came to write in German?

E.S.Ö.: It was during my time at the Schauspielhaus in Bochum when I was working for Claus Peymann. A Turkish friend of mine, a student, had given me a letter left in his possession by a former *Gastarbeiter* who had left Germany and returned to Turkey for good. It was in Turkish, eight pages long, densely type-written with scarcely a blank space. Why would a worker bother to use a typewriter, I wondered. I sensed that he had something he wanted to say to his people, to us Turks, and that he had typed the message so as to be taken seriously. At first I couldn't understand all his Turkish. The letter was full of facts such as when he had left his village in Turkey, when and where he had been in Germany, and so on. What I particularly liked about it was the fact that he at no point had anything bad to say about Germany. 'A worker has no home,' he said. 'Wherever there is work, that's his home.' I liked that very much. It was obvious, however, that he'd had problems with his wife. Unable to stand living in either Turkey or Germany, she had constantly commuted between the two countries, each time pregnant. Once, whilst in Germany, she told her husband that back in her home village she and her uncle had eaten some cherries together from the same tree. This incident so preyed on his mind that, leaving her behind in Germany, he set off on the three thousand kilometre journey home.

D.H.: Determined, like Karagöz in your play, to establish the truth, to find out who had first been standing under the tree?

E.S.Ö.: Exactly. This very erotic incident was just the germ of the worker's story, which then grew and grew. He couldn't express himself all that well, but he maintained that his life was like a novel. And I think he was right. His letter preoccupied me for some two years before I decided I would like to write a play on the subject. Eventually it was commissioned by the theatre in Bochum.

D.H.: Was that the sole reason why you wrote it in German? The fact that it was a commission?

E.S.Ö.: No. I was also attracted to German as a new language. You see, at that time, I often travelled back to Turkey by train, finding myself together with Greeks, Yugoslavs, Turks and Bulgarians, all migrant workers. Their common language was German. They would sing love songs and then try to translate them from their own language into German. They made mistakes, of course, but the German they spoke was devoid of clichés, and came out almost like poetry as they struggled to express the images of their mother tongues in this new language. And this, as I now realised, was the language of some five million *Gastarbeiter*. If I wanted to write a play about their experience, and I did, I knew it would have to be written in this new language.

My own language is of course Turkish, but it is no longer the language of my day-to-day experiences. In that sense, German is much more alive for me – whether it be a train conductor or a baker talking. It's also a physical thing. You must remember that my first encounter with German was via the theatre. I experienced the language as it were bodily, either by speaking lines myself or hearing them from the bodies of fellow actors. You could almost say that words themselves have bodies, and when they are spoken on stage they are especially beautiful. You are not afraid to rehearse and speak them there. And I suppose I have a gift for imitating others. In Turkey I used to ape my grandmother, and because I loved her very much, I could capture her tones of voice exactly. Of course, it is a very different matter when it comes to actually writing in a new language. There, I think being involved in plays by writers such as Kleist, Büchner and Brecht acted as stimulus. I used to be ashamed of myself, thinking I would live to the age of ninety without writing a word, whereas Büchner was only twenty-three when he died. I'm certain that these dramatists did a lot to lure my words out in the open.

D.H.: What you just said about German now being more alive for you interests me, because reading your short prose piece *Mutterzunge* I was struck by the fact that the first-person narrator, a Turkish woman living in Germany whom rightly or wrongly I associated with you, is more concerned with Turkish than German, desperately trying to recall a mother-tongue that she is conscious of losing in the foreign environment. Is this the case with you? Is it true that you were at first unable to understand much of the Turkish in the letter of the *Gastarbeiter*?

E.S.Ö.: Yes, but that was mainly because of the personal drama he was relating. Had he met me in person and told me his story, his eyes and body would have spoken to me too. But the grief of this Turkish peasant-cum-*Gastarbeiter* was stronger than the language available to him when he tried to write the 'novel' of his life. That was the problem. And when I wanted to show him that it really had become a novel – by inviting him to the première of *Karagöz* in Frankfurt, it was too late. He had died, aged forty-one, back in his home village, sitting in front of the shop he had set up with the money he had earned in Germany. Incidentally, he wasn't alone in calling his life a novel. My own father did so too. Most people's lives are.

D.H.: Did your father take an interest in your life, in your career when you left for Germany?

E.S.Ö.: Not really. My father never concerned himself with my career. With my health and well-being, yes. If we spoke on the phone he would always ask: 'Are you well?', not what I was doing. In Germany, it's quite different. It has to do with the much faster pace of life. In Germany people tend rather to ask: 'And what are you planning to do next?'

E.K.: How much of that slower pace of life, of elements of Turkish culture in general, has survived amongst Turks in Germany? In an area like Kreuzberg in Berlin, for example? Aren't Turkish customs and traditions beginning to disappear as those of the host country are adopted?

E.S.Ö.: As far as the first generation is concerned, I would say a great deal of the traditional culture still survives. Amongst younger people it's a different story. Of course they are losing touch, to some extent, with the traditions of their parents, but it doesn't matter so much, because they are also introducing new 'Turkish' elements of their own. You never know how these things will work out. It's not unknown, for instance, for children of Italian origin to develop into Mafia types of the 1930s. It also depends on individual circumstances and tastes. I myself, for instance, have largely adopted a German lifestyle, but that doesn't mean that I have cut myself off entirely from my cultural roots. Other factors can play a significant role in this. Love, for example, can bring different generations, say fathers and daughters, together again after years of estrangement.

E.K.: Amongst ethnic minorities in Britain, generational conflicts often arise because religious views remain dominant. This can cause great problems, especially for girls of the second generation.

E.S.Ö.: Of course. The revolution taking place in the role of women is bound to affect their situation. It is the same for Turkish girls in Germany. The wearing of head scarves is a case in point. They may have been largely discarded in Turkey as a result of Atatürk's reforms, but Turkish girls in Germany can now often be seen wearing them. In doing so they are primarily demonstrating a feminist attitude.

D.H.: I'd like to return briefly to the question of language, if I may. I understand now why you felt you had to write your play *Karagöz* in German. But your novel *Das Leben ist eine Karawanserei* is surely a different matter. There you are not trying to capture the language of *Gastarbeiter*. On the contrary, you seem to me to write a beautifully fluent, rhythmic kind of German prose.

E.S.Ö.: That may be true, but I was also very keen, on a secondary level, to retain some 'mistakes' in the book's language. Readers must be able to experience for themselves the process the writer has gone through linguistically. They have to be made to stumble, as it were.

D.H.: Did you write your novel directly in German, or were parts conceived in Turkish and then translated?

E.S.Ö.: Directly in German, I think. Yes, with one exception. The passage in verse about the visit to the shop to buy paraffin.[1] I had already written that earlier in Turkish. But I never remember consciously asking myself: 'Shall I write in German or in Turkish?'

I live with language, in reality with both languages. Sometimes, of course, Turkish images, metaphors or sayings get directly transposed into German, such as: 'He who sleeps with the blind will wake up squinting.' But my hand-written notes for the novel were all in German, about the plot sequence, the structure of the various ideas and motifs.

D.H.: If I can return to your play for a moment: by representing Turkish *Gastarbeiter* in the way you do on stage, don't you at times run the risk of re-enforcing the prejudices of some Germans in the audience? I am not thinking so much of the 'pidgin' German you have them speak, rather the jokes and anecdotes, such as the story of Turkish workers making the long journey home along the Yugoslav motorways and wedging a brick on the accelerator, or driving backwards.

E.S.Ö.: But that kind of thing happens! It is reality.

D.H.: I can well believe it, but isn't there nevertheless a certain risk involved in portraying it?

E.S.Ö.: It all depends how you read it, or how the audience perceives it.

E.K.: I'd be interested to know whether you are concerned to give your readers insights into specifically Turkish social structures? And are you also conscious of writing against prejudices of a terrible kind? Do you see your works, in this sense, as blazing a trail?

E.S.Ö.: I can't say that I have ever conceived of my writing in quite that way. Initially, I wrote my novel for myself. I had no idea what would become of it. I had no firm plans. It was more like a search for identity, but in a foreign country it is different from the process you undergo in your homeland. When you are in a strange land it is almost like an archaeological dig. You delve and you delve, right back to your origins in your mother's belly. My childhood in Turkey had already become a kind of fairy-tale for me. And diaries didn't help me in my search. My diaries ran to twenty-five volumes, but from all that material I used exactly one sentence in my novel. And, as I said earlier, there is a quite different pace to life in Germany. True, the pace of life is quick in Istanbul too, but if I go into a shop in Istanbul, before addressing the shopkeeper I say to myself: 'Hold on a minute, adjust yourself to his rhythm, pay attention to his body movements, otherwise there will be misunderstandings.' Similarly, in my novel, I wanted to slow down the pace I was living at in Germany, to re-capture the rhythm of my childhood which is a pre-industrial rhythm. I also wanted to re-awaken the memory of people I'd been in love with. You can bring people back to life by writing, and that was one of the things that gave me most pleasure.

E.K.: But introducing German readers to a whole new dimension of experience, a new rhythm of life as you put it, could have the effect of breaking down prejudices, couldn't it?

E.S.Ö.: I wanted primarily to waken feelings, to open up valves. That was my dream. After one of my readings a Turkish girl asked me: 'Was that really your life?' My reply was 'If I say yes, you don't have to believe me.' But she did. 'That was my life too, my street you were writing about,' she said. That pleased me no end. One German reader also told me it was like reading about Germany eighty years ago.

D.H.: Yet you have also consistently denied that your novel is closely autobiographical. Doesn't novel writing also involve 'telling tales' in the other sense, i.e., untruths? I am thinking of the incident in your book when the heroine makes up all kinds of false answers in reply to her grandmother's questions about what she is reading, and the grandmother calls her *orospu*, meaning literally someone who whores with her tongue.

E.S.Ö.: Yes, of course. As an author, you always indulge in a certain amount of cheating, but the feelings at least are true. And for them you need strongly dramatic enactment. You have to make your characters speak in such a way that their feelings become visible to the reader. Feelings don't lie. If a man, for instance, spends his life surrounded by women, you can see it in the way he speaks. Recently, I told a man: 'You've got a woman in your body.' Such instincts are important for a writer.

E.K.: I'd like, if I may, to switch now from your writing to questions of a more political nature. I'm interested in your reaction to the recent wave of xenophobia in Germany, culminating in the tragic events of Mölln and Solingen. How significant is this in your view? Is it true that a sizeable reservoir of intolerance persists under the apparently tolerant surface of German society?

E.S.Ö.: I don't know. Events can change things dramatically. Just think of the impact the taking down of the Berlin Wall had on relations between Germans in East and West. Or even on the behaviour of West Germans to one another. Suddenly even they began to talk to each other, in the train for instance! It was as if all at once they found themselves on an open stage and began talking. A play was to be performed and everyone wanted a part in it, but no-one knew what kind of play.

But, to return to your question, I'm not sure xenophobia is the right word. All sorts of people can be the targets of aggression in society, even thirteen-year-old children.

E.K.: Perhaps a better term would be 'willingness to use violence'?

E.S.Ö.: Yes. I find myself constantly wanting to say to people: 'Watch out, otherwise you too could be on the receiving end. You too could be a target of violence.' What I do find bad is the role of the media in these matters. They have painted a picture of Germany as a country where everywhere the SS is on the march again. And another thing: they have fostered an atmosphere in which any German, on seeing a foreigner, feels obliged to make a special effort to demonstrate that he or she is *not* xenophobic. Things were different before. Germans and non-Germans lived together as a matter of course. Now it's as if every German has been assigned the role of a doorman whose task it is to decide whether this or that non-German should be granted admission or not. They have to work at it. When confronted with such a situation myself, I have recently taken to staring into space, thus sparing people the effort.

E.K.: Is it really true that people accepted one another as a matter of course before?

E.S.Ö.: Yes. That is how I experienced it earlier, especially in big cities.

E.K.: I wonder whether guilty feelings aren't also involved to some extent. Take for instance the case of Germans and Jews. Since the Holocaust, Germans have been forced to live with guilt as an integral part of their existence. This makes them feel obliged to be especially friendly towards Jews. They are thus reluctant, even today, to face up to the reality of anti-Semitism in their midst. Isn't there a similar tendency to ignore xenophobia?

E.S.Ö.: Every country has its fascists. Turkey, the land of my birth, has more than Germany. And of course such people are interested in power. The state tends to use them for its own ends, rather than taking steps to positively remedy the situation. Why, for instance, are non-Germans not employed in television, as announcers and the like? Measures like that can have a positive effect on people's perceptions.

E.K.: Exactly. Many foreigners have been resident in Germany for forty years now, and still they haven't really gained acceptance.

E.S.Ö: It is true that the older colonial powers have managed the business of immigration much more successfully. The Germans came by their colonies relatively late in the day, and they have ended up creating new colonies on their home territory.

E.K.: Even in intellectual circles, of all things, non-Germans have not found acceptance. Why should this be?

E.S.Ö.: Germany has the most arrogant middle class in Europe, probably because the country, unlike France and others, never experienced a bourgeois revolution. The French, when they get up in the morning, sense that they are the fathers of *égalité*. In Germany, it's different. Karl Marx once said that in Germany every revolution was a counter-revolution. What happened in the East in 1989 has been described as a peaceful revolution, but most Germans don't see it that way. Since unification they seem to have been preoccupied with questions of identity.

E.K.: Were you conscious of differences in identity between East and West Germans before the wall came down?

E.S.Ö.: Yes. The wall that divided Germans wasn't one of stone, but of time. Whenever I crossed it during my spell at the theatre, although it was a journey of only two stops on the S-Bahn, I would say to myself 'How amazing, it's been snowing here too' or 'It's been raining here too.' I know of a woman from the former GDR who, going to West Berlin by bus for the first time after the Wall came down, was similarly surprised to see the sun shining beautifully there. This was because it was like moving between different time-zones. In many ways, time had stood still for Germans in the East. There too, the whole pace of life was slower; people moved differently. I feel something similar here in England. We used to sit and talk in East Berlin just as we are sitting here now. Often I found life in the West very tiring, and then I would cross over to the East, visit friends and recover for a while.

D.H.: To judge from what you say in your novel about the differences between life in eastern Anatolia and in Istanbul, moving between different 'time-zones' in that sense must have been nothing new to you.

E.S.Ö: True. There I talk of two different planets. I have often experienced such leaps in time in my life: between Malatya and Istanbul, between Turkey and Germany, between East and West Berlin. The experience can be rewarding. Once, when reading Jean-Luc Godard, I came across a sentence that I really like. In order to be creative, he said, you needed to leave your native country, indeed to betray it, and then you could be in two places simultaneously. That's how it really is, in my experience, when you are living in a foreign country. Whether you want to or not, you find yourself in two places at once. On the one hand you have the experience of your everyday existence in the new land, which is long and drawn out but has gaps in it; on the other hand you have sudden memories of the land you came from. But the whole thing runs like a simultaneous film in which images and yearnings merge without any gaps. When the two come together in this way, it makes for a beautiful encounter.

Notes

1. See E.S. Özdamar, *Das Leben ist eine Karawanserei*, Cologne, Kiepenheuer & Witsch, KiWi 334, 1994, p.134f.

CHAPTER 4

Emine Sevgi Özdamar
'Black Eye and his Donkey'
A Multi-Cultural Experience

Introduction and Commentary
by David Horrocks and Frank Krause

In 1992 the Hamburg weekly *Die Zeit* invited Emine Sevgi Özdamar to comment on the state of relations between Germans and non-Germans living together in the Federal Republic. 'I'll write something,' she replied, 'but something totally different from what you expect.' The following, re-printed with the author's permission, is the text of the article she submitted, together with an English translation:

Schwarzauge und sein Esel

Black Eye and his Donkey

Mein erstes Theaterstück war *Karagöz in Alamania*, 1982. Das bedeutet in Deutsch: 'Schwarzauge in Deutschland'. Ich habe es geschrieben, weil ich den Brief eines türkischen Gastarbeiters gefunden hatte. Ich hatte diesen Gastarbeiter nicht gekannt. Er war für immer in die Türkei, in sein Dorf, zurückgekehrt.

Das Wort 'Gastarbeiter': Ich

My first play was *Karagöz in Alamania*, written in 1982. In German it means 'Black Eye in Germany.' I wrote it because I had discovered the letter of a Turkish *Gastarbeiter*. I never knew the man personally. He had gone back to Turkey for good, to his home village.

'*Gastarbeiter*' is a word I love. When I encounter it I always

liebe dieses Wort, ich sehe vor mir immer zwei Personen, eine sitzt da als Gast, und die andere arbeitet.

Sein Brief war mit einer Schreibmaschine geschrieben. Das zweite, was mir auffiel, war, daß er an keiner Stelle schlecht über Deutschland sprach. Er sagte: 'Ein Arbeiter hat keine Heimat, wo die Arbeit ist, da ist die Heimat.' Er schrieb über seine Frau, die es weder in der Türkei noch in Deutschland aushalten konnte. Sie ging immer hin und her, und jedesmal war sie schwanger.

Die Frau hatte ihm in Deutschland einmal erzählt, daß sie mit seinem Onkel im Dorf in der Türkei vom gleichen Baum Kirschen gegessen hatte. Er war in die Türkei gefahren, 3 000 Kilometer weit, ließ seine Frau in Deutschland allein, nur, um seine Verwandten zu fragen, wer zuerst unter dem Kirschbaum gestanden hatte. Seine Frau oder sein Onkel? Wer war zum Baum gelaufen, und wer ist zu dem, der da Kirschen aß, gelaufen?

Er fragte im Dorf die Verwandten und Nachbarn. Die Sache wucherte und wucherte.

In Deutschland wurde er von türkischen maoistischen Studenten politisiert. Er verteilte mit ihnen zusammen vor einer Fabrik Flugblätter gegen die türkischen Faschisten. Die Faschisten kamen, die maoisti-

picture two people: one is just sitting there as a guest, and the other is working.

The letter was written on a typewriter. The other thing that struck me about it was that at no point did he say anything bad about Germany. He said: 'A worker has no home. Wherever there is work is home for him.' He wrote about his wife who could not stand the life either in Turkey or in Germany. She was always moving from the one country to the other, and on every occasion she was pregnant.

Once, whilst in Germany, his wife had told him that back home in their village in Turkey, she and his uncle had eaten cherries together from the same tree. Leaving his wife on her own in Germany, he had made the 3,000 kilometre journey to Turkey, merely in order to ask his relatives which of the two had first been standing under the cherry tree. Was it his wife or his uncle? Who had first gone to the tree, and who was it that had gone to join the other already eating cherries?

He questioned relatives and neighbours in the village. The whole affair grew out of all proportion.

Whilst in Germany he was politicised by Turkish students who were Maoists. Once he was with them outside a factory, handing out leaflets against the

schen Studenten verschwanden, ließen ihn allein. Die türkischen Faschisten schlugen ihn ins Gesicht, sein halbes Gesicht war gelähmt. Ich konnte in seinem Brief seine türkische Sprache nicht gut verstehen.

Ich wollte über ihn ein Drama schreiben und ihn nach Deutschland zur Premiere einladen. Ich wollte ihm zeigen, daß sein Leben ein Roman war – so wie er es auch in seinem Brief behauptet hatte. Deswegen fuhr ich mit dem Zug von Deutschland in die Türkei.

In Österreich stiegen auch Jugoslawen in den Zug. Bauarbeiter. Manche hatten ihre Finger absichtlich mit dem Hammer kaputtgeschlagen, um krankgeschrieben zu werden, und fuhren mit bandagierten Händen zu ihren Frauen nach Jugoslawien.

Es saßen Griechen, Türken und Jugoslawen zusammen im gleichen Zug, ihre gemeinsame Sprache war Deutsch. In Jugoslawien stiegen auch ein paar türkische Väter in den Zug, alte Männer. Sie waren mit leeren Särgen aus der Türkei nach Jugoslawien gekommen, um ihre toten Söhne und Töchter, die mit ihren Autos auf der Fahrt von Deutschland auf der Straße in Jugoslawien bei Autounfällen gestorben waren, in die Türkei zu holen. Die Väter rauchten Zigaretten, standen auf dem Zugkorridor

Turkish fascists. When the fascists arrived on the scene the Maoist students disappeared, and he was left standing there alone. The Turkish fascists punched him in the face, leaving one side of it paralysed.

I could not understand the Turkish he wrote in his letter very well.

I wanted to write a play about him and then invite him back to Germany for the première. I wanted to show him that his life was a novel, just as he himself had claimed that it was in his letter. So I made the journey from Germany to Turkey by train.

In Austria some Yugoslavs joined the train. Construction workers. Some of them had deliberately smashed their fingers with hammers to get a sick-note from the doctor and were now on their way home to their wives in Yugoslavia, their hands wrapped in bandages.

Greeks, Turks and Yugoslavs were sitting together in the same train, their common language German. In Yugoslavia, a few Turkish fathers, old men, also got on the train. They had journeyed there from Turkey with empty coffins in order to take back home the bodies of their sons and daughters, killed in accidents on the roads of Yugoslavia as they made their way back by car from Germany. Standing in the corridor, the fathers smoked cigarettes and

und sprachen leise über den Weg und über ihre toten Kinder. Einer sagte: 'Dieser Weg hat uns unsere fünf Seelen weggenommen.'

Die jugoslawischen Männer sangen Sehnsuchts- und Liebeslieder über ihre Frauen, zu denen sie zurückfuhren, und übersetzten diese für uns in ihrem gebrochenen Deutsch. Es entstand fast ein Oratorium, und die Fehler, die wir in der deutschen Sprache machten, waren wir, wir hatten nicht mehr als unsere Fehler.

In meinem Stück *Karagöz in Alamania* ist der Karagöz (Schwarzauge) ein türkischer Bauer. Er macht sich aus seinem Dorf mit seinem sprechenden Esel auf den Weg nach Deutschland und läßt seine Frau im Dorf zurück. Karagöz und der Esel erleben viele Stationen, bevor sie in Deutschland ankommen. Der Esel wird zu einem Intellektuellen, er zitiert Marx und Sokrates, trinkt Wein und raucht Camel-Zigaretten. Die Frau des Karagöz ist immer auf dem Weg zwischen der Türkei und Deutschland, weil sie es nirgendwo aushalten kann. Der Esel redet mit Karagöz' Opel Caravan über den kommenden Krieg. Das Auto wird böse und ruft seinen Besitzer Karagöz. Karagöz schlägt seinen Esel – der Esel kriegt einen Herzinfarkt und geht mit dem jugendlichen Ebenbild des Karagöz fort, das

talked in hushed voices about the journey and about their dead children. One of them said: 'This journey has robbed us of our five souls.'

The Yugoslav men sang songs of love and longing about the wives they were returning to, translating them for us in their broken German. The resulting conversation was almost an oratorio, and the mistakes we made in the German language were us. All we had were our mistakes.

In my play *Karagöz in Alamania* the figure of Karagöz is a Turkish peasant. He sets off for Germany together with his talking donkey, leaving his wife behind in the village. Before they reach Germany, Karagöz and the donkey experience many things along the way. The donkey turns into an intellectual, quoting Marx and Socrates, drinking wine and smoking Camel cigarettes. Karagöz's wife is constantly on the move between Turkey and Germany, unable to stand the life in either country. The donkey gets into a conversation with Karagöz's car – an Opel Caravan – about the impending war. The car gets angry, calling for its owner Karagöz. He beats the donkey who, suffering a heart-attack, leaves in the company of a figure who is the exact likeness of Karagöz in his youth. Karagöz

Karagöz nicht mehr kennt. Karagöz fährt wieder mit seinem Opel Caravan. Eine unaufhörliche Reise.

Ich inszenierte *Karagöz in Alamania* 1986 im Frankfurter Schauspielhaus. Weil meine Figuren im Stück mit ihren Geschichten und Auftritten behaupten, Stars zu sein, suchte ich auch Schauspieler und Laien, die Stars waren. Zum Beispiel fand ich einen älteren türkischen Arbeiter, Nihat, der früher Kebabsalonbesitzer gewesen war und ein sehr gutes Gesicht hatte, wie eine Mafiafigur. Eine wunderbare griechische Opernsängerin, deutsche, türkische, spanische Film- und Theaterstars. Wunderbare Gesichter – gute Schauspieler. Dazu hatten wir einen echten Esel, ein Schaf und drei Hühner. Das Schaf war während der Proben auf der Bühne ein schwarzes Lamm.

Am Anfang der Proben war auf der Bühne eine fast heilige Stimmung. Wir machen etwas Besonderes! Zum ersten Mal ein Theaterstück über Türken. Leise Stimmen – Liebesblicke. Langsame Bewegungen. Auch die Tiere waren miteinander befreundet. Esel, Schaf und Lamm schliefen im gleichen Stall nebeneinander. Die Schauspielerin, die auf sie aufpaßte, sagte: 'Wie die Tiere sich lieben!'

Das dauerte eine Woche.

no longer recognises his former self. He journeys on again in his Opel Caravan. His journey is endless.

I directed *Karagöz in Alamania* in 1986 at the Frankfurt Schauspielhaus. Because in their various stories and scenes in the play my characters claim to be stars, I looked for actors, professional and amateur, who were stars. For example, I found an elderly Turkish worker, Nihat, who had previously owned a kebab salon and had a good face, like a mafia type. Also a marvellous Greek woman, an opera singer, as well as German, Turkish, and Spanish stars of the stage and screen, all good actors with wonderful faces. In addition we had a real donkey, a sheep and three hens. A black lamb took the place of the sheep during rehearsals on stage.

At the start of rehearsals an almost sacred atmosphere reigned on stage. What we are doing is something special! For the first time, a play about Turks. Hushed voices – loving glances. Slow movements. The animals too, were friends with one another. Donkey, sheep and lamb lay down to sleep alongside each other in the same stall. The actress looking after them said: 'How they love one another, the animals!'

It lasted for a week. After one

Nach einer Woche fangen die normalen Schwierigkeiten der Probearbeit an.

Als die Schauspieler aufeinander böse wurden, fingen nach einer Weile die Tiere an. Der Esel trat das Schaf oder zeigte ihm die Zähne, das Schaf biß den Esel, das Lamm schrie zwischen beiden laut määää. Wir trennten die Tiere im Stall voneinander, damit sie sich in der Nacht nicht weiterschlugen. Der türkische Star wollte dem deutschen Star, der den Türken spielte, zeigen, wie man einen Gastarbeiter spielt. Der deutsche Star sagte zu ihm: 'Du Kümmeltürke, lerne zuerst einmal richtig Englisch.' Der türkische Star sagte zu ihm: 'Du SS-Mann, *you are SS-man.*'

Einmal brachte die deutsche Schauspielerin, die auf die Tiere aufpaßte, das Schaf und das Lamm mit zur Probe und rief: 'Wer hat hinter der Bühne auf den Kopf des Schafes gespuckt?' Daraufhin sagte der spanische Schauspieler: 'Du mit deiner deutschen Tierliebe – und die Menschen sterben in der Welt vor Hunger.'

Die deutsche Schauspielerin gab dem spanischen Schauspieler eine Backpfeife und sagte: 'Du eitler Spanier.'

Ein deutscher Star begrüßte mich jeden Morgen mit den Worten: 'Guten Morgen, Frau Chomeini.'

week the normal difficulties of rehearsal work begin.

A short while after the actors got cross with one another, the animals started in their turn. The donkey kicked the sheep or bared his teeth at it; the sheep bit the donkey; between the two of them the lamb uttered a loud baaaa. We separated the animals from each other in the stall so that they would not go on fighting during the night. The Turkish star wanted to show the German star, who was acting the part of the Turk, how to play a guest-worker. The German said to him: 'You caraway-chewing Turk, learn to speak English properly before you try to teach me anything.' The Turkish star said to him: 'You SS-man', adding in English: '*you are SS-man.*'

Once, the German actress looking after the animals brought the sheep and the lamb to rehearsals and shouted: 'Who has been spitting at the sheep's head backstage?' The Spanish actor responded by saying: 'You with your German love of animals, when the world is full of human beings starving to death.'

The German actress slapped the Spanish actor across the face, saying: 'You vain Spaniard, you.'

One of the German stars greeted me every morning with the words: 'Good morning, Mrs Khomeini.'

Nur Nihat, der ehemalige Kebabsalonbesitzer, lief zwischen den Schauspielern hin und her und rief: 'Was ist hier los? Was ist hier los?' Ein anderer türkischer Star legte eines Morgens einen Brief auf den Regietisch. Er schrieb mir, wenn ich den schwulen deutschen Star weiter mehr lieben würde als ihn, würde er bald in einer türkischen Zeitung seine Gefühle veröffentlichen.

Ich lud ihn zum Essen ein und kochte türkisch für ihn. Er aß, kritisierte mich, 'das Salz fehlt' usw., aß aber gerne, trank gezuckerten Kaffee. Dann erzählte er mir, daß sein Vater durch das ständige Gefühl, beleidigt worden zu sein, mit 36 Jahren gestorben wäre. Als der deutsche Star hörte, daß ich für ihn gekocht hatte, wollte er sich mit mir treffen. Er gab mir einen Termin um 23 Uhr in einem Lokal und kam zwei Stunden später. Er lachte und sagte: 'Oh, du hast auf mich gewartet.'

Eines Tages trug eine Schauspielerin, die eine Türkin spielte, in der Probe ein Kopftuch. Ich fragte sie, warum. Ein deutscher Schauspieler hatte ihr gesagt, sie sollte zu ihrem Türkischsein stehen. Einmal biß der Esel den türkischen Star in den Nacken. Er hatte den Kopf des Esels unter seinem

Only Nihat, the former kebab salon owner, ran to and fro amongst the actors, shouting: 'What's going on here? What's going on here?'

One morning, another Turkish star placed a letter to me on the director's table. In it he wrote that if I persisted in loving the gay German actor more than him, he would shortly make his feelings public in a Turkish newspaper.

I invited him for a meal, cooking Turkish food for him. He ate it, criticising me because it was not salted enough etc. But he ate it with relish, and drank sweet Turkish coffee. Then he told me the story of his father who had died at the age of thirty-six because he felt that he was the constant target of insults. When the German star found out that I had cooked for the Turk, he wanted to make a date with me. Having arranged to meet me at eleven o'clock at night in a restaurant, he turned up two hours late. He laughed, saying: 'Oh, you've been waiting for me.'

One day an actress who was playing a Turkish woman appeared at rehearsals wearing a headscarf. I asked her why. A German actor had told her that she ought to thus demonstrate her commitment to being Turkish. On one occasion the donkey bit the Turkish star in the back of his neck. He had been holding

Arm etwas festgehalten, so, als ob der Esel sein Freund wäre, mit dem er gerade scherzte. Der deutsche Bühnenbildner warf sich über den Esel, damit dieser den Nacken des Stars losließ. Wir brachten ihn ins Krankenhaus, wo er seine Spritze gegen Tollwut bekam. Ein türkischer Star sagte: 'Ein türkischer Esel würde so etwas niemals tun.' (Der Esel war ein Frankfurter Esel.) Ein deutscher Star: 'Ich verstehe mich mit dem Esel gut, er würde mir so etwas nie antun.' Dann trat ihn der Esel aber auch. Er kam zu mir und sagte: 'Ich werde mit dem Esel sprechen.'

Während der Proben starb der Vater der griechischen Sängerin, ihre Mutter und ihre Großmutter, einem deutschen Star seine hundertjährige Tante. So kamen wir mit vielen Toten und vom Esel Verletzten zur Premiere.

Ich wollte den Arbeiter, dessen Brief mich dazu gebracht hatte, das Stück zu schreiben, zur Premiere einladen. Er war aber auch gestorben – auf einem Stuhl, in seinem Dorf, vor seinem Laden. Herzinfarkt, 41 Jahre alt.

Der Intendant war ein netter Mann, er liebte die Arbeit. Als eine Schauspielerin sagen mußte: 'Ich bleiben zurück – / Mein Mann Alama-

the donkey's head fairly tightly under his arm, as if to show that the animal was a friend that he was joking with. The German stage designer threw himself onto the donkey to make it release its hold on the star's neck. We then took him to hospital where he was injected against rabies. One of the Turkish stars said: 'A Turkish donkey would never do a thing like that.' (The donkey was from Frankfurt.) A German star replied: 'I get on very well with the donkey. He'd never do anything like that to me.' But then the donkey kicked him too. He came to me and said: 'I'm going to have a word with the donkey.'

During rehearsals the father, mother and grandmother of the Greek opera singer all died, as did the hundred-year-old aunt of one of the German stars. We thus reached the première with several deaths in the cast, not to mention those wounded by the donkey.

I wanted to invite the worker whose letter had prompted me to write the play to the première. But he too had died – of a heart-attack, aged forty-one, in his home village, sitting on a chair outside his shop.

The theatre manager was a nice man who loved his work. When one of the actresses had to speak the lines: 'Me stay behind- / My husband stay

nia / Alaman Frau ficken – bleiben', sagte er: 'Bitte, sagen Sie das Wort nicht, sonst denken alle Deutschen, die türkische Poesie bestände aus solchen Wörtern.'

Daraufhin sagte die Schauspielerin in der Generalprobe: 'Mein Mann, Alamania, Alaman Frau fincken – bleiben ...'

Vor der Premiere ließ das Theater, ohne mich vorher zu fragen, aus Liebe zu diesem Stück an die Zuschauer ein Flugblatt verteilen, in dem das Theater versuchte, das Stück zu erklären: 'Manchmal werden Sie sich im Verlauf des Stückes fragen: Wo ist nun wo? Sind wir in der Türkei, sind wir in Alamania? ... Vielleicht haben Sie einige Mühe, sich die Szenen zu gliedern, sie sind nicht logisch geordnet wie in den uns vertrauten Theaterstücken ...'

Das ist sechs Jahre her – ich treffe immer noch Schauspieler, die dabei waren, oder sie rufen mich an. Sie erzählen dann über die anderen:

– Sie hat ein Kind, wußtest du das?

– Ich habe ihn in Berlin getroffen.

– Sie singt gerade an der Mailander Scala.

– Hast du was von ihm gehört?

– Jetzt kommt der Winter, ob sie wieder ihren langen Mantel anziehen wird?

Sie verfolgen sich wie die Liebenden.[1]

Germany / Fuck German woman.' he said: 'Please don't speak that word, otherwise the Germans will all think that Turkish poetry consists of such expressions.'

As a result, when it came to the dress rehearsal, the actress spoke the lines: 'My husband stay Germany/ Funck German woman.'

Before the première the theatre, out of love for the play and without asking my permission in advance, had leaflets distributed amongst the audience, in which it attempted to explain the work. 'In the course of the play you will occasionally wonder: Where are we now? Are we in Turkey, or are we in Germany? ... It may well be that you will have problems ordering the scenes in your mind. They are not logically structured as in the plays we are familiar with ...'

That was six years ago. I still meet with actors who were involved, or they ring me up. Then they talk about the others:

– She's got a child now, did you know?

– I met him in Berlin.

– Just now she's singing at La Scala in Milan.

– Have you heard anything of him?

– Winter is on the way. I wonder whether she'll put on her long coat again?

They pursue one another like lovers.

Commentary

'... something totally different from what you expect'. The first and most obvious point to make about Özdamar's text is that it is deliberately designed, as she had warned *Die Zeit* in advance, to thwart expectations. In an atmosphere of increasing xenophobia, marked by attacks on hostels housing asylum seekers and increased violence against individuals of foreign origin, the editors and readers of a quality newspaper might well have expected a writer of Turkish origin, resident in Germany, to come up with a reasoned statement, balancing condemnation of recent outrages with some attempt to analyse the causes of such hostility against ethnic minorities, and to influence public opinion in the direction of desirable solutions. Nothing of the kind. Instead, Özdamar chose to offer an account of the circumstances that led her to write her first play *Karagöz in Alamania* in 1982, a brief glimpse of that play's content, and a few anecdotes concerning the experiences of the multi-national cast and herself as director during rehearsals for the première in 1986 at the Frankfurt Schauspielhaus.

At first sight this seems tantamount to a simple evasion of the issue, but on closer inspection it becomes clear that Özdamar has elected to address it in an oblique fashion rather than head-on. Instead of employing the abstract rhetoric of an intellectual entering the political debate, she opts for a mixture of storytelling and dramatic enactment appropriate to her own spheres of activity as creative writer, actress and theatre director. Moreover, in thus seeking to persuade by presenting concrete examples of experience in a working situation, she implies that only from such experiences can practical lessons be learned, not from detached intellectual observation and analysis, and still less from pious injunctions to love one another. If this approach in itself constitutes a refusal to accept the basic premise of the newspaper's request for her opinion, it is compounded by a further refusal to consider the issue, as invited, in the clear-cut terms of relations between Germans on the one side and non-Germans on the other. Germans themselves are quite absent from the multinational gathering on the train south mentioned in the first part of the article, although broken German is the common language of the Greeks, Turks and Yugoslavs in the compartment and ironically constitutes their shared identity as they pass the long journey laughing and weeping together: '... die Fehler, die wir in der deutschen Sprache machten, waren wir, wir hatten nicht mehr als unsere Fehler.' ('...the mistakes we made in the German language were us. All we had were our mistakes.') In the second part, devoted to the preparations for the production of *Karagöz* in Frankfurt, Germans do figure prominently in the form of actors, set-designer and theatre manager, but they have no monopoly on national or racial prejudice and are clearly not seen to form a cohesive group apart from the other nationalities involved. In this respect, just like the Turkish *Gastarbeiter* whose letter originally inspired her to write *Karagöz*, Özdamar conspicuously avoids saying anything bad about Germany or the Germans as such.

Instead, what she offers in the second part of the article is a quite unsolemn, at times mischievously humorous, almost irreverent account of the interaction between the various nationalities – and animals – at work on her play. This begins with a 'honeymoon' period of just a week, characterised by an almost sacred atmosphere in which everyone communicates in hushed tones and exchanges loving glances, and even the animals involved lie down at peace with one another in the same stall. Here the biblical allusion suggests that such harmonious co-existence is the stuff of other-worldly idealism, at best a utopian dream. Real conflicts soon arise, but they are not presented as some terrible fall from grace or as moral lapses deserving of censure. On the contrary: they are 'die normalen Schwierigkeiten der Probearbeit.' ('The normal difficulties of rehearsal work'.) When the actors start to get cross with one another, the animals soon follow suit: 'Der Esel trat das Schaf oder zeigte ihm die Zähne, das Schaf biß den Esel, das Lamm schrie zwischen beiden laut määää.' ('The donkey kicked the sheep or bared his teeth at it. The sheep bit the donkey, and between the two of them the lamb uttered a loud baaaa.') The juxtaposition of the animals' physical aggression, which is also slightly anthropomorphised, with the verbal aggression of the human beings, suggests that both are in their nature and will inevitably out. Realism dictates that preventive measures be taken, and the animals at least are henceforth segregated at night. The 'honeymoon' is well and truly over.

The suggested parallel with relations in an ethnically and culturally mixed community becomes more obvious in the next few paragraphs, where Özdamar illustrates in a series of vignettes, themselves similar to short theatrical sketches, the way in which the aggressions of the actors, arising out of their work together, find expression in crude national stereotypes and clichés. These include identification of the individual with national eating habits, the insult 'Kümmeltürke' ('caraway-chewing Turk') – conforming to the same pattern as English usages such as 'Frog' or 'Kraut' – or with skeletons in the cupboard of the nation's political past – all Germans are SS-men at heart. Alternatively, the individual's behaviour is subsumed under some generalised disposition or character-trait: love of animals in the case of Germans, vanity in the case of Spaniards. In Özdamar's own case the generalisation is pushed even further. By virtue of her shared Muslim background with the then Iranian leader, and presumably because she presides over the whole enterprise with a degree of directorial authority, she suffers the indignity of being greeted every morning by one of the German actors with the words 'Guten Morgen, Frau Chomeini.' ('Good morning, Mrs Khomeini.') However, 'suffers' may be the wrong word, since in the absence of any direct comment by the author it is difficult to judge just how wounding are the insults traded by the cast. Only once does one of the human beings involved resort to physical violence, the German actress giving the Spanish actor a slap across the face. Otherwise the impression given is that the verbal exchanges have little lasting effect, and may even be regarded as a healthy way of working off tensions.

Fundamentally, too, these tensions are shown to have little to do with the ethnic or cultural prejudices that surface when they are verbalised. Rather, they derive from personal insecurities and petty rivalries that know no national boundaries. This is nicely illustrated by the vignette about the jealousy between the Turkish actor and his homosexual German colleague, both of whom vie for the affection of Özdamar as director. The Turk's problems are primarily of a psychological nature, as is demonstrated by the story he tells of his own father's premature death, brought about by the feeling that he was the constant butt of insults. The insult to his own manhood that he perceives in Özdamar's apparent preference for a homosexual merely finds an outlet in terms of an appeal to ethnic solidarity, albeit via the unpleasant blackmail involved in threatening to make public his feelings in a Turkish newspaper. Özdamar's solution to the problem is an eminently practical and pragmatic one. She panders to the actor's ethnic and cultural needs by temporarily assuming the role of the Turkish wife (or mother) and offering home-cooking, even having to put up with the customary criticism of the food in the process! Her consequent effort to placate the Turk's German rival results in a similar, culture-specific snub. When she agrees to a *rendez-vous* in a restaurant, he keeps her waiting for fully two hours. But the show goes on.

If, as stated above, Özdamar refrains from direct comment on, or overt condemnation of, these instances of prejudice, she nevertheless leaves the reader in no doubt as to their utter irrationality. Nowhere is this more apparent than in the farcical anecdote about the donkey where, in a *reductio ad absurdum* reminiscent of the burlesque humour of her own play *Karagöz*, national characteristics are even attributed to the animal. 'Ein türkischer Esel würde so etwas nie tun,' ('A Turkish donkey would never do anything like that,') claims one of the Turkish actors when the donkey – from Frankfurt – bites another Turkish colleague in the neck. The claim is then capped by a German who boasts that the beast would never do such a thing to him because he gets on well with it. However, he in turn receives a kick from the donkey, showing that it at least is incapable of ethnic discrimination. Undaunted, the German actor persists in his faith that communication can solve the problem: 'Ich werde mit dem Esel sprechen,' he declares. ('I'm going to have a word with the donkey.')

Evidence from elsewhere in the text suggests that such well-meaning approaches are not always as positive as they may seem, and by no means guaranteed to promote harmony and understanding. Thus the actress who one day appears at rehearsals wearing a head scarf, because she has been advised by a German colleague to enter whole-heartedly into the role of and show solidarity with the Turkish woman she is playing, can be seen to merely reinforce a cultural stereotype. Similarly, the theatre-manager's ostensibly sensitive request to an actress not to speak the word 'ficken' (fuck), because it might give German audiences the wrong impression that Turkish poetry consists of such terms, can be construed as patronising discrimination of a more positive kind, and it results only in the absurdly meaningless substitution 'fincken' (funck). Equally patronising is the pamphlet distributed to the first-night audience, in which the theatre management, without prior consultation with the author, deems it necessary to warn German theatre-goers that the scenes of Özdamar's *Karagöz* they are about to witness are not logically ordered 'wie in den uns vertrauten Stücken' ('as in the plays we are familiar with'). The gesture, however well meant, in practice encourages support for the stereotyped view of Western logic on the one hand, and Oriental, perhaps even feminine, irrationality on the other. In addition, the very wording encourages an 'us and them' approach to culture.

Common to the last two examples is the element of love, the very opposite of the hostility displayed in the insults mentioned earlier. The theatre manager who wants to cut the word 'ficken' is, we are told, 'ein netter Mann, er liebte die Arbeit' ('a nice man who loves his work'), whilst the explanatory pamphlet is issued to the audience 'aus Liebe zu dem Stück' ('out of love for the play'). Yet the effects of such loving care prove just as restrictive and reductive as hostile prejudice. The latter, to judge from the brief post-script to Özdamar's text, has no lasting consequences. The members of the multi-national cast are still in touch with her and each other six years after the event, and they show a lively interest in each other's lives, private and professional. Conspicuous by their absence from the brief snippets of mutual gossip quoted are all references to national identity or cultural difference. Simple pronouns of common humanity – 'sie', 'ihn', 'ihm' (she; him; him) – have taken their place. The conclusion seems positive. The rehearsals, read as a metaphor for the initial stages of cultural interaction, may have been fraught with difficulties, but they have proved to be rehearsals for genuine friendship. Or perhaps something more, since the final words of the text compare the former members of the cast to lovers, incapable of tearing themselves away from one another: 'Sie verfolgen sich wie die Liebenden.' ('They pursue one another like lovers.') The choice of the word 'verfolgen' (pursue) here may cast a slight negative shadow on the picture, but it too is consonant with Özdamar's generally realistic and unsentimental approach to the problem. In other words, what we are left with at the end, is no false dawn like the 'honeymoon' period that began the rehearsals.

The reference to lovers pursuing each other at the very end of the article is one motif that links the account of the cast's relationships with the details of the play's genesis in the first part. It recalls, for instance, the incident related by the real-life model for the character Karagöz, the Turkish *Gastarbeiter* who was prepared to travel the 3,000 kilometres back to his native village, merely in order to establish who had joined whom in eating cherries from the same tree, his uncle or his wife. The common denominator is love, together with its concomitant, jealousy. It is there too in the reference to the songs of yearning and love for their wives, that the Yugoslav workers sing on the train south. Another significant motif that unites both parts of the text is that of death as an ever-present factor of life.[2] The Turkish fathers on the train, taking back the coffins of their sons and daughters killed in car-crashes on the motorways of Yugoslavia, have their counterparts in the cast of the play who, as a result of various bereavements during the course of rehearsals, are said to arrive at the première 'mit vielen Toten' ('with many deaths'). Whilst not labouring the point, Özdamar thus suggests that the plain fact of mortality is another key factor that transcends cultural difference and can be a unifying force when jointly experienced.

A further linking motif, finally, is that of work. Here the picture painted has both negative and positive aspects. The damaging consequences of the working conditions of *Gastarbeiter* are amply demonstrated in the first half of the text with its references to the separation of husbands and wives, to endless journeying with not infrequent deaths on the road, and to cultural estrangement of the kind experienced by Özdamar's Karagöz, whose lifestyle changes so radically that he is incapable of recognising his former self. On the other hand, however, the words from the letter of the Turkish *Gastarbeiter* quoted at the outset indicate that work, with its potential for providing an alternative 'Heimat' to that of one's ethnic homeland, may have its beneficial aspects in terms of willingness to tolerate others, if only on material grounds: 'Ein Arbeiter hat keine Heimat, wo die Arbeit ist, da ist die Heimat' ('A worker has no home. Wherever there is work is home for him'), he writes, and it is he, as already pointed out, who pens not a word of criticism of Germany. Significantly too, the only participant in the rehearsals for the play who, Özdamar herself apart, does not join in the mutual ethnic insults, is Nihat, the former proprietor of a Kebab salon. When first introducing this man, Özdamar has described him as 'einen älteren türkischen Arbeiter' ('an elderly Turkish worker').

Subtly linked recurring motifs of the kind just discussed, combined with ambiguities, silences and a puzzlingly laconic conclusion emphasise the point, already made above, that Özdamar's text is pre-eminently literary in character. As such, rather in the manner of Bertolt Brecht,[3] it prompts an active and imaginative response from the reader rather than offering cut and dried solutions to a complex problem. *Die Zeit* asked for a statement of opinion. What it got was more in the nature of a thought-provoking parable.

Notes

1. *Die Zeit*, 25 February 1992, p.90.

2. A motif that, as we have seen in Chapter 2, is particularly prominent in Özdamar's novel *Das Leben ist eine Karawanserei*.

3. As can be seen from the biographical sketch in Chapter 3, Özdamar has considerable experience of Brecht's work, both as an actress and as an assistant director with Benno Besson. The whole emphasis on the practical lessons to be learned from the experience in working situations that we have noted in her article in *Die Zeit* may well owe something to the theory and practice of Brecht's own *Lehrstücke*, from the rehearsal and performance of which, in the first instance, the actors themselves were expected to learn things.

CHAPTER 5

Non-German Minorities in Contemporary German Society

Eva Kolinsky

At the beginning of the post-war era in 1945, non-German minorities had virtually no place in German society. Even before the National Socialists took to expelling and persecuting foreigners in their determination to create a Germany which would be inhabited only by Germans, successive German governments had restricted residency rights. In fact, non-Germans were normally admitted only as temporary migrant labour, accommodated in special compounds and forced to leave the country at the end of their contract period. They were essentially used as cheap labour and excluded from civic society. This approach came to a head in 1914 when 1.4 million migrant labourers were detained against their will to work in German agriculture and industry for the duration of the war.[1] During the National Socialist period, the same practice was radicalised into a system of forced and slave labour. In the build-up of the war economy and especially during the Second World War, over fourteen million so-called *Fremdarbeiter* were made to work in German industry and agriculture, of whom only half survived to be liberated in 1945.[2] In addition, several million concentration-camp victims and prisoners of war were used as slave labour in the German economy and many of them died from starvation, exhaustion or disease.[3]

This dark hour of German history, the heinous exclusion from civil rights and a public policy of physical destruction cast a shadow over the post-war era and served as an impetus for change. The changes of policy and practice which were put into place were complicated by the division of Germany and the different political and social systems in the two German states.

In East Germany (GDR), official government policy proclaimed a complete break with National Socialism and Germany's past history. Anti-fascist by its own definition, the East German state claimed to espouse international friendship, the acceptance of foreigners and special protection of minorities.[4] Behind the proclamations, however, lay a different reality. German cultural minorities could retain some of their identity, provided they acquiesced in party control. Non-German minorities had no place in the GDR. Access of foreigners to the country and their freedom of social participation remained severely restricted. At the time of its collapse, the population of the GDR included 1.2 percent foreign nationals, most of them short-term contract workers, accommodated in hostels and excluded from civic society. Compared with the situation in Imperial Germany, the status of non-German minorities had hardly changed and fewer foreign nationals than in 1939 lived in the territory which had been the GDR.

In West Germany, the past cast a different shadow. At the time of unification, over eight percent of the population were members of various national minorities, many of them long-term residents. In some cities such as Frankfurt/Main, Berlin or Stuttgart, one in five inhabitants was a foreigner; in some districts, the majority of residents were non-German. As will be shown later in this chapter, the emergence of democracy in West Germany ensured that non-Germans were included (at least partly) into civic society. The tradition of exclusion, however, persisted in the guise of restricted residency rights, various policies to encourage foreigners to leave or compel them to do so, a concept of citizenship based on German origin and the absence of an immigration policy. This chapter sets out to show inclusion and exclusion, social opportunities and their denial, as potent and contradictory forces which determine the place of non-German minorities in German society to this day.

Immigration and German Citizenship

Both German states and the new Germany since unification in 1990 have clung to a concept which makes citizenship dependent on blood ties (*jus sanguinis*). Historically, this concept dates back to the late emergence of a nation state in Germany and the fact that state boundaries and cultural boundaries never matched. Given the complex migration patterns and political structures of Central Europe, people of German origin and of a German cultural orientation always lived outside the territory which constituted the German state. For this reason, people of German origin, wherever their place of residency, have been considered German nationals and enjoyed an automatic right of citizenship.[5]

By contrast, immigration of non-Germans does not constitute a tenet of German policy. Successive governments have stressed 'Germany is not a country of immigration and shall not become a country of immigration in the future'.[6] In East Germany, non-immigration and the exclusion of foreigners could be enforced as part and parcel of socialism from above. In West Germany, non-immigration and the exclusion of foreigners conflicted with two distinct policy commitments which turned it into a country of immigration against its will: the policy of admitting asylum seekers and the policy of recruiting foreign labour into the post-war economy. Together, these two policies produced a sizeable population of non-German migrants in a country which officially has no immigrants.

The first of the two policies, the acceptance of asylum seekers, can be traced directly to Germany's dark past and the determination in the immediate post-war years to make amends. While Nazi Germany had forced millions into exile, post-war Germany was to become a haven for everyone who suffered persecution on political grounds. Article 16 of the Basic Law granted the right of asylum to political refugees and the right to all refugees to remain in Germany until their case had been decided. In the early post-war years, only a handful of asylum seekers entered West Germany, most of them from Eastern European countries and at least half of them certain of automatic recognition and an entitlement to stay. In 1971 for instance just over 5,000 persons applied for political asylum and 57 percent were successful. By 1990, numbers had soared to over 100,000 annually but recognition plummeted to 5 percent. In 1993, only 3.2 percent of the 323,000 applications for political asylum were approved. In July 1993, the commitment of the immediate post-war years, to make Germany a refuge and allow asylum seekers to stay in the country until their case had been decided, was rescinded. Under the influence of hostile public opinion and the inability of the admission bureaucracy to cope with mass migration or to force rejected applicants to leave after a period of investigation which could take up to eight years to conclude, the Federal Parliament amended the Basic Law and the legislation governing political asylum. The main aim of these amendments was to prevent refugees from entering the country unless they arrived directly from the state whose nationality they held and where they were persecuted. A list of so called 'safe' states from which asylum could not be sought was attached to these changes. Given Germany's geo-political location in the centre of Europe, only asylum seekers who arrived directly by plane or ship from the country from which they sought to escape were not turned back at the border and could expect to have their case at least examined.[7]

The asylum issue occupied the lime-light of German *Ausländerpolitik* in the 1990s until the change of legislation in 1993. Given the low recognition rates, however, the overall number of foreigners who have entered Germany as asylum seekers and gained settlement rights totals only about 150,000 since 1950, although the number who have sought political asylum and whose applications have been processed by German authorities amounts to well over 2.5 million.[8]

The second tier of policy which led to migration of non-Germans into the non-immigration country Germany concerns the recruitment of foreign workers, the so-called *Gastarbeiter*. In line with German tradition, non-German labour was drafted in at times of labour shortage. As will be shown later in this chapter, such a labour shortage began to emerge in the mid-1950s and ended in 1973 when labour recruitment stopped. Also in line with German tradition, the original intention had been to employ cheap labour and replace it after twelve months if demand persisted. The twin pillars of temporary residency and rotation were to ensure that only working people would come to Germany, that none would settle, and that no commitment beyond a limited contract arose for employers or for society.

Contrary to German tradition, the policy of exclusion proved impossible to enforce: at times of labour shortage, employers were keen to retain skilled and reliable labour while the trade unions insisted on integrating non-German labour into the regular structure of pay and benefits.[9] At times of economic crisis – in 1966, in 1973 and again in 1982 – the government tried to ease unemployment among Germans by excluding non-Germans from the labour market or by devising incentive schemes to encourage them to return home of their own free will.[10] Some did, although many did not. However, contrary to the German tradition, West Germany had given certain rights to foreigners, enabling some to remain in the country. The erstwhile *Gastarbeiter* became a non-German member of the labour force, an *ausländischer Arbeitnehmer*. In the course of the 1970s, Germany's non-German population was transformed from labour migrants to semi-permanent and permanent residents. In Germany today, one in three children under the age of ten, and one in five young people under the age of eighteen are 'foreigners', i.e., they do not hold German citizenship (although many were born in the country). The self-perception of the Federal Republic as 'German' in citizenship and culture no longer reflects its nationally diverse and increasingly multi-cultural reality.[11]

German Migration and the Reconstruction of Post-War German Society

German society in the immediate aftermath of the Second World War has been called a 'mobilised' society,[12] a term coined to describe an unprecedented degree of upheaval, dislocation and migration. Ten million or so Germans had been evacuated and sought to return to their home towns, more still had lost their homes and were seeking shelter with relatives or in makeshift accommodation. Four million German prisoners of war had returned home by 1950. Dislocation also refers to the ten million former *Fremdarbeiter* and concentration camp inmates who had been liberated and found themselves in Germany. From the outset these so-called 'Displaced Persons' were the administrative responsibility of the military governments, and at no time did Germany consider offering residency rights to the people who had been deported or imprisoned by the National Socialists.[13] By 1950, all but 400,000 of the erstwhile *Fremdarbeiter* had been repatriated, often against their will into hostile countries. At the insistence of the United States, the Federal Republic finally agreed to grant residency rights in the early 1950s to those who had become stateless as a result of their deportation, and had nowhere to go.[14]

The 'mobilisation' which recast post-war German society was caused by German migration, not by absorbing former victims of National Socialism in compensation for their suffering.[15] The main population movement occurred from east to west, as Germans fled or were expelled from areas which had been occupied by the Nazis and resettled with Germans, or which Germany lost as a result of the war.[16] The flight and expulsion of Germans from the east had commenced as the Russian armies advanced, and became official policy at the Potsdam Conference in August 1945. By 1946, over five million expellees had reached occupied Germany; by 1950, their number had swollen to twelve million.[17] About nine million had settled in the Western Zones which were to become the Federal Republic of Germany, some three million in the Soviet Zone, although many of these later fled to the West. In rural areas such as Schleswig Holstein or Lower Saxony, where bomb damage had been less severe, up to sixty percent of the post-war population consisted of expellees.

In both Germanies, one in four inhabitants was an expellee and the challenge of integration was considerable. Until the mid-1950s, expellees in West Germany bore the brunt of unemployment, poverty and homelessness although a series of social-policy measures had been put into place to secure material compensation, pension entitlements and re-employment.[18] By the end of the decade, the social disadvantages of former expellees had largely been overcome. In the West, former expellees enjoyed their share of the economic miracle; in the East, their living standards were as low as those for the population as a whole. Given the different social systems, the first decade of the post-war era saw in both Germanies the successful integration of expellees into the labour market and the fabric of each society.[19]

In addition, West German society absorbed the East Germans (some of them former expellees) who fled the Soviet Zone of occupation and later the GDR. Between 1945 and 1961, when the Berlin Wall sealed the German-German border, East-West migration amounted to 3.4 million people.[20] By December 1989, when the collapse of the Berlin Wall had effectively removed the border between the two German states, 4.4 million East Germans had moved West. At least sixty percent of these refugees were young, skilled, and readily integrated into the German labour market. In West Germany, one of the main sources of skilled labour during the period of intensive economic growth in the 1950s was East Germany, which in turn experienced a severe labour shortage as the exodus continued.

The first decade of post-war reconstruction, therefore, can be called a decade of German social reconstruction. The main challenge of this reconstruction consisted of the integration of Germans who had been socially dislocated, expelled or become refugees as a result of the war and its aftermath. Population movements within Germany, and migration into Germany consisted first and foremost of German migration.[21] East and West Germany together received nearly twelve million expellees from the eastern territories, of whom at least ten million eventually settled in the West. West Germany also received 4.4 million refugees from East Germany. In addition, it received 'resettlers' i.e., people of German origin who had continued to live in an Eastern European country after the Second World War and who considered themselves German by origin and cultural background. Between 1950 and the mid-1980s, some two million of these *Aussiedler* (resettlers) arrived from Eastern European countries in West Germany (Table 5.1). After the collapse of the Iron Curtain, up to 400,000 per year claimed their citizenship and residency rights. By 1995, close to 3.5 million resettlers had come to live in Germany with a further three million hoping to do so.[22]

Table 5.1: German Migration into the Federal Republic, 1945–1995

From the beginning of the post-war period until 1995, the overall numbers of German migrants into the Federal Republic (West Germany) were:

Expellees	Refugees [a]	Resettlers	Total German/ German migration
12 million	4.4 million	3.5 million	19.9 million

Note: a) From May 1945 to December 1989. After the opening of the Berlin Wall in November 1989, East Germans moving west were no longer counted as refugees but included in internal migration statistics.

Sources: Compiled from various volumes of *Statistisches Jahrbuch für die Bundesrepublik Deutschland* and *Datenreport 1994* ed. Statistisches Bundesamt. Bonn: Bundeszentrale für politische Bildung 1994, pp. 20ff.

As mentioned earlier, all newcomers of German origin have always been entitled to citizenship. In practical terms this entails financial support, housing allocation, language tuition and other measures to aid social integration.[23] In East Germany, in-migration ceased after the first post-war wave of expellees, and the country lost population to West Germany throughout its history. Even during the existence of the GDR, German-origin resettlers from Eastern Europe used their claim to citizenship to go to the West; the GDR was never a recipient country for migrants.

In West Germany and in unified Germany, migration has been based on the *jus sanguinis*, targeted at German nationals and intended to include those of a homogenous culture into a homogeneously German society. Successive federal governments have devised social policies and material compensation to encourage German-German migration, facilitate the social integration of German migrants into society, and thus make that society as German as possible in its composition.

The Emergence of Non-German Minorities in Contemporary Germany

The social and economic dislocations came to an end in the 1950s. With growth rates of up to ten percent annually, the West German economy experienced the so-called 'economic miracle', a period of structural modernisation, expansion and full employment which lasted from the early 1950s to the early 1970s. Economic success, rising living standards and improved social opportunities were of paramount importance for the acceptance of political democracy by the German population, for the social and political integration of more expellees and refugees, and for the development of the contemporary welfare state and social policy net. Then as now, Germans have been especially proud of their economic achievements and tend to link their confidence in the political system with confidence in its economic success and ability to protect living standards.[24]

Labour migration into post-war Germany started, as it had always done, as recruitment at government level to alleviate shortages in specific areas. Between 1955 and 1968, the Federal Republic concluded intergovernmental contracts with eight Mediterranean countries (Table 5.2), although seasonal agricultural labour had been recruited to south-western Germany from Italy since the early 1950s. This Italian migration was caused by a combination of low agricultural wages and buoyant industrial and business development, which created shortages of unskilled labour in a region where French military government had refused to admit German expellees. Elsewhere, unemployment of former expellees and refugees remained high. When negotiations began in March 1955 on recruiting Italian workers on one-year contracts, unemployment in West Germany stood at more than one million; when the first *Gastarbeiter* arrived in the November it had fallen by one quarter. By 1960, full employment had been achieved, and vacancies outnumbered applicants. To alleviate labour shortages, Germans tended to take the recruitment of non-German labour in their stride, although it was also greeted with hostility. A CDU member of parliament expressed a view held by many: 'The very last German has to be in employment before such a thing [the recruitment of foreign labour, E.K] should at all be considered. We beseech the government to force industry to move to those regions where unemployment remains high.'[25]

Table 5.2: Intergovernmental Contracts for
Labour Recruitment 1955–1968

Country	Year	Date of Contract
Italy	1955	22 November
Spain	1960	29 March
Greece	1960	30 March
Turkey	1961	30 October
Morocco	1963	21 June
Portugal	1964	17 March
Tunisia	1965	18 October
Yugoslavia	1968	12 October

Source: Compiled from Verena McRae, *Gastarbeiter. Daten - Fakten - Probleme*. Munich, Beck, 1980, pp. 13 f.

Non-German labour migration was to alleviate a range of unfavourable developments. By the mid-1950s, German agriculture and industry feared labour shortages as the low birth-rate of the war and post-war years reduced the cohort of school leavers, while increased educational participation and earlier retirement further curtailed the overall size of the potential labour force. Moreover, the shift towards white-collar employment and higher qualifications of the German workforce induced fears among German employers of a labour shortage at the unskilled and semi-skilled levels. It has been argued that the recruitment of non-German labour was designed, above all, to supply Germany with a relatively cheap unskilled blue-collar workforce at a time when wages for unskilled work in Germany had already begun to rise faster than wages overall, and manpower shortages seemed imminent.[26] In East Germany, the manpower shortages of the 1950s were alleviated by integrating women fully into the labour force. In West Germany, women's family roles and employment remained in conflict, while manpower shortages were reduced by recruiting *Gastarbeiter*. The term *Gastarbeiter* itself implies 'rotation', a non-permanent stay. The non-German labour force, as created through intergovernmental contracts during the 1950s, was to consist only of persons who were active in the labour market, who would not normally draw on social services or other support networks, and who would not need to be integrated into society in terms of housing, pensions, schools, family provisions, leisure pursuits or cultural background. *Gastarbeiter* would normally be under the age of forty, male, on twelve-months contracts, and living in dormitories or other purpose-built accommodation.[27] *Gastarbeiter* were to be what foreign workers had always been throughout German history, a mobile labour force outside civic society, economically necessary and socially excluded.

Labour Recruitment

This tradition may have continued into the post-war era but for three unexpected developments: wage equality, the Berlin Wall and legislative change which gave some access to civil rights. The first of these developments originated with the German trade unions. They insisted on integrating *Gastarbeiter* into the wage structure pertaining to the German workforce in order to ensure that their recruitment would not depress wage levels unduly.[28] Although recruited at the unskilled end of the labour market, *Gastarbeiter* became eligible from the outset for the social benefits and employment rights of their German colleagues, including statutory holidays, unemployment benefit, sickness pay and pension entitlement. Secondly, when the Berlin Wall cut off the supply of highly skilled manpower which had come to West Germany from the GDR, the recruitment of *Gastarbeiter* took on a new urgency, and additional contracts were signed with Turkey, Morocco, Portugal and Tunisia (see Table 5.2), before post-war Germany's first economic recession in 1966 led to mass dismissals of *Gastarbeiter* and the forced return to their home countries (Fig. 5.1). In the absence of East German refugees, however, *Gastarbeiter* had begun to be perceived as an essential labour force whom employers wished to retain, a labour force which was increasingly irreplaceable by Germans. By 1966 when some 300,000 foreign workers lost their jobs, a substantial number of employers had already issued longer-term contracts to their foreign workforce and were determined to keep them. The 1966/1967 recession was short-lived and the ensuing economic boom could only be sustained by an intensification of labour recruitment from outside Germany. A new recruitment contract was signed with Yugoslavia in 1968. From 1969 onwards, Turkish workers arrived in greater numbers. Although the contract with Turkey dated back to the days of the Berlin Wall in 1961, it had hardly been activated until the end of the decade (Table 5.3).

Fig. 5.1 *Gastarbeiter* 1960–1975

by country of origin

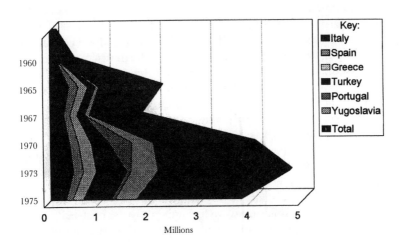

Table 5.3: Non-German Labour Force in Germany
by Country of Origin, 1955–1990

Non-German Labour	1955	1960	1965	1967	1973	1980	1990
(in 1,000)	80	279	1,217	991	2,595	2,015	1,740
as a % of labour force	0.4	1.3	5.5	4.4	11.9	9.5	7.9

Non-German Labour Force by Country of Origin (in % of non-German labour force)

Country of Origin	1955	1960	1965	1967	1973	1980	1990
Turkey	nil	nil	11	13	23	29	34
Yugoslavia	nil	nil	5	10	21	17	18
Italy	9	44	31	27	17	15	10
Greece	1	5	15	14	10	7	6
Spain	1	3	15	12	7	4	4
Others	89	48	23	24	22	18	28

Sources: Calculated from *Statistical Yearbooks* and Klaus J. Bade, *Vom Auswanderungsland zum Einwanderungsland? Deutschland 1880-1980*, Berlin, Colloquium Verlag, 1983, p. 70.

1973 saw the introduction of an *Anwerbestopp*, a ban on recruitment in the wake of the oil-shock and the onset of endemic mass unemployment in West Germany. It was accompanied by a programme of financial incentives to motivate *Gastarbeiter* to leave Germany. Within two years, an estimated 400,000 had done so. Despite the ban on labour recruitment, which continues to this day, the overall number of non-Germans in Germany increased.[29] Indeed, the recruitment ban changed the national composition and the social structure of Germany's non-German population as labour migrants became residents. Until the early 1970s, Germany's foreign workers were *Gastarbeiter* – a migrant labour force without clear intentions to settle in Germany. After the early 1970s, those unwilling or unable to return to their home country resolved to stay and bring their families to Germany. Migrants were recast into minorities. When the *Anwerbestopp* was imposed, 11.6 percent of Germany's labour force and 6.4 percent of the population were foreigners. By the mid-1980s, 7.7 percent of the labour force and 7.4 percent of the population were of non-German origin.[30] Until the mid-1960s, the largest cohorts of foreign workers came from Italy, Spain and Greece, the first countries with whom intergovernmental contracts had been signed. From the mid-1960s onwards, recruitment from Yugoslavia and in particular from Turkey gained pace. When the recruitment of foreign workers was halted, Turkish nationals constituted one quarter of the non-German labour force. At the time of unification, their share had increased to one third. Table 5.3 shows the increasing significance of Turks among the non-German labour force, as labour market participation from traditional recruitment countries diminished.

The most recent arrivals, *Gastarbeiter* from Turkey, were the least willing to leave and the most likely to settle and reunite with their families. From a national group at the margins of Germany's foreign population and workforce, they soon rose to prominence. (Table 5.4) In the early 1960s, one percent of non-Germans in Germany had been of Turkish origin; ten years later, sixteen percent; a further decade later over thirty percent. In the early 1990s, close to two million Turkish citizens lived in Germany [31] (Table 5.5).

Table 5.4: Germany's Non-German Population and Turkish Minority, 1961–1992.

Year	Non-German Population	%	Turkish Minority	%
1961	686,200	1.2	6,700	1.0
1970	2,600,600	4.3	249,400	16.5
1987	4,240,500	6.9	1,453,700	34.3
1989	4,845,900	7.7	1,612 600	33.3
1990 [a]	5,342,500	8.4	1,675,900	32.0
1991 [b]	5,882,300	7.3	1,779,600	30.3
1992	6,495,800	8.0	1,854,900	28.6

Notes: a) Data from 1961-1990 for the 'old Länder'; b) data from 1991 for the 'old' and 'new' Länder together.

Sources: *Statistisches Jahrbuch für die Bundesrepublik Deutschland*, 1992: 71: *Statistisches Jahrbuch für die Bundesrepublik Deutschland*, 1994.

Table 5.5: Non-German Population in Germany
by Country of Origin, 1992

Country of Origin	Population (in 1,000)	% of non-German Population
Turkey	1,855	41
Ex-Yugoslavia	916	21
Italy	558	12
Greece	346	8
Poland	286	6
Romania	167	4
Spain	134	3
Portugal	99	2
Iran	99	2
Morocco	80	1
All countries listed	4,540 [a]	100

Note: a) The table highlights former recruitment countries and does not list all countries of origin of Germany's non-German population in 1992.

Source: *Der Spiegel*, 23, 1993, p. 19.

Workers into Residents

Initially, seventy percent of Germany's non-German minorities were in employment; after the *Anwerbestopp*, labour market participation fell to just over fifty percent as the number of children, young people, and women increased. Recasting the former *Gastarbeiter* population into a resident non-German minority entailed what may be called a 'normalisation' of social structure. In actual terms it involved women and children joining men who had already moved to Germany in the context of labour recruitment programmes, a shift from short-term to long-term residency, and the emergence of established non-German minorities within German society. Between 1974 and 1988, the number of men of non-German origin declined by 18 percent, the number of women increased by 17 percent, that of children under sixteen by 39 percent. More specifically, the number of non-Germans from traditional recruitment countries such as

Spain, Portugal, Greece, Italy and also Yugoslavia decreased by up to 46 percent, while the Turkish population in Germany nearly doubled. [32]

Table 5.6: Non-German Population and Turkish Minority in the German Länder, 1992

a) Old Länder

Land	Non-German Population (in 1,000)	Turkish Minority (in 1,000)	as % of non-German Population
Baden-Württemberg	1,190.8	324.5	27
Bavaria	995.9	244.4	25
Berlin [a]	382.8	129.8	34
Bremen	75.7	29.7	39
Hamburg	235.5	60.3	26
Hesse	745.9	184.4	25
North-Rhine Westfalia	1,812.3	639.1	35
Lower Saxony	425.8	121.4	29
Rhineland Palatinate	258.9	68.0	25
Saarland	68.2	12.6	18
Schleswig Holstein	125.9	38.6	31

b) New Länder

Brandenburg	55.0	0.6	1.1
Mecklenburg-Pomerania	22.5	0.2	1.0
Saxony	50.8	0.5	1.0
Saxony-Anhalt	33.9	0.4	1.0
Thuringia	20.3	0.3	1.4

Note: a) includes East Berlin.

Source: Calculated from data in *Statistisches Jahrbuch für die Bundesrepublik Deutschland* 1994.

Traces of *Gastarbeiter* regional recruitment from the 1960s remain visible to this day (Table 5.6). Regions with previous labour shortages in manufacturing industries, such as Baden-Württemberg or North-Rhine Westphalia, attracted larger *Gastarbeiter* populations and developed larger non-German minorities than rural parts of Germany such as Schleswig-Holstein. For the latecomer Turkish recruits, unskilled labour in car manufacturing and mining, and low-level jobs in public services such as refuse collection and street or office cleaning were first destinations and determined where they could live. Berlin, Bremen and North-Rhine Westphalia became their main settlement areas. In 1992, 93 percent of Germany's foreigners lived in the old Länder (Table 5.6). Of the few foreigners in the East, only one percent were of Turkish origin. The GDR policy of exclusion left the former GDR virtually *ausländerrein* – bare of foreigners – and even more *türkenrein* – without Turkish residents.

Between Inclusion and Exclusion

There is general agreement in the literature that the 1973 policy of excluding foreign workers from German society had the unexpected consequence of turning migrant labourers into long-term residents. If the 1960s faced a challenge of integration, this challenge concerned the labour market and extending equal pay and conditions to Germans and non-Germans alike. Social integration did not appear to be required for a population of workers with few families and children, with few permanent homes, whose stay in Germany was assumed to be of limited duration, a stepping stone to building a better future for themselves and their families back home. Yet, the 1960s brought important adjustments to the legislation governing the rights foreign nationals enjoyed in German civic society. Without these adjustments, the 1973 *Anwerbestopp* would have resulted in the eviction of non-Germans from Germany, and not in the paradox that a policy of exclusion should become the challenge of inclusion and multi-cultural development which has occupied German society since the mid-1970s.

During the first decade of *Gastarbeiter* recruitment, the social and legal status of foreigners in Germany was determined by a law dating back to 1938. Although freed from its more racist overtones, this law remained in force until 1965. It was based on the assumption that foreigners working in Germany were contract labour without freedom of movement or residency rights. In keeping with authoritarian traditions, up to the mid-1960s the legislation on foreigners admonished employers to ensure that their foreign workers would receive a change of straw to sleep on every three months, and that bed linen should be washed in the interest of hygiene.[33] The new *Ausländergesetz* of 1965 did not appear to advance the civic rights of foreigners. Non-Germans remained essentially contract labour, permitted to remain in Germany for the duration of their employment. As in the past, foreign workers could only be taken on if no German national could be found to take the job. Foreigners whose contract came to an end, or who lost their jobs, had to leave the country. The law stipulated that any foreigner would be deported who depended on social security payments or other benefits. Residency permits were conditional and temporary, and the right to remain permanently in Germany was virtually unattainable.

Yet, the letter of the law was vague enough to allow *de-facto* settlement, and prepare the ground for the transformation of the *Gastarbeiter* into a resident population.[34] The 1965 law left it to local and regional authorities to interpret its meaning. At that level, employers' interests in retaining their non-German labour force, party-political sensibilities concerning the place of foreigners in German society, and a pragmatic adaptation to preferences among the non-German population to make Germany their home, produced a situation whereby the law seemed to preclude settlement, while its application did not. The situation was further obscured by the fact that local and regional decision makers tended to be guided by regular social legislation and include non-German applicants in benefit provisions, while the letter of the foreigners' law stipulated that those in need of support should be made to leave the country. Since residency and work permits were decided at local and regional level, the administrative processes played a significant role in creating social space for non-Germans in Germany. The political diversity of Germany's federal system produced conservative and social-democratic answers. The former tended to be more restrictive, the latter more inclined to include rather than exclude.

The political culture since the early 1970s has been characterised by an ambivalence towards the former *Gastarbeiter* and their descendants. Forces to the right of centre, and in particular the extreme right, portray foreigners as unwanted competitors for jobs, a burden on the public purse, and a threat to German national identity and the fabric of society.[35] It could be argued that the introduction of the *Anwerbestopp* was an attempt by Willy Brandt's SPD-led government to mollify the right and silence xenophobic sceptics without fully giving in to them. The political culture among the educated, younger generations with left-of-centre orientations had moved away from exclusion and tended to regard cultural diversity and the presence of non-German (and other) minorities in German society as a precondition of democracy. With regard to foreigners, Willy Brandt's call from the early 1970s 'to dare more democracy' meant assisting those who had already settled in Germany to improve their living conditions and social opportunities.

This duality of exclusion and inclusion, of hostility and acceptance has prevailed to this day. In the early 1970s, the balance seemed to tilt in favour of inclusion; a decade later, exclusion had gained ground, and open hostility had come to dominate among lower skilled and lower educated Germans. After unification, the non-acceptance of foreigners in East Germany further shifted the balance towards exclusion, although by that time, over 60 percent of non-Germans had lived in the country for more than ten years, and had established a place in German society. By that time also, national and regional governments were committed to including non-German minorities in their policy provisions, and a network of support agencies had developed to advise and assist the social integration and orientation of foreigners.[36]

If the *Anwerbestopp* had been intended to rid Germany of foreigners, it was a resounding failure. Forced to choose between returning to their country of origin and enduring the harsh living conditions which drove them to seek work in Germany in the first place, the majority of former *Gastarbeiter* opted to remain. In the first two years after the *Anwerbestopp*, overall numbers declined, as half a million people left and few newcomers entered; after an initial disorientation, however, ex-*Gastarbeiter* began to draw on their right of family reunion. Family reunion effected a significant shift in the age structure of the non-German population, and in particular among the Turkish minority. Once family reunion got under way, one in three Germans and non-Germans were children or young people under twenty-one, although among the Turkish minority, this young age cohort constituted 38 percent (Table 5.7). By 1987, the proportion of young Germans under twenty-one had fallen to 23 percent, that of young non-Germans remained stable at 31 percent, and that of young Turks had increased to 42 percent. In the mid-1970s, 60 percent of the new arrivals from Turkey were under the age of eighteen.[37] As procreative behaviour, life-expectancy and family size has changed, the German population has been ageing, and a majority is aged forty or over. Among non-German minorities, and in particular among the Turkish minority in Germany, the young continue to predominate, since family sizes have remained larger – non-German women tend to have 2.6 children on average, German women 1.3 – and the former *Gastarbeiter* generations are still below retirement age.

Table 5.7 Age Distribution of Germans and Non-Germans, 1977–1987 (in %)

Age Group	Non-German Population		Turks	
	1977	*1987*	*1977*	*1987*
0–6	11	7	15	10
6–10	6	6	7	8
10–15	6	8	7	2
15–18	3	5	4	7
18–21	4	5	5	7
21–35	37	27	34	24
35–45	21	21	23	16
45–55	8	14	4	13
55–65	3	6	1	3
65+	2	3	*	*

Source: Calculated from *Statistisches Jahrbuch für die Bundesrepublik Deutschland*, 1987. More recent yearbooks no longer provide data on the age distribution of different national groups.

On the face of it, the right of family reunion suggests that humanitarian principles have prevailed. Yet even in this realm, German minority policy, alongside a pragmatic acceptance of residency, has never abrogated exclusion. Despite the *de-facto* emergence of a resident non-German minority, German policy makers and German society continue to look for means of preventing or obstructing settlement and, of course, curtailing or prohibiting new arrivals. The social integration of German expellees and refugees in the 1940s and 1950s had been helped by social policies and a general acceptance, although many newcomers were greeted with hostility when they first arrived. With regard to non-German minorities, Germany never advocated acceptance without also advocating exclusion. The practicalities of family reunion can serve an example of this. Although family members have been permitted to come to Germany if the applicant can provide proof of employment and housing of a sufficient size, they themselves have not been allowed to take up employment until four years after their arrival. Family reunion, therefore, has meant that people of working age have had to refrain from employment and remain financially dependent on the 'breadwinner' who initiated the reunion. The ban on employment turned family reunion into social hardship and prevented women and young people in particular from obtaining vocational qualifications or earning a living. By the time their employment ban ran out, they were already disadvantaged in their occupational opportunities. Barbara John quotes the following case from her work as Commissioner for Foreigners in Berlin:

> A young woman of Turkish origin, born in Berlin, who wants her husband to join her in Germany has to, first of all, move out of the parental home. Why? Because it is deemed too small. In order to permit her husband to join her, her living accommodation must be of a certain square footage per person. (...) She is lucky and finds a flat, allowing her husband to join her. This husband is now banned from taking up employment for four years. The couple already have a child. The woman, therefore, starts work as a cleaner while the husband stays at home to care for the child. He would like to work but cannot obtain a work permit. He would, however, be allowed to help in his father-in-law's grocery shop, since no work permit is required for this. You see [Barbara John said to her audience] how complicated the foreigners' law is, especially if one is affected by it. Assisting family members do not normally require a work permit. But our husband is unlucky: although he is a member of the family and would like to help in the shop, the law stipulates that he would have to live in the same household with his father-in-law to permit him to do so. This condition, however, the young couple was unable to meet, since the husband could not have joined his wife in her parental home. This law [Barbara John concludes] is full of snares and full of suspicion against newcomers and the members of their families who are born in Germany.[38]

The political debate as to whether Germany should impose an age limit on entry, and exclude anyone except children under the age of six and spouses, has never subsided. To date, children up to the age of sixteen are permitted to join their families, although a newly married husband or wife has to wait for one year before being allowed to settle in Germany. Until 1990, the majority of foreigners who lived in Germany did not hold unrestricted residency rights, but were required to apply to the relevant authorities and seek an extension of their stay. Although there is no evidence that permits were withheld wilfully, the very fact that non-Germans could not obtain the right of permanent residency after ten years but only the right to reapply, has exacerbated a status of insecurity and points to non-acceptance by the host society. Imposing such conditional status on long-standing members of a society suggests that their presence in that society is regarded as conditional and threatened by exclusion. In 1990, an amendment of the foreigners' legislation made it possible to apply for a permanent (rather than a conditional) residency permit after eight years.

Yet, the majority of non-Germans in Germany cannot be regarded as temporary residents by any standards. Of Germany's foreign population in 1993, over 40 percent had lived in Germany for over fifteen years, one in four, even, over twenty years. By the time the *Anwerbestopp* took effect, 60 percent of the *Gastarbeiter* cohort had already brought their families to Germany and begun to settle permanently. Of the Turkish minority in 1973, 38 percent lived with their families in Germany, and the majority sought reunion. Table 5.8 shows that compared to other national groups, Turks have lived for a shorter time in Germany. Since family reunion was more significant for Turks than for other national groups, and continues to influence the structure and residency of the Turkish minority, their duration of stay underlines their motivation to remain and not, as is often alleged, their low level of integration. When deciding whether or not to settle in Germany, the most qualified were the most likely to remain.[39] Measured by educational and vocational qualifications in their country of origin, Turks, Greeks and Yugoslavs were the most qualified and motivated to make their way in Germany. The in-migration of family members confirms this determination and the intended permanency of their stay. Nevertheless, 80 percent of Turks in the early 1990s only held conditional residency permits. The overall

number of non-Germans who have been living in Germany for
less than four years has been boosted by the recent influx of
asylum seekers from many countries, including Turkey, whilst
the influx of refugees from war-torn Bosnia and Croatia has
made for a particular increase in the number of Yugoslavs in
the same category (Table 5.8).

Table 5.8: Non-Germans by Country of Origin and Duration of Stay
in Germany, 1993 (in % of national group)

Years	Spaniards	Greeks	Italians	Yugoslavs	Turks	All Non-Germans
20 and over	60	44	41	36	19	25
15–under 20	19	16	16	19	25	16
8–under 15	10	12	19	13	27	19
4–under 8	5	7	10	5	11	12
under 4 [a]	7	22	14	26	18	28

Note: a) This category includes asylum seekers who gained permission to stay
and newcomers in the context of family reunion.

Source: *Sozial- und Wirtschaftkunde, Arbeitsmappe*, no.9, 1993, Berlin, Schmidt
Verlag, 1993.

Foreign nationals who have been resident in Germany for ten
years or more are entitled to apply for German citizenship,
provided that they can demonstrate to the German authorities a
good command of the language and an assimilation to German
culture. Since Germany does not accept dual citizenship, those
who opt to become Germans have to renounce their original citizenship. To date, few foreign nationals have availed themselves of
this opportunity: while an estimated 70 percent would be eligible,
less than 0.5 percent annually take out German citizenship, one
in five of them from the Turkish minority.[40]

The revised foreigners' law of 1990 stipulates that foreign
nationals born in Germany are entitled to become Germans
when they reach the age of eighteen. Although they will still be
required to give up their non-German nationality, bestowing
German citizenship as a right, not a privilege to be granted or
refused by scrutinising authorities, is a step towards inclusion.

In the early 1980s, the Bundesrat had vetoed a similar proposal. It could be argued that German policy makers were persuaded towards inclusion in order to distance themselves and the Federal Republic as a polity from the ground swell of xenophobia and violence which was directed against foreigners in Germany, including long-term residents. The concession on citizenship also responded to sentiments voiced during candle-light demonstrations against xenophobia and right-wing extremism. A demonstrative signal seemed to be needed inside and outside Germany that integration and inclusion were at the heart of German policy. Given the German view of nationhood, offering the right of citizenship to foreigners who were born in Germany constituted a significant compromise. Some ambiguities, however, remain which imply exclusion within inclusion. One of the criticisms levelled at Germany's foreigners by the proverbial man-in-the-street, but also by prominent leaders such as Chancellor Kohl, concerns their alleged distance from mainstream German culture and their lack of willingness to integrate: 'It is also up to the foreigners themselves who live here whether they can successfully integrate or not. They must not remain isolated and mix only with their own kind, but they have to actively approach Germans and fit into our public and social life'.[41] Including young non-Germans through citizenship was also meant to assuage concerns that an ever-increasing cohort of young people was living in the country whose foreign nationality might produce or sustain distance from Germany's political system and cultural traditions. In this perspective, the concession on citizenship borders on non-acceptance and can be seen as an attempt to dilute minority cultures and protect German society against unwanted diversity.

The Social and Economic Position of Non-German Minorities Today

Twenty years after the former *Gastarbeiter* settled to become a resident minority of various nationalities, the legacy of labour recruitment is still evident. Originally hired as unskilled or semi-skilled labour, most remain as unskilled or semi-skilled labour. While economic modernisation has transformed the occupational structure in Germany with a significant shift from blue-collar to white-collar employment, from production to administrative and managerial tasks, from manufacturing to service sector functions, the employment of non-Germans reflects, as if in a time-warp, an outdated model. Non-Germans tend to work in manufacturing industry or construction (67 percent), Germans in white-collar employment and the public sector (59 percent).[42] In Germany generally, socio-economic modernisation has gone hand-in-hand with a decrease in blue-collar employment. In 1992, just 36 percent of the German, but 83 percent of the non-German workforce were blue-collar workers; among Germans most belonged to the so-called elite of *Facharbeiter*, skilled workers. Although fewer non-Germans were in unskilled and more in skilled blue-collar work in the 1990s than ten years previously, the dominance of blue-collar employment has remained in place. At the white-collar end of the labour market, non-Germans have been able to double their share of administrative and managerial positions, but this still only amounts to 6 percent compared with 37 percent for Germans (Table 5.9).

Even more strongly than non-Germans generally, Turks in Germany depend on blue-collar employment (85 percent in 1992) and appear to be particularly disadvantaged. Yet, upward mobility among this group is evident from an increase of skilled workers (from 13 percent to 22 percent), higher level white-collar employment (from 2 percent to 5 percent) and self-employment (from 2 percent to 8 percent). Amidst a general social position at the lower end of the German occupational structure, non-Germans improved their occupational status in the course of the 1980s. The status gap between Germans and non-Germans was larger at the beginning of the decade, but persists. The proportion of Germans trapped at the unskilled and semi-skilled level remained nearly stagnant, while some non-Germans improved their employment situation.

In the second generation, those who were born in Germany or settled there before reaching adulthood, a similar development towards higher skilled and qualified positions is evident as the number of unskilled blue-collar and basic white-collar workers decreased. More second-generation than first-generation non-Germans have obtained advanced positions in their occupational sector, and there has also been a shift towards administrative and managerial positions, but the occupational gap to their German peers remains as wide for second-generation non-Germans as it was for their elders.

Table 5.9: German and Non-German Labour Force
by Occupational Status and Generations, 1984–1992
(in % of national group [a])

Occupational Status	Non-Germans 1984	Non Germans 1992	Germans 1984	Germans 1992
Unskilled worker	25	17	4	4
Semi-skilled worker	45	40	12	11
Skilled worker	20	26	18	21
Basic white collar	4	3	9	5
White collar: higher	3	6	33	37
Self-employed	4	7	12	12

2nd Generation [b]

Unskilled worker	25	12	8	2
Semi-skilled worker	25	39	12	10
Skilled worker	30	29	22	30
Basic white collar	14	5	17	4
White collar: higher	4	13	29	44
Self-employed	2	2	3	4

Turkish Minority

Unskilled worker	37	21
Semi-skilled worker	42	42
Skilled worker	13	22
Basic white collar	4	3
White collar: higher	2	4
Self-employed	2	8

Notes: a) Since Civil Servants are excluded from the table, percentages may add up to less than 100;

b) For Germans, the data refer to the age cohorts 16-25.

Source: Own calculations from *Datenreport* 1994, p. 590.

Living Conditions and Incomes

The successful socio-economic integration of German expellees and refugees in the early post-war years, for instance, benefited from the privileges arising from citizenship, but it also benefited from the buoyant economic development at the time. By comparison, the integration of German resettlers in the 1980s and 1990s proceeded sluggishly, and frequently failed to meet the expectations of the newcomers, although living conditions had been much worse in the countries left behind.[43] Non-German minorities had to carve out their space in German society after the economic miracle had come to a halt, unemployment had become endemic, public spending cuts had curtailed the provision of subsided housing and exacerbated competition at the lower end of the housing market, while changes in household structure and family size generated a new demand and new shortages. The housing situation is a good example of the obstacles to finding a foothold in German society. When non-Germans entered the housing market in greater numbers, they were economically weak clients in a market in which low-cost housing was in short supply. Forced to secure housing in order to obtain residency permits, they had to live where they could. A 1991 report on the housing situation of foreigners in Germany sums up the difficulties:

> The housing situation of foreigners is predominantly poor. Many families are the last remaining tenants in dilapidated and condemned buildings. One reason may be that they do not wish to spend much money on rent. At least as important, however, is the fact that they are turned down by German landlords on the open market because of prejudice. Even in co-operative housing developments foreigners who have fully assimilated to the German way of life find it very difficult to obtain an apartment alongside Germans. (…) One of the consequences of the housing shortage has been that foreigners tend to live in ghetto-like inner-city areas, which in turn produces further problems with schooling and with adjusting to life in German society.[44]

Non-Germans tend to live in rented accommodation (92 percent) and predominately in cities with over 100,000 inhabitants.[45] Here they have been concentrated in former working-class tenements or inner-city areas. The average housing quality is poorer for non-Germans than for Germans: more overcrowded and less well equipped with heating, bathrooms or toilets, although average rents tend to be high for the type of property.[46] In Berlin for instance, nearly half the non-German population of the city lives in only three districts, Wedding, Kreuzberg and Neukölln, former working-class areas with pre-war, unmodernised tenement buildings which have been vacated by Germans in exchange for post-war, state-subsidised *Neubauten*. The housing concentration in Berlin applies to the Turkish minority in particular: in 1989, 64 percent of non-Germans in Wedding, 70 percent in Kreuzberg and 60 percent in Neukölln were Turks.[47]

Table 5.10 Germans and Non-Germans in Berlin
by Income Groups, 1993 (in % national group)

Income Group (in DM)	Non-Germans	Germans
under 600	10	6
600–1,000	11	9
1,000–1,400	8	12
1,400–1,800	7	11
1,800–2,200	8	12
2,200–2,500	6	8
2,500–3,000	7	9
3,000 and over	8	14
without income	35	19

Source: Landesamt für Statistik, Berlin, *Statistisches Jahrbuch Berlin*, 1994, p. 93

Table 5.11 Germans and Non-Germans in Berlin
by Source of Income, 1993 (in % of national group)

Main source of income	Non-Germans	Germans
Employment	38	46
Unemployment Benefit [a]	7	4
Pension	3	20
Investment Income etc.	-	(0.3)
Parents/Spouse	40	24
State Benefit [b]	12	6

Notes: a) Includes *Arbeitslosengeld* and *Arbeitslosenhilfe;* b) includes *Sozialhilfe* and educational grants (*Bafög*)

Source: Statistisches Jahrbuch Berlin, 1994, p. 94.

Given the prevalence of employment in blue-collar occupations and the relatively lower wages attainable in these fields, it is not surprising that the income distribution is less favourable among non-Germans than among Germans. In 1993 in Berlin, one in three non-Germans (31 percent) with an income received less than DM 1,000 per month; among Germans, 18 percent of income-earners fell into this bottom bracket. With a poverty line of DM 800, most of these low income earners can be regarded as poor.[48] Yet, one in five non-Germans in Berlin (compared with 29 percent of Germans) earned DM 2,500 or above per month and can be considered affluent. Since the category 'non-Germans' includes foreign diplomats, academics and professional people, a further analysis would be needed to show that the former *Gastarbeiter*, their descendants, and accredited asylum seekers dominate in the lower income brackets, while the material circumstances of other non-Germans is more varied. Table 5.10 reveals a further disadvantage of non-Germans: one in three (35 percent) have no income of their own (Germans 19 percent). Non-income earners include children, but they also include resident foreign nationals without work permits.

Households of non-Germans tend to be larger than those of Germans. One in three (30 percent) of the former and only 8 percent of the latter consisted of four or more people, but non-German households depended more often on just one income.[49] For 40 percent of non-Germans and just 24 percent of Germans in Berlin, parents or spouse were the main source of financial support (Table 5.11). Income from employment and pensions were more important for German Berliners, income from unemployment and state benefit more important for non-German ones.

Unemployment

Since the late 1970s, unemployment has affected non-Germans more severely than Germans. As with income levels, employment opportunities are linked to qualifications and occupational status, and the non-German workforce tends to be concentrated in areas of the labour market where the risk of unemployment is highest. On the eve of unification, 14 percent of Berlin's population but 18 percent of the unemployed were non-Germans. Since unification, unemployment has emerged as a major problem and a key source of social discontent for

Germans in the East. Although disadvantaged in comparison with West Germans, East Germans have remained more secure in their employment than non-Germans East or West. In December 1993, 27 percent were unemployed (Table 5.12). Unemployment statistics, however, conceal the real extent of the problem. Since school leavers without completed vocational training are not permitted to claim unemployment benefit until they reach the age of twenty, they remain unrecorded, as do married women who are looking for employment but do not qualify for benefit. It has been estimated that 24 percent of Germans who are unemployed are not entitled to benefit and do not appear in the statistics. They constitute the 'silent reserve'. Among non-Germans, the exclusion of new arrivals from employment, and the difficulties encountered by young people in securing training make for an even greater 'silent reserve' of 34 percent.[50]

Table 5.12 Employment and Unemployment in Berlin, 1993 (in % of German and Non-German inhabitants)

Status	Non-Germans West Berlin	Non-Germans East Berlin	Non-Germans Berlin (all)	Germans West Berlin	Germans East Berlin	Germans Berlin (all)
Employed	73	72	73	89	86	88
Unemployed	27	28	27	11	14	12
Population overall (in 1000)	328.6	44.2	372.8	867.7	593.3	1461.0

Source: *Statistisches Jahrbuch Berlin*, 1994, p. 92

Second-Generation Prospects

There is some evidence that social exclusion has become a greater threat for non-Germans in the 1990s than in earlier years. In Germany generally, social conditions have become harsher, not merely since unification exposed East Germans to market forces and committed West Germans to transfer payments. By the mid-1980s, the economic and social modernisation in West Germany which had boosted living standards and social opportunities for a majority of people, produced a sizeable minority of losers. The unskilled and uneducated in blue-collar occupations were not only the most vulnerable to unemployment, they were also the least likely to see their standard of living increase in line with that of other sectors of society. Regardless of nationality, Germany produced its own reality of social exclusion. In some cases, of course, social exclusion is defined as the gap between reality and expectation, and constitutes a subjective category. Perception of disadvantage, however, may be as forceful a social and political motivation as objectively measured disadvantage. An increasing number of people in Germany, however, meet objective criteria of social exclusion such as low income, homelessness, unemployment, and poverty. Despite its affluent mainstream society, Germany also includes another society outside that of·affluence. Before unification, its size had been estimated at one-third of German society; since unification, the East-West tensions of thwarted expectations and uneven development have added another dimension.

By all criteria which contribute to social exclusion, non-Germans in Germany live in or near that other third of society. In 1978, non-Germans constituted 4 percent of all recipients of social security benefit, i.e., state support to subsistence level. In 1991, non-German recipients of benefit constituted 29 percent. In 1978, just 5 percent of recipients received monthly payments; in 1991, 32 percent did. Between 1987 and 1990, the number of Germans on 'welfare' increased by 9 percent; that of non-Germans nearly doubled.[51] In his 'Poverty Report', Walter Hanesch argued that poverty (or affluence) is defined by a number of factors which contribute to the subjective well-being, and material life-chances and opportunities of a person. Among the constituent elements of poverty today, income, housing, education including vocational training, and employment emerged as the most important determinants of social opportunities or social exclusion (Table 5.13). On all four counts, poverty existed among West Germans and East Germans, albeit not in the same areas and with equal intensity. Non-Germans, however, fared worse than either East or West Germans on all counts. Thirty-seven percent had experienced poverty in two or more of the key areas.

'Social exclusion' as under-provision in key areas is a problem for non-Germans as well as Germans. Disadvantage varies between areas. Thus, East Germans benefited from comprehensive education and vocational training which left them better equipped on these counts than West Germans in the same areas, while access to employment or quality housing was worse in the East than in the West. For non-Germans, the analysis in Table 5.13 consolidates our earlier observations about low income levels, poor housing conditions and labour market constraints. It also highlights education and vocational training as major deficits.

Table 5.13: Social Exclusion of East Germans, West Germans and Non-Germans in Key Socio-Economic Areas, 1992 (in % of population group)

	Income	Housing	Education (schools)	Vocational Training	Employment	Social Exclusion [a]
East	13	16	1	10	21	10
West	7	11	4	24	6	7
All Germans	8	12	3	21	10	8
Non-Germans	17	44	27	58	11	37

Note: a) This column gives the index of under-provision as analysed by the Socio-Economic Panel.

Source: Walter Hanesch et al., *Armut in Deutschland*, Reinbek, Rowohlt, 1994, p. 175.

In Germany, educational and vocational qualifications have been major trajectories of improved social opportunities. The educational reforms of the 1960s paved the way for women to equal men in participation, and even to overtake them in results at secondary level, to narrow the traditional gender gap at tertiary level and make significant gains in the labour market. While women have yet to enjoy equal treatment in the world of work, bastions of inequality are crumbling, not least since policy makers and public opinion no longer condone sex discrimination unchecked.[52] Young people in Germany and women in particular, have experienced a silent revolution of educational progress with a majority now completing advanced secondary education where over 70 percent had to make do with elementary education in the past.

The recast educational opportunities have hardly extended to non-Germans. In the early 1990s, 85 percent of young people without German nationality who had left school in Germany had only attended the lowest possible level: *Hauptschule*, an improvement of only 5 percent since the early 1970s. For German children, the name 'main school' has become a misnomer and the term *Restschule* – 'remainder school' a better match, since only one in three obtain no higher educational qualifications. For young non-Germans, this level has remained the main school, the most advanced they will ever encounter. Of their German peers, just 10 percent fail to complete the *Hauptschule* with a leaving certificate which indicates that they have achieved the required academic standards in all or a majority of subjects. Among non-Germans, 30 percent leave school without qualifications.[53] One of the key reasons can be found in the German school system itself, which requires children to achieve a prescribed standard at the end of each school year before progressing to the next level. Children with language difficulties, from socially or educationally deprived environments, children who cannot afford the additional coaching which the majority of German eight year olds already receive, will not normally progress fast enough from one form to another to complete the whole programme and gain a certificate. Moreover, depending on regional and local practice, non-German children are often taught in separate classes, ostensibly to help them overcome language difficulties, but in practice also excluding them from participating in the mainstream curriculum on which the leaving certificate is based. The concentration of non-German residents in a limited number of districts exacerbates the problem. In 1986, 50 percent or more of the children in infant and junior schools in the Berlin districts of Wedding and Kreuzberg were non-Germans, while the local selective secondary schools (*Gymnasien*) included 25 percent non-German nationals among their pupils. At the A' level stage, the proportion had fallen to below ten percent.[54]

Compared with the 1970s, when the children of former *Gastarbeiter* first entered the German educational system, much has been accomplished. All non-German school-age children attend school and obtain some formal education. This may mean that even those who do not obtain a school leaving certificate overtake their parents, who often had no formal education in their country of origin. For the third generation of non-Germans, however, improvements cannot readily be measured by looking back to another country. Language barriers, which may have constituted a major obstacle in the past, have decreased in relevance as 60 percent of non-German children are born in Germany and an increasing number have never lived anywhere else. The majority of second-generation non-Germans have a good and improving command of spoken German.[55] In 1990, one in four second-generation non-Germans thought of themselves as German.[56]

Turks, again, fare worst. Of the former *Gastarbeiter* national groups, Turkish children are the most disadvantaged (next to Italians) in educational terms. They are also the least likely to secure a vocational training place in a company, a precondition in Germany for all skilled and often even semi-skilled occupations. In 1990, descendants of former *Gastarbeiter* were as successful as German applicants in gaining places in the coveted dual system of vocational training, although many of these places were in declining occupational fields such as metal or foundry work. Half a decade earlier, the training gap between Germans and non-Germans had been 20 percent. Only Turks failed to benefit from the improved opportunities and remained the most disadvantaged of the erstwhile *Gastarbeiter* cohorts.[57] Given the centrality of qualifications in the German economic and social system, educational and qualification deficits translate into economic and social disadvantages, and produce a spiral of social exclusion for non-Germans, especially for the Turkish minority in Germany.

Lives Apart

Non-Germans have remained strangers in the country in which they live. If anything, feelings of segregation have increased, although most have lived in Germany for many years, or intend to stay. Even among the second generation, more than half do not have social contacts with Germans, although they attended German schools and met Germans as work mates or colleagues. Inside German schools, conflicts are rare, but so are contacts. During breaks and after school, German and non-German children do not normally mix. The same holds true for adolescents and adults. Again, members of the Turkish minority remain more segregated, less likely to have social contacts with Germans and less likely than members of other minorities to regard themselves as part of German society. Compared with the 1960s, acceptance of foreigners in German society has generally increased. In 1966, 66 percent of the population thought that foreigners should leave Germany and return to their own country; in 1978, that figure had fallen to 39 percent but by 1989, 56 percent again wanted foreigners to leave.[58] For adherents of the extreme right, a rejection of foreigners, and even physical violence against foreigners, constituted the core of their ideology: 90 percent of Republican voters declared in 1989 that foreigners should leave, but so did 66 percent of CDU voters.

By historical chance, German unification coincided with an unprecedented wave of non-German migration, as asylum seekers sought refuge. The uncertainties about economic and social prospects in the East, and misgivings in the West about the cost of unification, and the unexpectedly different Germans who now claimed their share of affluence, may go down in history as another instance of German national hopes falling flat in the face of political and social realities.

For non-Germans, the consequences have been alarming. In the East, arson attacks and physical violence against newcomers, who in socialist times would never have been admitted or allowed to move about freely, began as soon as the first groups of asylum seekers were distributed to the new Länder.[59] In the West, opinion polls recorded sixty or more percent of the population concerned about the *Ausländerproblem*, i.e., problems caused by the presence of foreigners, their arrival, and also the boost this gave to right-wing extremists.[60] While the East took the lead in attacking foreigners, West German right-wing extremists soon committed more xenophobic offenses, including several murders. Anyone of non-German appearance was at risk, including Jews, Africans, and Vietnamese. The aggressors did not trouble themselves with distinctions, although asylum seekers and Turks faced the most ardent hostility. Among non-Germans of all nationalities, and regardless of their duration of residency in Germany, this outburst of open aggression created a climate of acute fear. In Solingen, where the house of a Turkish family was burnt down with the loss of three lives, some even tried to form vigilante groups to protect themselves.

Restricting the right to asylum, curtailing the influx of asylum seekers, banning some neo-Nazi groups and passing harsher sentences on right-wing extremist offenders have calmed the situation. The images of Germans applauding in public, as asylum seekers were driven out of their burning hostels are not easily forgotten. For many Germans, exclusion remains an acceptable alternative. Ursula Mehrländer's observation that 'the German population has never endorsed the integration of foreigners as a key aim, but has remained reserved or plainly negative' dates from the early 1980s but has lost none of its pertinence.[61]

Notes

1. K J. Bade, 'Labour, Migration, and the State: Germany from the Late 19th Century to the Onset of the Great Depression', in *Population, Labour and Migration in 19th and 20th Century Germany*, ed. K J. Bade, Oxford, Berg, 1987, pp.76–7.

2. E. L. Homze, *Foreign Labor in Nazi Germany*, Princeton University Press, 1967, p.153.

3. It has been estimated that at the end of the war, 714,000 concentration camp inmates were utilised for forced labour; testimony provided during the Nuremberg Trials suggested that between 20 and 30 percent of those deported to Auschwitz were allocated to forced industrial labour at the camp; in addition, German industry employed at least 400,000 concentration camp victims at any one time. The survival rate for each prisoner was estimated by the SS themselves at a maximum of nine months. In addition, about half of the Russian prisoners of war died of starvation or neglect, or through hard labour. The information on these effects of Nazi inhumanity against minorities is scattered across several studies of the period. See for instance E. Kogon, *Der SS Staat. Das System der deutschen Konzentrationslager*, Frankfurt/Main, Fischer, 1965; H. Krausnick, H. Buchheim, M. Broszat and H.-A. Jacobsen, *Anatomy of the SS State*, London, Collins, 1968, pp.460–504 and U. Hörster-Philipps ed., *Wer war Hitler wirklich? Großkapital und Faschismus 1918–1945. Dokumente*, Cologne, Pahl-Rugenstein, 1978, pp.311–319.

4. On the minority status of the Sorbs, see W. Oschlies, *Die Sorben – Slawisches Volk im Osten Deutschlands*, Forum Deutsche Einheit no. 4, Bonn, Friedrich Ebert Foundation, 1990; on the minority status of Jews in East Germany, R. Ostow, *Jews in Contemporary East Germany. The Children of Moses in the Land of Marx*, Basingstoke, Macmillan, 1989; S. T. Arndt, H. Eschwege et al., *Juden in der DDR. Geschichte. Probleme. Perspektiven*. Duisburg, Brill, 1988.

5. Since 1990, a political debate has developed in Germany about the validity of *jus sanguinis* and a reform of legislation governing citizenship. Demands to liberalise the approach and grant a right of citizenship, including dual citizenship, to all children born in Germany have originated especially among the Greens, but also within the SPD and FDP. For a good summary of the party positions, see L. M. Murray, 'Einwanderungsland Bundesrepublik Deutschland? Explaining the Evolving Positions of German Political Parties

on Citizenship Policy', in *German Politics and Society*, no. 33, Fall 1994, pp. 23–56.

6. *Bevölkerungsbericht der Bundesregierung*, July 1994 quoted in B. Hof, 'Möglichkeiten und Grenzen der Eingliederung von Zuwanderern in den deutschen Arbeitsmarkt', in *Aus Politik und Zeitgeschichte*, vol. 48, 1994, p.16; see also H. Korte, 'Guestworker Question or Immigration Issue? Social Sciences and Public Debate in the Federal Republic of Germany', in Bade, ed., *Population, Labour and Migration*, pp.163–188.

7. For an overview see B. Marshall 'Germany's New Refugee Policy – a critical assessment'. Paper presented at Chatham House, March 1995.

8. Based on own calculations from various issues of the *Statistisches Jahrbuch für die Bundesrepublik Deutschland*, which publishes annual application numbers and recognition rates. The figure does not include asylum seekers whose applications were turned down and who remained illegally in Germany. Data on these illegal 'immigrants' are not available, but rumour has it that about 60 percent of the original applicants never leave, amounting to 1.5 million people.

9. Details in E. Klee ed., *Gastarbeiter. Analysen und Berichte*, Frankfurt/Main, Suhrkamp, 1975 esp. the chapter by H. Anagnostidis, 'Gewerkschaften und Ausländerbeschäftigung', pp.104–136.

10. D. von Delhaes-Günther et al., 'Rückwanderung – eine Perspektive für ausländische Arbeitskräfte' in *Aus Politik und Zeitgeschichte*, B 32, 1984, p. 31. The authors show that many returners were unemployed in their home countries.

11. A powerful defence of multi-culturalism in D. Cohn Bendit and T. Schmidt, *Heimat Babylon. Das Wagnis der multikulturellen Demokratie*. Hamburg, Hoffmann & Campe, 1993.

12. The term was coined by D. Hilger, 'Die mobilisierte Gesellschaft', in *Die zweite Republik. 25 Jahre Bundesrepublik Deutschland – Eine Bilanz*, ed. R. Löwenthal and H.-P. Schwarz, Stuttgart, Seewald, 1974, p.95ff.

13. J. Wetzel, '"Displaced Persons" Ein vergessenes Kapitel der deutschen Nachkriegsgeschichte', in *Aus Politik und Zeitgeschichte*, B 7–8, 10 February 1995, pp.34–39; W. Jacobmeyer, *Vom Zwangsarbeiter zum heimatlosen Ausländer*, Göttingen, Vandenhoeck und Ruprecht, 1985.

14. C. Kleßmann, *Die doppelte Staatsgründung. Deutsche Geschichte 1945–1955*, Göttingen, Vandenhoeck und Ruprecht, 1982, p.44.

15. Of the 200,000 Jewish concentration-camp survivors in Germany, few wished to remain there. Their property and belongings which had been taken from them by the Nazis remained in German hands; most had nowhere to go and had to wait in Germany until the creation of the State of

Israel in 1948 allowed them to leave. Waiting meant for many living in camps, often in the same camps where they had been imprisoned. Similar to the former slave labourers, these survivors of Nazi persecution were not perceived by the German authorities or by the German population as members of their post-war society in the same way in which the expellees and refugees of German origin were. They had been excluded from mainstream German society by the Nazis and continued to be excluded as Displaced Persons in the post-war years.

16. For a recent overview of developments and numbers see A. Theisen, 'Die Vertreibung der Deutschen – ein unbewältigtes Kapitel europäischer Zeitgeschichte' in *Aus Politik und Zeitgeschichte*, B 7–8, 1995, pp.24–27.

17. A.-M. de Zayas, *The German Expellees. Victims in War and Peace*, Basingstoke, Macmillan, 1993, p.150.

18. Widespread in Germany is the perception that the suffering of German expellees has been ignored by the world and unjustly overshadowed by the suffering of Nazi victims. Many of the accounts of expellees highlight testimony of atrocities against German civilians fleeing from the East or the suffering and deaths endured en route. None of these books, however, places these events in the context of the Nazi expulsion and resettlement policies in the East, from which many of the Germans benefited who were later expelled, or the treatment of local populations at the hands of Nazis and Germans.

19. The integration of former expellees in the GDR has not been the focus of specialist research until after unification. Contrary to the FRG, expellees in the former GDR were not permitted to retain their identity, form associations or articulate claims to regain their former homes. See J. B. Bilke, K. Lau and M. Wille, *Die Vertriebenen in Mitteldeutschland*, Deutschlandpolitische Schriften no. 10, Bund der Vertriebenen, Bonn, 1991. For West Germany, the detailed study by Lemberg still presents the most informative account of dislocation and social integration.

20. Data on East Germans from D. Staritz in *Sonderband DDR*, Frankfurt/Main, Fischer, 1990, p.134.

21. A. Lehmann, *Im Fremden ungewollt zuhause. Flüchtlinge und Vertriebene in Westdeutschland, 1945–1990*, Munich, Beck, 1991.

22. Up to the mid-1980s, about half the *Aussiedler* came from the Soviet Union, one third from Poland, 13 percent from Romania and the remainder from elsewhere in Eastern Europe. By 1991, the balance had shifted to 66 percent from the former Soviet Union, 19 percent from Poland, 14 percent from Romania and 1 percent from other countries. In order to control the inflow, the German government restricted entry from July 1990 to those who had supplied proof of their German origin prior to departure. On arrival, *Aussiedler* are entitled to financial support, housing, language tuition

and assistance with labour market integration. See S. Schwab, *Deutsche unter Deutschen. Aus- und Übersiedler in der Bundesrepublik*, Paffenweiler, Centaurus, 1989; G. Gugel, *Ausländer, Aussiedler, Übersiedler. Fremdenfeindlichkeit in der Bundesrepublik*, Tübingen, Verein für Friedenspädagogik, 1992.

23. For a complete list see B. Malchow et al., *Die fremden Deutschen. Aussiedler in der Bundesrepublik*, Reinbek, Rowohlt, 1990, pp.56–63.

24. The first major study was G. Almond and S. Verba, *The Civic Culture*, Boston, Little Brown & Co., 1963; a follow-on survey was published by D. Conradt, 'Changing German Political Culture', in G. Almond and S. Verba eds, *The Civic Culture Revisited*, Boston, Little Brown & Co., 1980, pp.212ff.

25. Taken from a speech by the CDU member of the Bundestag Niederalt and quoted from Cohn-Bendit and Schmidt, *Heimat Babylon*, p.83.

26. A concise analysis in K.J. Bade, *Vom Auswanderungsland zum Einwanderungsland? Deutschland 1880–1980*, Berlin, Colloquium, 1983.

27. For details of the early living conditions see Klee, *Gastarbeiter. Analysen und Berichte*, pp.195ff.

28. Initially, the trade unions opposed the recruitment of *Gastarbeiter* and saw it as a device by German employers to halt progress in improving wages and working conditions which had commenced in the 1950s. The trade unions' insistence on including *Gastarbeiter* in the general wage agreements was intended to protect their German members. A good summary in P. Katzenstein, *Policy and Politics in West Germany*, Philadelphia, Temple UP, 1987, pp.222–225.

29. *Statistisches Jahrbuch* 1994.

30. R. Erichsen, 'Zurückkehren oder bleiben? Zur wirtschaftlichen Situation von Ausländern in der Bundesrepublik', in *Aus Politik und Zeitgeschichte*, B 24, 1988, p.15.

31. Citizens of the former Yugoslavia took second place, including former *Gastarbeiter* who had arrived in the 1960s and refugees from the war-torn regions of Bosnia or Croatia.

32. Details in D. Thränhard, 'Die Bundesrepublik Deutschland – ein unerklärtes Einwanderungsland', in *Aus Politik und Zeitgeschichte*, B 24, 1988, p.5. Between 1974 and December 1988, the Turkish population in Germany increased by 44 percent.

33. Quoted in Klee, *Gastarbeiter. Analysen und Berichte*, p. 27.

34. H. Rittstieg, 'Einführung in das Ausländerrecht', in *Deutsches Ausländerrecht*, 7th edition, Munich, Beck Texte, dtv, 1990, pp.10–13; for the text of the law itself, see Ibid, pp.22ff.

35. For a detailed analysis of contemporary developments see W. Bergmann and R. Erb eds, *Neo-nazismus und rechte Subkultur,* Berlin, Metropol, 1994, and H. Willems, *Fremdenfeindliche Gewalt. Einstellungen, Täter, Konflikte,* Opladen, Leske & Budrich, 1993.

36. W. Benz ed., *Integration ist machbar. Ausländer in Deutschland,* Munich, Beck, 1993 presents a range of detailed case studies of the work of support agencies for foreigners at national, regional and local level and at the workplace.

37. M. Frey, 'Ausländer in der Bundesrepublik. Ein statistischer Überblick' in *Das Parlament,* 26 June 1982, p.9. Also M. Frey and U. Müller, *Ausländer bei uns – Fremde oder Mitbürger?* Bonn, Bundeszentrale für politische Bildung vol. 186, 1982.

38. From *Einigkeit, Asylrecht, Freiheit. Ein Gespräch zur Ausländerfrage der Nation mit Barbara John, Wolfgang Thierse, Renate Wilsen und Johann W. Gerlach,* Berlin, Dokumentationsreihe der Freien Universität, no. 17, 1992, pp.7–8.

39. A good summary in H. Esser, 'Ist das Ausländerproblem in der Bundesrepublik ein "Türkenproblem?"' in *'Fremde raus?' Fremdenangst und Ausländerfeindlichkeit,* ed. R. Italiander, Frankfurt, Fischer, 1983, pp.169–179.

40. *Datenreport 1994,* p.37; *Statistisches Jahrbuch 1994.*

41. From Kohl's *Regierungserklärung,* 16 June 1993, quoted in *Innere Sicherheit,* no. 4, June 1993, p.3.

42. In 1992, 67 percent of non-Germans and 41 percent of Germans were employed in the manufacturing and construction industries; of the non-Germans (23 percent) and Germans (59 percent) in white-collar employment, half were in public employment (12 percent and 29 percent respectively), although the majority of non-Germans held low status positions as refuse collectors etc., while German public servants would normally be administrators or civil servants. Calculated from *Datenreport* 1994, p.592.

43. See B. Koller, 'Aussiedler in Deutschland. Aspekte der sozialen und beruflichen Eingliederung' in *Aus Politik und Zeitgeschichte,* B 48, 1993 and Malchow et al., *Die fremden Deutschen,* pp.66ff.

44. *Bericht der Beauftragten der Bundesregierung zur Integration der ausländischen Arbeitnehmer und ihrer Familienangehörigen,* Liselotte Funke, Bonn, March 1991, p.11.

45. Forty-two percent of Germans and just 8 percent of non-Germans own their own home.

46. For details see C. Koch-Arzberger et al., *Einwanderungsland Hessen? Daten, Fakten, Analysen,* Opladen, Westdeutscher Verlag, 1993, pp.39ff.

47. Statistisches Landesamt Berlin, *Statistisches Jahrbuch Berlin 1990,* p.71. Unless indicated otherwise, the data in the following sections are taken

from the Statistical Yearbooks for Berlin. These include census data from 1987 and 1993 on the socio-economic position of non-Germans. Comparable data are not contained in the Statistical Yearbooks for the Federal Republic.

48. In 1993, average incomes in West Germany and West Berlin stood at DM 1,760; in East Germany and East Berlin at DM 1,230 (*Datenreport 1994*, p.452). Since the majority of non-Germans in Berlin live in the Western part of the city, comparison should be made with the West German pay levels. The poverty line is located around DM 800 per month.

49. In 1990, non-German households in Berlin included on average 2.6 persons, German households 1.8. *Statistisches Jahrbuch Berlin 1990*, p.91.

50. P. Czada, *Wirtschaft. Aktuelle Probleme des Wachstums und der Konjunktur*, Opladen, Leske & Budrich, 1984, p.194. Citing findings of the socio-economic panel of 1990, 1991 and 1992, W. Hanesch et al., *Armut in Deutschland*, Reinbek, Rowohlt, 1994, p.153 conclude that the 'Silent Reserve' has grown rapidly to 2.5 million people as unemployment in the old Länder persisted. The authors estimate that the 'Silent Reserve' in 1992 amounted to ten people for every sixteen on the unemployment register.

51. Calculated from *Statistisches Jahrbuch für die Bundesrepublik Deutschland*, various years, and specialist reports on social security benefit published in *Wirtschaft und Statistik*.

52. For a fuller discussion of the changes see E. Kolinsky, *Women in Contemporary Germany. Life, Work and Politics*, Oxford, Berg, 1993, esp. chaps 4 and 5.

53. G. Jungblut, 'Zugewanderte Kinder und Jugendliche in hessischen Schulen', in Koch-Arzberger et al., *Einwanderungsland Hessen?*, p.87.

54. Statistisches Landesamt Berlin, *Statistisches Jahrbuch Berlin 1986*, pp.108–109.

55. In 1987, 80 percent declared their command of spoken German was good; in 1991, 90 percent. From a longitudinal survey reported in *Datenreport 1994*, p.596.

56. Ibid. In 1988, 13 percent of second-generation non-Germans had expressed a German identity.

57. Jungblut, 'Zugewanderte Kinder und Jugendliche', p.90, and *Statistisches Jahrbuch Berlin 1986*, pp.111, 113.

58. From *Journal für Sozialforschung* no.1, 1983 and *Journal für Sozialforschung* no.4, 1992. Similar conclusions emerged in other surveys, see e.g., M. Küchler, 'Germans and "Others"' in *German Politics*, vol.3, no.1, 1994, pp.47ff.

59. A detailed analysis in E. Kolinsky, 'Foreigners in the New Germany. Attitudes, Experiences, Prospects', *Keele German Papers Research Series*, ed. T. Scharf, no.1, 1995.

60. W. Bergmann, 'Anti-Semitism and Xenophobia in the East German Länder', *German Politics*, vol.3 no.2, 1994, pp.265–276; also P. Merkl, *The Neo-Nazis are not the Old Nazis*. Paper delivered at the APSA Annual Conference, Washington DC, 2–5 September 1993.

61. U. Mehrländer, 'Ausländerpolitik und die sozialen Folgen', in *Der gläserne Fremde. Bilanz und Kritik der Gastarbeiterforschung und der Ausländerpädagogik*, ed. H. M. Griese, Opladen, Leske & Budrich, 1984, pp.98–99.

CHAPTER 6

The Turkish Minority in German Society

Elçin Kürsat-Ahlers

After the construction of the Berlin Wall in 1961, workers from so-called *Anwerbeländer*, recruitment countries, played an important role in satisfying the demand for labour which had previously been met largely by the westward migration of refugees from East Germany. In the course of the decade, social improvements such as a reduction in working hours, an entitlement to paid vacation, a reduction of the retirement age and access to education and training programmes began to take effect.

The principle of *rotation* which had dominated when recruitment commenced, included an obligation on the side of the worker to return to his home country. This was displaced by the principle of *integration*, a motivation spearheaded by employers to keep the workforce they had trained, and adopted by successive German governments.[1] The right of foreign workers to bring their families to live with them in Germany and to apply for long-term residency constituted one tier of a policy which also included the determination to keep the foreign workforce 'flexible', to limit contracts and to encourage or require foreign workers to leave. The recruitment ban of 1973, *Anwerbestopp*, was passed in response to the macro-economic situation at the time, but fits into a policy approach in which exclusion and the principle of *integration* have always been in conflict. Thus, 'integration' was defined in contradictory terms as preserving the home-land culture of a minority in order to facilitate re-migration, but also contained an expectation that non-German minorities should adapt to the culture of the host country Germany.

The contradictory nature of this policy approach has tended to give priority to macro-economic considerations at the expense of the social aspects of integration. This approach may be called 'social engineering' since it does not concern itself with assisting foreigners to develop a socio-psychological identification with their new environment. To that extent, German policy towards minorities has failed.

Only in the late 1980s did the concept of a *multi-cultural society,* which had earlier emerged in the United States and Australia, begin to appear in German political discourse. Migration, of course, had its own twenty-year history in post-war Germany, and the discourse of *multi-culturalism* was not intended to recast the German concept of nation or produce a new blueprint for socio-cultural change. It was basically a question of *semantic* change.

This attempted re-definition of terms was designed to gain acceptance of the fact that foreigners were no longer *Gastarbeiter* but had in reality become unwanted immigrants. Some differences between various concepts of *multi-culturalism* should not be overlooked. In the United States and in Britain, notions of *multi-culturalism* went hand-in-hand with equal rights and anti-discrimination policy, and with affirmative action.[2] In Germany no such movement and no such political purpose were ever intended. Even after a decade or more of public debate, there are to this day, no legal sanctions against face-to-face discrimination and no means to enforce equal treatment. Despite recent outbursts of xenophobia and violence against foreigners, German policy makers maintain that their country does not require specific legislation, since the equality of all persons, regardless of sex, race, language, country of origin, religion or political belief is guaranteed as a human right in the Basic Law, the German constitution, while discrimination on any of these grounds is deemed anti-constitutional and thus outlawed. The fact that the constitutional principles which define the relationship between citizens and state have not resulted in concrete and enforceable rights of the individual, or protected minorities from xenophobic action and discrimination goes unheeded.

Why an Equal-Rights Strategy Matters: Some Basic Points

Before analysing the social situation of the Turkish minority in Germany, I should like to summarise in four points how the absence of an equal-rights and equal-opportunities strategy in Germany exacerbates the exclusion of minorities and makes it a nonsense to call a society *multi-cultural* merely because it includes non-Germans among the population.

1. In the absence of an equal-rights strategy, existing differences in cultures are used to justify unequal access to political and social resources such as education, housing, health care or employment. Real differences in social power are thus condoned or masked by references to cultural differences between migrants and Germans.

2. Migrant cultures tend to be defined as essentially backward, exotic, foreign, static and incapable of dynamic transformation. They are perceived as resistant to change and opposed to social or cultural mixing.

3. Culture serves as an irrevocable demarcation line between migrant groups and the host society. Cultural differences are seen as biological in origin and therefore as an unalterable deviation on the part of the migrants from mainstream society. In Germany, culture and national identity together create the national self-image. Since the onset of German nationalism in the nineteenth century, German culture and identity have been perceived as being in stark contrast to other national groups.[3] This constellation has persisted despite the influx of non-German residents.

4. Germans have tended to interpret multi-culturalism as a model to facilitate the preservation of their own German culture and shield it from contact with (or contamination by) migrant cultures. The resulting society is indebted to the tradition of the nation state, culturally homogeneous and socially partitioned into a dominant culture and isolated migrant cultures. In this perspective, multi-culturalism constitutes a defensive strategy against ethnic and cultural heterogeneity. Paradoxically, public-opinion leaders within the Turkish minority readily adopted this concept of cultural segregation, since it enhanced their social influence within the Turkish community.

Excluded or Accepted?
Aspects of Turkish Community Life in Germany

In several key areas, the Turkish minority differs from migrants in other Western democracies. Almost all Turkish migrants in Germany are foreign citizens. Very few have been naturalised because the official requirement that naturalisation should be preceded by a degree of cultural assimilation makes it an unattractive option for Turks, who remain attached to their culture and country of origin. Calls to introduce dual citizenship conflict with the German concept of nationhood and, although the debate continues, political decision makers have so far reaffirmed their objections to such a policy.

Due to the geographic proximity of Turkey and Germany, cultural transfer and influence from the country of origin has remained considerable among the Turkish minority. A distinctive Turkish migrant culture in Germany with its own political developments, social movements, cultural modes and fashions has been slow to emerge. Rather, a culture has developed that draws on both German and Turkish contexts, and the contradictions between the two. The majority of second-generation Turks in Germany appear to have developed emotional and cultural ties to the country of origin of their parents, Turkey, and also to the country where they live and intend to remain. A study of young Turks aged between sixteen and twenty-five found that 70 percent had decided to settle in Germany permanently, whilst 30 percent envisaged returning to Turkey in the future.[4]

Most Turkish migrants and their families pay yearly visits to their relatives back home. Even in Germany, Turks from the same village or area often live in the same city and contacts between them constitute a major factor of social life. The concentration of Turks in certain urban districts tends to restrict their range of contacts to their own minority group. This social cohesiveness among Turks can also been seen as a response to the reluctance of Germans to develop social contacts with Turks, who are perceived to be of low social status and who have been the butt of prejudice. Half of the Turkish population in Germany have relatives living near their own home, 38 percent meet them daily, and 39 percent several times a week.[5]

Through chain-migration, that is to say through encouraging friends and relatives to settle in the same area, Turks have created a climate of emotional security for themselves and a social solidarity within their communities, which partly compensates for welfare-policy deficits such as the lack of kindergarten places or leisure facilities. Mehrländer found in the early 1980s that young Turks who lived in predominantly German residential areas were more likely to want to return to Turkey than those who lived in ethnic enclaves.[6]

Most Turks in Germany live in two divergent cultures with contrasting behaviour codes and patterns of belonging. At work or school, German culture tends to dominate, while during leisure time social networks divide along ethnic lines. In the first generation of migrants, social networks were almost exclusively Turkish, in the second and third generation the demarcation line remains as effective as ever. Everyday life is a continual 'border-crossing'; a continual switch between cultural environments. This bi-polarity can be culturally enriching, but may also produce psychological stress and a high degree of ambivalence for members of minority groups in Germany.

Most Turks, even those of the second generation, live in ethnically homogeneous friendship networks and are more segregated from Germans than other national groups. In 1991, for instance, 78 percent of first- generation and 65 percent of second-generation migrants had only Turkish friends. In the case of Yugoslavs, ethnically homogeneous contacts amounted to 62 percent among the *Gastarbeiter* generation and only 26 percent among their children.[7] In Berlin, 34 percent of young Turks had no contacts and a further 30 percent only occasional contacts with Germans in their leisure time, while 36 percent reported frequent contacts.[8] Yet another survey found that 30 percent of young Turks had daily contacts with Germans, 27 percent each reported meeting Germans socially many times a week or once a week, while 19 percent had no contact at all with Germans.[9]

A similar duality of integration and segregation is evident in the use made of mass media. The majority of young Turks in Germany have recourse to both German and Turkish mass media. Three in four watch German television and 60 percent read a German newspaper, while 54 percent watch Turkish television programmes and 51 percent read Turkish newspapers that are on sale in Germany.[10]

The cultural identity of Turks in Germany is built around their religious identity as Muslims. Ethnic or national backgrounds play a comparatively secondary role. The most active organisations in the Turkish community, and the most cohesive and influential groups within it are Islamic groups. Their impact and social-leadership function stems from their role as social-welfare institutions and support systems where they fill a vacuum left in migrant communities by social and public policy. Centred around mosques are various associations and self-help groups whose activities range from free meal distribution to the poor, or extending credit to people who want to set up their own business, to putting on courses for women or offering rehabilitation for the increasing number of drug addicts among Turks in Germany. Even in Turkey itself, the process of secularisation has not succeeded in penetrating all social strata or regions. It is all the more understandable that for Turks in Germany a sense of inse-curity, lack of orientation and even social desperation have encouraged a higher level of identification with Islam.

Turkish middle-class formation in Germany remains extremely weak. The majority of Turkish *Gastarbeiter* came from rural and economically underdeveloped regions. Those from urban working-class backgrounds (one third) had only recently migrated from the countryside and did not have an established history of urban integration before leaving Turkey. Even in the 1990s, many industrial workers in Turkish cities are first or second-generation migrants from rural areas.[11]

The weakness of the middle class results in the near-absence of a Turkish intellectual elite in Germany, which could spearhead cultural development. Without such an elite, Turkish migrant culture in Germany remains backward-looking and contributes to the hiatus between host-country and migrant community. This situation has been aggravated by the emergence among Germans of a negative view of Turkish culture. The existence of a Turkish middle class might break this vicious circle. Its virtual non-existence, however, tends to re-enforce the discrimination and inequality encountered by Turks at work, in education, housing, social welfare and in their legal status.

Residency Uncertainties

The Turkish minority numbered close to two million in 1994, or 28 percent of all foreign nationals in Germany. Of the former *Gastarbeiter* and their descendants one in two was of Turkish origin.[12] As shown in the previous chapter, the size of the Turkish minority in Germany continued to increase even after the recruitment ban of 1973 due to family reunion, marriages with partners from Turkey and a high birth-rate.[13] Turks in Germany today are a young population with two out of three under the age of thirty and only 19 percent over forty-five.[14] Two in three were also born in Germany and can hardly be regarded as 'foreigners' even though they remain so officially. Long-term residency among Turks, as among other non-German minorities, has become the dominant trend.[15]

Initially, most Turks appear to have imagined that they would return to Turkey before too long. In reality, a different picture emerges: the number of Turks who declare that they wish to remain in Germany for good has increased sharply and is now larger than that of would-be permanent residents from other nationalities. (Table 6.1).

Table 6.1 Between Staying and Returning: Residency Preferences among Non-German Minorities in Germany, 1993 (in %)

Preference	Turks	Yugoslavs	Italians
Return planned	31	18	25
Wish to return, without date or time	12	13	20
Undecided	14	29	20
Decision to stay in Germany for good	43	40	35

Source: *Ausländer in Deutschland*, no.4, 1993, p. 4, Reporting findings from an Emnid survey of 1993.

Many of those who remain undecided, or wish to return without committing themselves to a time and date, are likely to put off making a final decision in order to keep the hope alive that they may be reunited with their families and return to their place of origin in Turkey which, from afar, has taken on a nostalgically idealised glow. There are ready explanations for remaining in Germany: children who have to complete their education or training, the need to save money for their children's dowry, or the wish to stay close to their children who have themselves decided to stay.

The exclusion in principle of foreigners from German citizenship (unless they apply for naturalisation and can provide evidence of cultural assimilation and linguistic fluency) has produced a paradoxical situation for the Turkish minority. In early 1994, only about one in four (537,000) Turks enjoyed unrestricted residency rights in the form of an *Aufenthaltsberechtigung* which normally protects non-Germans against expulsion. In addition 409,000 Turks held what Germans call an *Aufentshaltserlaubnis,* a residency permit which is unlimited in theory but may be cancelled at any time when the continued stay of the foreigner is deemed not to be in the public interest.[16] For 293,000 Turks, the permit itself was of limited duration. What might constitute a reason for expulsion is broadly defined in the legislation, but interpreted and put into practice by state authorities at various levels of the federal system. On paper at least, the German government is entitled to expel any foreigners who are dependent on welfare benefits, commit a traffic offence or suffer from a psychiatric or an epidemic illness. Naturalisation, however, has not been perceived as an alternative to the uncertain status of a foreigner. Of the Turks in Germany, only 0.4 percent have taken this course.

Table 6.2: Changes in the Household Income of Germans, Non-Germans and Turks, 1984 and 1989

| | | Turks | | | non-Germans | | | Germans | |
	1984	1989	% change	1984	1989	% change	1984	1989	% change
Household Income in DM	2,417	2,921	20.9	2,526	2,977	17.9	2,812	3,235	15.0
Income per person	738	843	14.2	998	1,110	11.2	1,170	1,489	27.3
Equivalent income [a]	970	1,097	13.1	1,131	1,264	11.8	1,313	1,656	26.1

Note: a) weighted in accordance with the age structures of family members in order the allow for different consumption need. This equivalent income category is taken from the Federal Law on Social Benefit.

Source: *Sozio-ökonomisches Panel,* Welle 1-6, 1990.

Households and Incomes

During the course of the 1980s, the average size of German families decreased from 2.8 to 2.5 people. That of Turkish families increased from 4.1 to 4.3. Turkish households are larger than German households and include more non-earning members, thus the overall household income has to be divided between more members than in German families. Given that German household income has been higher than that of Turks (although the rate of increase among Turkish household incomes has been greater than that of Germans), each member of a German household in the late 1980s had nearly twice as much income per month as a member of a Turkish household. (Table 6.2) The prosperity gap between Germans and Turks not only remains in place, but it has widened since the early 1980s.

Fig. 6.1 Income Development, 1984–1989:
Non-Germans and Germans

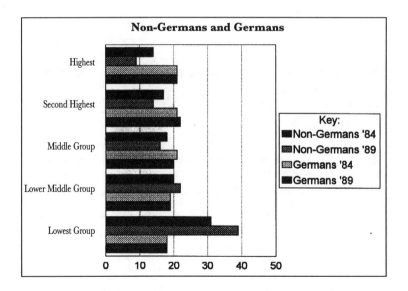

Source: Sozio-ökonomisches Panel, Welle 1–6, 1990. The income groups or *Quintile* are arrived at by dividing the whole income range into five equal percentage slices. The Lowest Income Groups comprises the bottom 20% of incomes, the Lower Middle Groups, incomes in the 20–40% range etc. The x-axis shows the percentages of non-Germans and Germans for the two years in the relevant income group.

At the end of the 1980s, nearly two-fifths of non-German households in Germany were concentrated in the bottom 20 percent of incomes. During the decade, the share of non-Germans in the highest groups declined from 15 percent to 10 percent. Among Turks the relative decline in income was particularly marked, as three in four of those in the highest income group in the early 1980s subsequently slipped into a lower one. German households in the higher brackets succeeded in maintaining their position. At the lower end, mobility was in the opposite direction. Half the Germans in the lowest bracket were able to improve their income level; among non-Germans generally, one in three managed an improvement, among Turks just one in five (see Fig. 6.1). Despite their longer-term residency and their motivation to settle in Germany for good, Turks have thus fallen behind in terms of household incomes both compared with Germans and with other non-German minorities.

Poverty among minorities, a much under-researched subject in Germany, has affected Turks more than others. Poverty tends to be defined in comparison with average income. For the purposes of this chapter, I have adopted the measure that an income below 50 percent of average earnings constitutes poverty. By this yardstick, 13 percent of Germans and 14 percent of non-Germans, but as many as 30 percent of Turks were living in poverty in 1984. By 1989, poverty among Germans had decreased to 11 percent but had risen to 17 percent among all non-Germans and to 38 percent among Turks (see Table 6.3).

Table 6.3: Poverty among Germans, Non-Germans and Turks, 1984 and 1989 (in %)

Groups of Affected by Poverty	1984	1989
Non-German Poor	21	24
Non-German Poor in Employment	15	22
Turkish Poor	30	38
Poor of other Nationalities	14	17
German Poor	13	11
German Poor in Employment	9	8

Source: W. Seifert, 'Am Rande der Gesellschaft? in *Informationsdienst zur Ausländerarbeit*, no. 3/4, 1994, p. 19.

Employment has not proved an effective shield against poverty. For Germans, employment normally means a decreased risk of poverty. For non-Germans, however, employment has offered only limited protection. In the course of the 1980s, the proportion of non-German poor in employment increased from 15 percent to 22 percent, while that of Germans fell from 9 percent to 8 percent (Table 6.3). Although poverty has become endemic throughout Germany, non-Germans have been three times as likely to be affected by it than Germans.[17]

For non-Germans in Germany, poverty not only means material uncertainty but exacerbates the uncertainties of status and residency rights mentioned earlier. The fear that they may be compelled to leave the country where they have spent all or much of their lives, prevents many from seeking public assistance. Through such status uncertainties the German welfare state maintains the possibility of excluding non-Germans from the support functions that a modern state should offer to all its inhabitants.

Low incomes translate into material need or poverty in retirement. In Germany, the level of retirement pension depends on the wage level and on the number of years in employment, when contributions to the national pension scheme were made. Foreign workers who came to Germany at a later age and received lower average wages than Germans are faced with a dual disadvantage. In the early 1990s, the monthly pensions of Turkish men amounted to just over half of those received by Germans, DM 898 compared to DM 1,543.[18] To date, the number of former *Gastarbeiter* above the age of sixty has remained small. First estimates, however, suggest that their social circumstances are considerably worse than those encountered by Germans. Poverty in old age among non-Germans constitutes a growing problem since it is projected that by the year 2030 the demographic structure of non-Germans will resemble that of Germans with 37 percent aged sixty or over.[19]

Housing Conditions

One of the main spheres of life to be influenced by low income is housing. At the time when they first settled in Germany, discrimination against foreigners in the housing market and a shortage of low-cost rental accommodation forced most to live in conditions which were considerably worse in terms of size and quality than those of Germans. Of all the national groups,

Turks were least able to escape social discrimination in the housing market.[20] In 1989, Germans lived in accommodation with, on average, 1.9 rooms per person. Taking this level as the norm, a definition of poor housing would imply that one person has one room or less to live in. In 1984, this applied to 40 percent of Germans but 81 percent of non Germans; in 1989, poor housing among Germans had declined to 34 percent but remained at 80 percent for non-Germans.[21] By the housing standards familiar in German society, one in three Germans, but four out of every five non-Germans live in over-crowded conditions.

Segregation and the emergence of districts with a high concentration of foreigners has increased rather than decreased. In 1980, 41 percent of non-Germans lived in areas where more than 12 percent of the inhabitants were foreigners. By the mid-1980s, their share had risen to 45 percent for non-Germans generally and 49 percent for Turks.[22] Expectations that non-Germans would successfully blend into German society and that enclaves of non-German residential districts would give way to a social mix in line with the duration of stay, have not been fulfilled.

Low income is not the sole cause of housing discrimination. There is little evidence for claims, repeatedly made in the literature, that the housing conditions of Turks are determined by their unwillingness to pay more rent, by their primary concern to save as much as possible rather than invest in better housing, or by their free decision to opt for segregation and live in a Turkish neighbourhood. On the contrary, recent evidence points to ethnic discrimination as the main cause for poor housing and the exclusion of Turks from housing integration in German society.

The most comprehensive study of the housing conditions of Turks in Germany was conducted in the mid-1980s among 43,343 German and 9,676 Turkish members of the workforce at Ruhrkohle AG in the Ruhr industrial region.[23] The average income of Turkish workers at Ruhrkohle, many of whom worked at the coal-face, lay 9 percent above that of Germans, and many (59 percent) were even willing to pay higher rents in order to improve the quality of their housing. One in three Turks (30 percent), but only one in six Germans (16 percent) lived in flats without a bathroom. Ninety-three percent of Turks compared to 48 percent of Germans wished to have a larger home. In addition to the discrepancies in housing quality, various studies have revealed that Turks have to pay 20 percent more rent than Germans for property of the same standard.

The study of housing conditions among the Ruhrkohle workforce also showed that most Turks were interested in developing social contacts with Germans. Thirteen percent preferred to live in a segregated neighbourhood, 53 percent in a mixed neighbourhood, while 33 percent even expressed a preference for neighbours who were solely German.[24] The 1985 survey showed that a mere 9 percent of Turks, given the choice, would have opted for a predominantly Turkish neighbourhood.[25] Despite these findings, the myth has persisted among Germans that Turks opt for Turkish neighbourhoods and for segregation. In turn, this is held against them as evidence of an unwillingness to integrate sufficiently into German society and the German way of life. The allegation that Turks exclude themselves from German society and culture serves to exonerate Germans from harbouring prejudice, whilst appearing to make discrimination against them the fault of Turks themselves.

Table 6.4: Unemployment among Non-Germans from former Recruitment Countries, 1980–1994 (in %)

Year	Labour Force overall	All non-Germans	Turks	Yugoslavs	Italians	Greeks	Spaniards	Portuguese
1980	3.5	4.8	6.3	2.8	5.5	4.1	3.2	2.1
1985	8.7	13.1	14.8	9.0	14.7	11.4	8.7	7.6
1990	6.6	10.0	10.0	6.0	10.6	9.7	6.8	5.5
1994	8.8	15.5	18.9	9.8	17.0	16.2	11.2	11.2
Total unemployed at 30.8.94	391,648	141,851	45,141	38,339	22,643	6,837	6,036	

Source: Compiled from statistics published by the Bundesanstalt für Arbeit for the relevant years.

Employment

When the employment of *Gastarbeiter* was regulated by recruitment contracts, their underprivileged place at the unskilled end of the labour market was all but compensated for by relative job security. This no longer applies. The second and third generations face the full competitive force of the labour market. Low achievement at school, limited access to vocational qualifications and their exclusion from other cultural resources coincided with a rapid transformation of the German economic structure, a decline in manufacturing, notably in the metal-working sector, and a drastic drop in the demand for unskilled or semi-skilled labour, the type of labour most frequently offered by Turks in Germany. From the early 1980s onwards, employment opportunities contracted sharply, and unemployment among non-Germans rose faster than among Germans (Table 6.4). In 1994, the unemployment rate among Turks was twice the national average and had trebled since 1980.

In the early years of recruitment, foreign workers were concentrated in manufacturing industry. By 1993, employment in manufacturing had declined to 42 percent for non-German workers generally; among Turks it still constituted 53 percent. Conversely, service-sector employment had increased from 7 percent in the 1980s to 26 percent in 1993. Among Turks, 19 percent worked in the service sector (Table 6.5).

The economic modernisation which has transformed labour-market opportunities and occupational status in Germany benefited non-Germans less than Germans, and Turks least of all.[26] Turks tend to be employed in jobs which are dirty and potentially damaging to health, in shift or piece work and often in plants with a fluctuating workforce and little job security.[27] In certain branches such as plastic production (16 percent of the workforce), foundry work (24 percent), car manufacturing (13 percent), in hotels and catering (25 percent), in cleaning services (20 percent), fish processing (34 percent) and leather processing (28 percent), Turkish and other foreign workers are particularly strongly represented.

In 1993, 35,000 Turks ran their own businesses and between them had created 13,500 jobs. Overall, just over 200,000 non-Germans were self-employed. The slow emergence of a non-German middle class, including a small Turkish sector, had begun, although most of these business were on a small scale and frequently employed family members. In many cases, unemployment had led to setting up in business in an attempt to reduce economic insecurity. Some Turkish business men, however, also stressed that their key motivation had been to achieve independence (73 percent), higher income (60 percent), higher status (62 percent) and more security for their families (50 percent).[28]

Table 6.5: The Employment of Non-Germans and Turks
by Economic Sector, 1993 (in %)

Economic Sector	Non-Germans	Turks
Agriculture/Fisheries	1.0	0.8
Mining/Energy	1.2	2.8
Manufacturing	42.2	53.4
Construction	19.0	7.6
Trade/Commerce	10.4	8.9
Transport/Communication	4.8	4.5
Banking/Insurance	1.1	0.4
Public Services	2.5	1.9
Private Services	25.7	18.9
Charities	1.5	1.0
Total (N)	2,150,114	619,053

Source: Bundesanstalt für Arbeit, *Arbeits und Sozialstatistik*, 31 December 1993.

White-collar employment remains the exception for non-Germans. In 1990, only 19 percent held white-collar jobs compared to more than 50 percent of Germans. The *Gastarbeiter* legacy of low-status, low-income blue-collar employment continues to haunt the next generations. The old structures persist. In the early 1990s, for instance, 47 percent of all apprentices in Germany were training for white-collar, and 53 percent for blue-collar employment. For all trainees in Germany the mismatch between training and employment produces problems of transition into the labour market, as many skilled blue-collar workers cannot find employment opportunities in the area of their skills. Non-Germans are even more affected by this discrepancy. Of those who had secured vocational training places, a prerequisite in Germany for skilled employment, 25 percent were training for white-collar, and 75 percent for blue-collar occupations. Among young non-German women in vocational training, nearly half were in blue-collar occupations compared to only 25 percent of young German women. Generally speaking, non-German women face additional disadvantages compared to men. In the early 1990s, nearly half the apprentices in Germany were female, i.e., in terms of numbers and formal participation rate, women had closed the age-old gender gap of vocational qualifications. Among non-German apprentices, only one in three were women, while 70 percent were men. Access for young non-German women to qualifications and employment opportunities is even more fraught with difficulty than for their male peers.

Underprivilege Perpetuated: Turkish Children at School

It has been argued that the influx of *Gastarbeiter* into the German economy and their employment at the unskilled and semi-skilled end of the labour market increased the occupational mobility of Germans. As low-status jobs were taken up by foreigners, Germans were free to move from blue-collar to white-collar, from low-paid to higher paid employment. In education, a similar pattern established itself. Although two thirds of non-German children were born in Germany, their educational opportunities differ sharply from those of their German peers with a heavy concentration at the lower educational levels. From the mid-1970s onwards, the presence of non-German children in the educational system improved the chances of German children to gain advanced educational qualifications. The lowest tier of a selective school system which would at best equip for low-status employment in the future was increasingly populated by non-German children.[29] The low socio-economic status of parents was perpetuated across the generations through the low educational opportunities of their children.

In 1994, one in four young non-Germans and only six percent of young Germans failed to gain a school leavers' certificate. Without such a certificate, employment is hard to find and vocational training unobtainable. Today, an estimated one in three Turks below the age of twenty-five are out of work while 65 percent have not found vocational training.[30] Since completed vocational training constitutes a recognised entry ticket to the German labour market – even if trainees cannot find employment in the field in which they qualified – remaining without a completed apprenticeship results in unskilled employment or no employment at all in the future. The few studies which focus on vocational training opportunities for non-Germans suggest that employers have been reluctant to take on non-German apprentices partly because they may themselves be prejudiced and partly because they are afraid that the presence of foreigners may unleash social tensions at the work place.[31] Most employers assumed that their business partners or their employees would react negatively to non-German members of the trainee and workforce. Moreover, German applicants normally find a training place though personal contacts and networks. The children of non-Germans have no such contacts and networks at their disposal and their parents lack the influence German parents can exert on potential employers.

Table 6.6: German, Non-German and Turkish Pupils in German Schools, 1991 (in %)

Type of School	German and Non-German pupils	Non-German pupils	Pupils from recruitment countries	Turkish pupils
Junior	37	37	36	37
Main	17	26	29	29
Middle	11	9	10	8
High	20	10	8	6
Special	4	6	6	7
Auxiliary [a]	10	11	11	13

Overall number of pupils	9,133,000	800,241	600,480	360,912

Note: a) Auxiliary School (*Hilfsschule*) is a special school for slow learners. Transfer into this school type is obligatory when pupils fail to pass the academic requirements of any one school year for the second time. Figures in table are rounded up and may not total 100

Source: Calculated from *Bundesbildungsbericht*, Bonn, 1991.

It could be argued that the political will to combat discrimination against ethnic minorities can best be demonstrated by the state itself and its recruitment to public-sector employment. The

German state, however, far from using this method to counteract the unequal opportunities in the private sector, has simply perpetuated inequality. In 1994, 5 percent of German applicants but only 1.5 percent of non-German applicants (1,829 individuals) were accepted for public-sector employment.[32]

In the selective education system of Germany, Turkish children fare worst (Table 6.6). Not only have intermediate and advanced levels of schooling, the entry roads to further studies and professional qualifications, been less accessible to them than to their peers of German or other national origin, they have also been more likely than others to be deemed educationally subnormal and compelled to attend special schools. The data on educational qualifications are data on educational inequality: only 28 percent of German but 44 percent of Turkish pupils leave school with the lowest educational qualification, the *Hauptschulabschluß;* 28 percent of young Germans and 6 percent of young Turks pass the *Abitur* and gain the right to study at university. Overall, 3.8 percent of pupils in Germany, but 6.7 percent of Turkish children attend special schools. There can be no explanation for this other than an unintentional structural discrimination, or even an intentional discrimination against foreign children at school. A complex set of mechanisms is at work: continuing difficulties with the German language and with cultural adaptation, often because kindergarten places and pre-school education are not available; lack of parental support with homework in an educational system which presupposes that parents play an active part in studying with their children; the lack of study space for children in overcrowded flats; and, for the same reason, difficulties with concentration at school due to the restrictions on play and motion. For the children, cultural and emotional stress resulting from social stigmatisation and isolation from class mates makes school a problem place, while teachers react with impatience and an unwillingness to cope with 'problem children' who demand more attention and energy than they wish to invest. Moreover, the intelligence tests that are used to determine the ability range of pupils and a possible transfer from a regular to a special school are biased in favour of the mainstream culture, thus disadvantaging members of non-German minorities.

Even for those who, succeeding at school against all the odds, complete their *Abitur*, equal opportunities remain elusive. Young non-Germans, including those who have been born in Germany and manage to obtain university entrance qualifications there, are deemed to be foreign applicants and have to compete with others from abroad for the places reserved for non-German students in the German university system. In 1990/1991 for instance, the number of students at German universities totalled 1.85 million, 1.75 million of them Germans and just over 99,000 non-Germans. Of these, 14,500 were Turks who had completed their *Abitur* in Germany. To put it another way: 0.8 percent of students at German universities were Turks with German educational qualifications. Not their education, but the national origin of their parents determined their access to university education. Given that university education has become the required route to the professions and to elite positions, even the best educated young Turks in Germany continue to be penalised because of the background of their parents.

Outlook

For Turks in German society, both those of the first generation who arrived as *Gastarbeiter* and those of the second or third generations who were born in Germany or joined their families there, intentional or unintentional patterns of discrimination perpetuate disadvantage and low economic and social status, whilst curtailing social advancement. Despite their long-term residency, Turks continue to face hostility. In fact, hostility against them has intensified since the mid-1970s when the erstwhile *Gastarbeiter* opted for residency. In Germany today there is an undercurrent of xenophobia in public opinion and an open emphasis on xenophobia in right-wing and neo-Nazi organisations, groups and youth cliques. More than other former *Gastarbeiter* and their descendants, Turks have been exposed to such hostility. The wave of xenophobic violence that saw offenses treble between 1991 and 1993, claimed several Turkish lives and revealed just how excluded and vulnerable non-Germans have remained in German society.

In German law, discrimination against a member of an ethnic minority is not regarded as a criminal offence, nor is it the focus of legislation. Only murder, incitement to murder or to racial violence are classified as criminal offenses before the law, while the whole gamut of offensive and discriminatory action that exudes xenophobia but falls outside the narrow definitions of the criminal code tends to go unpunished. German policy makers have persistently refused to admit that a political and social climate in which discrimination against minorities is endemic may encourage acts of harassment or even violence against members of these minorities. Admitting such a link, however, would be a first step towards an anti-discrimination law. Without such a law, the goodwill of Foreigners' Commissioners and other institutional or personal initiatives can only be of limited effect. In order to improve the opportunities of Turkish and other non-German minorities and halt the perpetuation of disadvantage, a concerted action of government and the judicial system seems called for, to implement anti-discrimination programmes and to outlaw discrimination of any kind. Only then can peaceful social relations between Germans and non-German minorities be assured in the long term. Minorities who remain deprived of political rights, social opportunities and cultural participation have been singled out for hostility in the past and continued treatment of them in this way may constitute a threat to democracy in the future.

Notes

1. K.J. Bade, 'Paradoxon Bundesrepublik: Einwanderungssituation ohne Einwanderungsland', in *Migration in Geschichte und Gegenwart*, ed. K.J. Bade, Munich, Beck, 1992, p.393.

2. O.J. McCrudden et al., *Racial Justice at Work*, London, Policy Studies Institute, 1991; N. Glazer, *Affirmative Discrimination: Ethnic Inequality and Public Policy*, New York, Glazer Books, 1978; E. Kürsat-Ahlers, 'Appelle an das Gewissen der Mächtigen reichen nicht aus: Verspätete Gleichstellungsrechte für Migranten', in *Utopie Kreativ* no. 39/40, January–February, 1994, pp.23–40.

3. N. Elias, *Studien über die Deutschen*, Frankfurt/Main, Suhrkamp, 1990; E. Kürsat-Ahlers, 'Das Stigma des Einwanderers – Über die Macht, Kultur und Abwehr in Einwanderungsprozessen', in *Die multikulturelle Gesellschaft: Der Weg zur Gleichstellung?*, ed. E. Kürsat-Ahlers, Frankfurt/Main, IKO, 1992, pp.41–93.

4. *Berliner Jugendliche türkischer Herkunft in Berlin*, ed. Die Ausländerbeauftragte des Senats von Berlin, 13 January 1992, p.8. Of the 30 percent intending to leave, 39 percent gave as a reason for their decision the increased hatred against foreigners in Germany; 11 percent felt generally uncomfortable and insecure, while 31 percent declared that they saw Turkey, not Germany as their homeland. In the survey, 43 percent of young Turks

had experienced discrimination of some kind, 19 percent of them at work, 14 percent in public offices, 14 percent in the street, 12 percent at schools and 8 percent in shops. One in three stressed that attacks and direct insults had increased since 1990. It appears that most xenophobic criminal offenses are committed outdoors in an atmosphere of anonymity. Between five and seven percent had personally experienced verbal abuse or physical attacks.

5. U. Neumann, *Die Erziehung ausländischer Kinder*, Düsseldorf, Schwann, 1981.

6. U. Mehrländer, *Türkische Jugendliche: Keine beruflichen Chancen in Deutschland?*, Bonn, Friedrich Ebert Foundation, 1983.

7. H. Alpheis, 'Erschwert die ethnische Konzentration die Eingliederung?', in *Generation und Identität*, ed. H. Esser and J. Friedrichs, Opladen, Westdeutscher Verlag, 1991, p.172.

8. *Berliner Jugendliche*, p.14.

9. *Ausländer in Deutschland*, ed. Isoplan-Institut, no.1, 1990, p.5.

10. *Berliner Jugendliche*, p.11.

11. E. Kürsat Ahlers, 'Einwandererfamilien, ihr Struktur- und Funktionswandel im Migrationsprozeß', in *Neue Lebensformen – Zeit-Krankheiten und Psychotherapie*, ed. P. Buchheim, Th. Cierpka and T. Seifert, Berlin / Heidelberg / New York, Springer, 1994, pp.78–106.

12. *Ausländer in Deutschland*, ed. Bundesministerium für Arbeit und Sozialordnung, no.2, 1994, p.2.

13. Ibid., p.8. In 1994, 45,000 children were born to Turkish mothers, which constituted 13 percent of all births. Non-German births in the same year totalled 103,064.

14. *Ausländer in Deutschland. Statistiken*, no. 4, 1993, p.2ff.

15. Two out of three have lived in Germany for ten years or more. See also Chapter 5.

16. 'Daten und Fakten zur Ausländersituation', in *Mitteilungen der Beauftragten der Bundesregierung für die Belange der Ausländer*, Bonn, October 1994, p.41.

17. F. Hamburger, 'Migration und Armut', in *Informationsdienst Ausländerarbeit*, no. 3/4, 1994, shows that in 1984, 11.8 percent of Germans and 25 percent of non-Germans lived in poverty. With some fluctuations during the course of the 1980s, poverty in 1992 affected 8.9 percent of Germans but 24.5 percent of non-Germans, i.e., among the former the risk of poverty decreased, among the latter it remained stagnant at its higher level.

18. M. Dietzel-Papadyrkakou, 'Ältere ausländische Menschen in der Bundesrepublik Deutschland', in *Expertisen zum Ersten Altenbericht der Bundesregierung*

III: Aspekte der Lebensbedingungen ausgewählter Bevölkerungsgruppen, Berlin, 1993, p.82.

19. Statistisches Bundesamt, *Modellrechnung*, Wiesbaden, 1986.

20. *Die Situation der ausländischen Arbeitnehmer und ihrer Familienangehörigen in der Bundesrepublik Deutschland. Repräsentativuntersuchung 1985*, ed. Bundesminister für Arbeit und Sozialordnung, Bonn, 1986.

21. W Seifert, 'Am Rande der Gesellschaft?', in *Informationsdienst Ausländerarbeit*, no. 3/4, 1994, p.21.

22. U. Mehrländer, *Die Situation der ausländischen Arbeitnehmer und ihrer Familienangehörigen in der Bundesrepublik Deutschland*, Forschungsbericht im Auftrag des Bundesministers für Arbeit und Sozialordnung, Bonn, 1981; and P. König, *Die Situation der ausländischen Arbeitnehmer und ihrer Familienangehörigen in der Bundesrepublik Deutschland*, Forschungsbericht im Auftrag des Bundesministers für Arbeit und Sozialordnung, Bonn, 1986, p.345.

23. H. Korte, V. Eichener, C. Koch and K. Schmidt, *Die Wohnsituation der ausländischen Mitarbeiter der Ruhrkohle AG. Forschungsbericht*, Bochum-Essen, 1981; H. Korte ed., *Die Wohnsituation ausländischer Mitarbeiter der Ruhrkohle AG*, Schriftenreihe Landes- und Stadtentwicklungsforschung des Landes Nordrhein-Westfalen, Dortmund, 1984.

24. Korte et al. Eds, *Die Wohnsituation*, 1981, and M. Borris, *Ausländische Arbeiter in einer Großstadt*, Frankfurt/Main, Europäische Verlagsanstalt, 1975, p.159.

25. König, *Die Situation der ausländischen Arbeitnehmer.*

26. Bundesanstalt für Arbeit, *Arbeits- und Sozialstatistik – Hauptergebnisse 1993*, Nuremberg, 1993 shows that in 1993, 38 percent of Germans worked in manufacturing, 22 percent in the service sector, while white-collar employment had displaced manufacturing as the largest employment sector among Germans but not among non-Germans.

27. E. Kürsat-Ahlers, 'Die Fabrik als Präge- und Zivilisierungsinstanz der Migration', in *Spannungsfeld Personalentwicklung*, ed. S. Laske and S. Gorbach, Vienna, Manz, 1993, p.334.

28. *Selbständige Ausländer in Deutschland*, ed. Zentrum für Türkeistudien, Opladen, Leske & Budrich, 1991, p.79.

29. *Untersuchungen zur Bildungsbeteiligung ausländischer Kinder in Bielefeld*, ed. Zentrum für Lehrerbildung der Universität Bielefeld, Projektleiter F.O. Radtke, Bielefeld, 1992.

30. *Ausländerbericht der Stadt Bielefeld*, Bielefeld, 1995, p.18. Before moving to the University of Hanover, the author was Commissioner for Foreigners in the City of Bielefeld, and in this capacity she contributed to preparing the above report.

31. *Arbeits- und Ausbildungssituation ausländischer Jugendlicher: 'Zukunft ohne Beruf'*, ed. Deutscher Gewerkschaftsbund, Bildungswerk des DGB, Düsseldorf, 1990, p.15.

32. *Ausländer in Deutschland. Statistiken*, no.3, 1994.

CHAPTER 7

Turkish Everyday Culture in Germany and its Prospects

Dursun Tan and Hans-Peter Waldhoff

Introduction

Turkish everyday culture in Germany is a heterogeneous affair, and writing about it means highlighting its main characteristics and putting them into some sort of order. This chapter, therefore, focuses on common trends and typical developments in Turkish everyday culture, while its many divergent tendencies and facets can only be hinted at in passing.

At the time of writing, Turkish everyday culture in Germany is undergoing a profound structural change. The former *Gastarbeiter* are gradually turning into permanent residents, a transformation which is evident in a number of things such as naturalisation, changes in language, in manners and consumer behaviour, in the living environment, or in setting up institutions to meet specific needs.

Generations and Families

The first *Gastarbeiter* generation is about to reach pensionable age. Many of them are beginning to examine their life stories and in particular the story of their migration in order to determine whether their hopes and aims of yesteryear have been fulfilled. They are taking stock of their lives so far. In doing so, old, forgotten and previously unsolved problems move more sharply into focus again and may, as they mingle with current problems, produce a sense of stress. A major and recurring topic of conversation among first-generation migrants is the question as to whether they have achieved what they aspired to before emigrating, what price they have had to pay for it and whether in the final analysis it has all been worthwhile in material and non-material terms. The outcome of this stock-taking is likely to leave its mark on attitudes and behaviour. An individual Turk may wonder whether he or she was right to be open and generally positively inclined towards the German social environment. Another may resolve to cut him- or herself off more deliberately from the German setting and turn back to the ethnic and cultural roots left behind in the homeland. Some may participate actively in social or political affairs, others may seek or dismiss inter-cultural contacts with persons of different social and national backgrounds.

Taking stock also affects the nature of inter-generational relations and of relations within families. Although the stock-taking exercise constitutes only one of several factors, it tends to shape the aims for the future which are passed on to the children and which the children are expected to meet. Are these aims framed with the country of origin in mind, and intended to be realised there, or do they pertain to life in the country of immigration? Parents whose own aims were focused on their country of origin and who originally hoped to realise them there, but were prevented by adverse circumstances from doing so, are more likely to want their children to achieve in the country of origin what they themselves were not able to achieve. Parents whose plans were geared to life in Germany will expect their children to make their way in Germany. These aspects are important for the structure of authority and the general patterns of relationships within families.

The family structure of migrants has frequently been seen as a distinct type, a 'migrants' family' with special characteristics. Common to all migrant families has been the experience of geographical, linguistic, cultural and environmental change and the special challenges these bring. In the early stages of migration, traumatic fears of separation are a common occurrence, exacerbated by uncertainties about the success of migration, the splitting-up of families and changes in the structure of power and authority within and between families. In contemporary society, these conflicts erupt as disagreements over issues of upbringing, moral codes, educational styles and norms between the various agencies involved in the educational process, not least between parents and their children.

Similar conflicts surround vocational training. What kind of training do parents expect their children to obtain? Do they choose on the basis of criteria derived from their country of origin or from the German society in which they are living? Are the parents aware of these criteria or do they choose subconsciously? Are the children interested in the type of training which their parents envisage for them?

Linked to these questions is the issue of jurisdiction and authority within the family. In principle at least, fathers tend to suffer a loss of jurisdiction and authority as head of family in the course of migration, while mothers may gain economic influence and children often acquire greater social and cultural power. No migrant family escapes a transformation of its established pattern of authority and structure. Such a transformation normally breeds conflicts. These problems may overlap with and/or take the same form as the usual conflicts between generations, but those directly involved frequently perceive them in 'ethnic' terms and tackle them accordingly. Indeed, migration itself and living as a minority in Germany is frequently cited as the dominant reason for any kind of problem, be it family-based or rooted in society more generally. Researchers often confirm such arguments, or even propose them themselves in lieu of more probing explanations.[1]

Migration involves a relocation from one social system to another and from one system of symbols to another. Such a relocation also entails a sudden change of familiar status and power relationships, a devaluation of traditional skills and roles. The effect of these changes goes right across all migrant families. The various stages of the migration process can be linked to various members of the migrant family.[2] The children import the norms of German society into the family and interact with their parents according to these norms, i.e., following the model they have derived from their German environment. Such behaviour includes teenage protests against the parent generation or against society. Many parents, on the other hand, having themselves been brought up in an atmosphere dominated by pressures to succeed, will not tolerate dissent. They prefer their children to follow reliably in their footsteps and support the collective effort to accomplish better living conditions. Thus, parents tend to stress values such as obedience, tidiness and diligence. In addition, many parent-child relationships come under stress from the physically demanding, monotonous shift work of the parents and the dual burden of the mother. The increased emphasis on Islamic customs and social rules, the insistence on traditional cultural values and norms, and the strong reference back to one's place of origin, may in many instances be interpreted as an attempt by Turkish parents to recoup some of the authority they have lost through migration and to inhibit further changes. 'Retaining religious customs and an Islamic upbringing after migration provides a means for some Turkish families and in particular some Turkish fathers and brothers to protect the traditional family structure from unwanted social influences. Here, "lived Islam" becomes a device to legitimise and prop up the patriarchal family'.[3]

Relations between families in kinship networks and neighbourhoods also influence social behaviour. On the one hand, kinship networks and neighbourhoods constitute an important informal support system, on the other hand they exercise massive social control and constitute a rigid and conformist environment in which any kind of deviation elicits fierce punishment. The control exercised by Turkish males over female members of their families is also intended to prevent a potential loss of honour, since the standing of a family and the esteem in which it is held is presumed to depend above all on the blameless behaviour of its female members. This notion of 'honour' is the 'weak point' and at the same time the means by which the migrant community can force families to remain loyal and conform to the group norms.

These tensions and dynamics in Turkish migrant families can of course only be understood with reference to the relationship developed by Turks with Germans, which has been characterised as a confirmation of 'The Established and the Outsiders'.[4] This configuration explains why many families remain close to their supportive kinship networks despite intolerable conditions and seriously disrupted relationships. As long as the outside world they perceive as German appears to be hostile, there is little chance of individual families shrugging off the traditional notions of authority and ignoring its guardians. On the contrary, the guardians of tradition are all the more likely to put social pressures on families in order to make them comply with their claims of dominance.

Religion

Seen from the outside, Islam appears to be an undifferentiated and monolithic whole. In reality, however, the Muslim religion is as varied in its internal structure and as fragmented into denominations as the Christian. The complexity of Islam tends to go unnoticed since the way 'Christian-Germans' perceive it is determined by a group of Muslims who set themselves demonstratively apart from non-Muslims and 'errant Muslims', by means of their dress, their conduct and the religious symbolism of many of their everyday activities. Among the two million Turks in Germany, this group constitutes only a minority, but it has managed to monopolise the debate about the status and nature of Islam in the country.

While secular Muslims regard Islam and religion generally as a personal and private matter which they do not parade in public, fundamentalist Muslims make a conscious effort to proclaim their religious convictions and thus turn them into a public matter. Their basic attitude towards the 'modern' German environment can be called 'culturally defensive'.[5] Since they condemn German society as 'decadent' and distance themselves from it, each deliberate or unintended conflict with that society serves to reinforce the internal stability of their own group. Other practising and conservative Muslims are often mistaken for fundamentalists although they merely seek the protection of religion and hope to achieve a balance which will allow them to live by their Muslim identity and beliefs in Germany.

Of course, the boundaries and dividing lines between these various groups – fundamentalist, conservative and practising Muslims – are not sharply drawn. Conservative and practising Muslims tend to be interested in compromise, are looking for dialogue with other denominations, and favour an harmonious co-existence with other social groups, religions and ideologies. These 'Muslims who wish to make Germany their home'[6] are the ones most likely to spearhead the emergence of a European Islam. There are many signs of such developments. Islamic religious meeting houses in Germany, for instance, do not just serve as venues for the prescribed daily prayers, as is customary in Turkey, but have become community centres of sorts, ministering to both spiritual and social needs. Most centres have a dining hall, stalls for market traders, a *hallal* butcher and a hall for funeral ceremonies. In addition, many Islamic meeting houses have sports facilities and offer vocational training for young people.

The liberal strand of Islam in Turkey, so-called *Alevites,* are beginning to develop similar organisations and attempting to shape social developments in their country of immigration. In their conduct and appearance, these liberal Muslims are perceived as less alien by Germans than fundamentalists, and are therefore taken to be more Europeanised and integrated. Prevalent among Germans, however, is an image of Turks as fundamentalists, which means that Turks or Muslims in western dress and with apparently western lifestyles are seen as exceptions who have strayed from the fold. Even some researchers are prone to encourage ethnic stereo-typing. The German academic Annemarie Schimmel for instance, a convert to Islam, used the award of the Peace Prize for Literature to accuse the Indo-British writer Salman Rushdie, who faces a death threat over his book *Satanic Verses,* of having offended all Muslims.[7] By contrast, Europeanised Turks and Muslims stress that their Turkish or Muslim identity does not prevent them from supporting democracy and human rights. In their view, a European and a Muslim identity, however understood, do not contradict each other.

Doctrinally at least, past history shows that there is nothing in Islam to prevent migrants from developing a modern European strand of religion. Every religion tends to absorb aspects of the social practices and cultural orientation of the society in which it exists and becomes itself part of that society. Varieties of Islam – Arab, African, Indian and Asian Islam – have already developed over the centuries and an American and European Islam have begun to take shape.

Language

Language competence plays a central and complex role in all migration processes. It constitutes a special challenge to this chapter to portray in English some of the linguistic effects of Turkish-German migration. By drawing on specific examples, we should like to sketch some developments which, in our view, are characteristic of modern migration from the periphery to the centre, a phenomenon relevant not only for Turks in German society, but currently the focus of attention world-wide.[8]

For the majority of first-generation Turks, the Turkish language at the time of their migration remains the key reference point. In both languages, German and Turkish, this generation has inadequate competence. First-generation Turks in Germany have thus far enjoyed few opportunities to develop their command of Turkish beyond its original level, or to adapt to recent changes in language use. Since this first cohort of migrants originated predominantly from rural or impoverished urban milieus, had not received a formal education and had only known local dialects, their language competence in Turkish had never gone beyond a restricted colloquial level.

In the country of immigration, many were engaged in shift-work which made heavy demands on their physical strength and left them little time to develop their mother tongue or to expand their knowledge of German as a second language.[9] In the beginning, both motivation and opportunity to study were missing. Since migration had been envisaged for an interim period only, the main aim was to use the time to work and to save enough money to set up in business back home. At that time, longer term goals for a life in Germany seemed out of place. Employers were only interested in migrant labour and the short-term benefits of *Gastarbeit*. In this perspective, organising language courses at the workplace would have only been an unnecessary expense. In any case, the majority of migrant workers were employed in piece-work production where tasks were monotonous, requiring no specialised skills or linguistic competence.

Outside the workplace, few opportunities presented themselves to develop the mother tongue or make progress in German. Cultural events or radio and television broadcasts in Turkish had hardly begun. Meeting places such as tea or coffee houses, restaurants or prayer halls were able to satisfy the need to communicate with like-minded people from a similar background, but since the participants all came from the same social strata neither language skills nor social contacts were extended.

Public places or squares, which migrants had known in their country of origin and which might have offered opportunities to enter into conversation with Germans and in German, had no place in German urban planning or in the urban environment of the 1960s and 1970s. In any case, Germans showed little interest in communicating with the *Gastarbeiter*, of whom they had an essentially negative image. Only the arrival of video recorders and satellite transmission offered first-generation migrants the opportunity to experience the elaborated code of their mother tongue and to share – in Turkish – events in their home country and in world affairs. Printed media had a much more limited impact. Until the arrival of visual media, first-generation Turks depended on re-translations from the German by their children, by professional translators or by social workers. The command of German among first-generation migrants was no less restricted. Only with the help of their children – who had grown up in Germany – translators or social workers, could first-generation Turks communicate with the 'German world' in which they lived.

Second and third-generation migrants, together with an influx of educated political exiles from Turkey, have done much to change the situation. Although Turks remain firmly located in the bottom social strata, first signs of an emergent middle class and a distinctive intellectual development are evident. It is possible, for instance, to identify a variety of 'linguistic currents' among Turks presently living in Germany: a Turkish language scene with a relatively high linguistic competence in Turkish; a scene with high competence in both German and Turkish; a scene with limited command of Turkish but an impressive command of German, and a scene were both languages merge to produce a new linguistic melange.

A similar diversification exists in German-Turkish culture. Works of music, film, theatre, literature, painting and academic research are aimed at Turkish-speaking migrants in Germany, at German-speaking Turks, at Germans or more broadly at all of these groups. In addition, innumerable avant-garde works seem to owe little or nothing to the background of the artist, and Turkish origin no longer appears to matter.

One of the most interesting facets of cultural transformation concerns the language use of second and third-generation Turks who, in contrast to their parents, have a firm command of German. Most speak German better than Turkish. When they speak Turkish, it is often with a German accent or even modelled on a German dialect. Some modify their Turkish by adding German grammatical and syntactical structures. By and large, these generations learn Turkish in their parental home, in their neighbourhood and their community.[10] Some attend the classes in Turkish offered at their local school, others study Turkish as a foreign language, a subject now on offer in many German schools. In some German Länder, Turkish has even been approved as a subject to be studied for the *Abitur*.

The second generation speaks a mixed language in which either Turkish or German is the dominant component. Language formation reflects the wide variety of ways in which the Turkish and German life-styles touch or overlap and constitute the social environment and milieu for that generation. Concepts, ideas and patterns of feeling from the two spheres merge to produce their own peculiar mix of linguistic symbols and expressions. This applies to grammar and phonetics, and even to pitch, breathing and intonation. Some people prefer to use Turkish only to express certain experiences or feelings, using German for a different set of purposes. Many, for instance, who are fluent in German switch to Turkish when it comes to counting, whereas they will continue to speak German in a political debate, even if the topic is wholly specific to Turkey. Others think and write in German but opt for Turkish when caressing their children, partners or pets. Others again will change language on specific occasions, for instance switching to Turkish at dances and musical events, banquets and drinking sessions, or in situations such as states of fatigue, intoxication, intense joy, mourning, anger or rage. Such code-switching may occur during a conversation, sometimes even in mid-sentence; it usually happens automatically without a conscious decision by the speaker. To outsiders who are not familiar with both languages, the constant jumping from one to the other language can be irritating. Not surprisingly, its speakers are frequently deemed to have only a partial-command of language, what is known as *Halbsprachigkeit*.

Those who know both languages well enough to cope with this style of communication do not interpret code-switching as restricted competence. On the contrary, they see it as an additional freedom of choice, enabling them to say what they intend to all the more precisely. Speakers who switch code have an increased capacity for expressing fine nuances of language, and are better able to cross linguistic, cultural, logical and emotional boundaries. When conversing with others, such people can redefine at will which feelings, which ideas, which images they wish to use in which language in order to intensify their impact. The speaker of such a mixed language does not perceive his or her communicative ability as *Halbsprachigkeit* – as a deficiency – since both languages together constitute the linguistic repertoire and cannot be separated. This pattern of speech and communication is a specific form of bi-lingualism and not the restricted code of semi-competence.

In the third generation, even body language, facial expressions, gestures and posture have visibly changed. These changes suggest that the individual's emotional and cognitive reference points have also changed from the culture of origin to the German host culture.[11] The physiological mode of language production, the creation of sound as well as the use of the tongue, expression and gesture have been moulded so strongly by the German language that many complain of producing too much saliva and of muscle pains in the mouth area when they have to engage in longer conversations in Turkish.

Since Turks first settled in Germany in the 1970s, the Turkish language in Germany has incorporated many German terms, while Turkish has made little impact on German. With the exception of a few terms relating to food, virtually no term or concept has entered German from Turkish. Moreover, of the few metaphors and symbols to find a place at all in colloquial German the majority appear to carry negative meanings.

For Turks in Germany, the situation is quite different: many everyday activities and events are expressed in a mix of German and Turkish. On bidding farewell and on concluding a telephone conversation, many Turks now use the German 'Tschüß' (bye-bye) instead of the Turkish 'hoscakal' or 'allahaismarladik'. This can cause friction. If for instance the custom of saying 'Tschüß' is adopted at the end of a telephone call to Turkey, it may be understood to mean 'Tschüsch' – 'you donkey' and cause offence. 'Such little things can cause serious rifts which are not easily smoothed over.'[12]

Another typical linguistic development consists of mixed sentences such as 'Krank yapiyorum' – 'I have a sick note from my doctor' or 'Urlaub aldim' – 'I have taken a holiday'. These sentences violate the grammatical rules of both languages; they are German-Turkish, which is increasingly different in terms of semantics, phonetics and syntax from the Turkish spoken in Turkey. Özata's study of Turkish in Germany contains many examples such as: 'I often hear Turkish kebab sellers ask their Turkish customers: "scharf (spicy) *mi olsun?*" instead of the correct Turkish *Acili mi olsun?* (Do you want it spicy?) or "Soße (gravy) *mi olsun?*" instead of *soslu mi olsun?* (Do you want it with gravy?).'[13]

Occasionally, Turkish is spoken according to the logical pattern of German. In correct Turkish, the expression 'you are right' would be: 'haklisin', but it has been all but displaced by 'hakli konusuyorsun', which translates as 'you are speaking correctly'. Often, Turkish sentences employ the German auxiliary verb 'haben' (to have). Since Turkish does not have auxiliary verbs or an equivalent form, using a German auxiliary is a serious language mistake as well as an infringement of the rules governing vowel harmony in the Turkish language. Certain metaphors also tend to be transposed in a linear fashion from one language to another.[14]

Diminutives of names are another example of language mix. In Turkish, a diminutive is achieved by adding the suffix 'cik' or – to indicate possession – 'cigim'. Thus Ahmet becomes Ahmet*cik* or Ahmet*cigim*. In German, of course, the equivalent form is the suffix 'lein', which has made its appearance in Turkish. Ahmet*cigim* becomes Ahmet*lein* and sometimes the two diminutives are even added together to make Ahmet*ciklein*, little Ahmet in Turkish-German.

In colloquial language, Turkish and German expressions are increasingly intertwined. The German 'komm her' – 'come here' – has acquired a Turkish ending 'komm her, *lan*', taken from the Turkish phrase 'gel buraya, lan' – 'come here, man'. An example from teenage speech would be the melange 'amma da *affen geil*, be' which may be translated as 'that's fucking great'. Here the implant of German teenage jargon – 'affengeil' is the current semi-obscene equivalent of 'great' or 'super' – into a part-Turkish sentence, and the elevation of this mixture to a commonly understood phrase highlights the blend of cultures and the change of the Turkish language in Germany.

In articulation and stress, Turkish rules have been modified to conform with German practice. The 'r' for example is pronounced in a short and rolling manner in Turkish, whereas in German it is round, softer and longer, especially in final position. Increasingly, this German 'r' dominates even within Turkish words. German words, however, also get adapted to Turkish manners of speaking:

Sometimes German place names, names of buildings or streets are changed to fit the Turkish language structure and phonetic traditions. Sometimes the German is replaced altogether by a similar Turkish name. Thus the *Görlitzer Bahnhof*, the train station named after the German town of Görlitz, becomes *Gülüzar Bahnhof*, after a Turkish girls' name. The German *Hermannsplatz* turns into a *Harmanplatz* after the Turkish 'harman', meaning threshing. For the *Gedächtniskirche* in Berlin, a new Turkish name has been invented, *Yikik Kilise* or destroyed church.[15]

Culture

All aspects of Turkish life in Germany are undergoing major changes. The Turks in Germany are becoming German-Turks or Turkish-Germans as their Turkish identity acquires more and more German traits and they in turn import Turkish features into German life. This is most apparent in forms of artistic expression such as music, dance, theatre, film and literature. In all these fields, cultural changes are clearly visible, and unplanned social experiments are under way, creating a cultural synthesis. Young Turks, for instance, are more likely to opt for break-dancing or discos than for Turkish folk dances, although some add traditional Turkish elements to these modern dance-styles, thus creating their own blend of western and oriental cultures.

Similar developments have occurred in music. Young Turks of the second and third generations have adopted 'rap' or 'hip-hop' from American sub-cultures and turned them into a multi-faceted protest against the dominant German culture, against the culture that dominates within the Turkish community and against the discrimination they feel they suffer.[16] These young Turks are rebelling against both their culture of origin and the majority culture of the host society, and they articulate this rebellion musically in their 'rap', giving it force and shape. Accordingly, 'rap' is for the most part sung in two languages, Turkish and German, with a rich dose of intrinsically Turkish themes and tunes.

Alongside the expression of protest through rap, a whole range of experimental, avant-garde works are being created in an attempt to communicate what it means to live a migrant's life. In German film, for example, the Turkish-born and German-trained director Teyfik Basar occupies a secure place with two major works on the situation of Turks in Germany, *Forty Square Metres of Germany* and *Destroyed Paradise*.

The synthesis of Turkish and German themes or forms of expression is however always characterised by a key discrepancy: the uneven weight of the cultures which are brought together. 'Culture' itself may be regarded as an expression of a power struggle. Globally, the most important cultural centres in international terms are located in the most powerful societies which themselves constitute the centre in a centre-periphery constellation.[17] Societies near or at the periphery in the first instance usually have no other option but to base their activities, whether positively or negatively, on the cultural models and standards of the centre. Only rarely do their spokespersons succeed in attracting attention to themselves or even less in kindling a more profound interest in their own societies on the part of those nations that constitute the global elite.[18] This lack of recognition, which is often accompanied by desperate attempts to gain acceptance in the world order, can give rise to isolationist thinking, to feelings of uniqueness or ultimately to notions of a supernatural world mission. Past developments in Russia, Germany and Turkey provide ample evidence for these connections.

The established centres of civilisation and culture have a tendency – often unintended – to exaggerate differences and distort meanings. Thus, the literature of Eastern countries and less powerful states in general is scanned for its 'typical' contents, for its exotic characteristics and its traditional and folksy, ostensibly 'authentic' traits.[19] Representatives of these literatures who resist pressures of this kind to confine them to a status of cultural under-development, and fight for recognition on an equal basis and according to universal standards of quality in world literature are likely to have their demands dismissed as arrogant. In this respect, Turkish literature shares the same fate as other literatures of near-peripheral and peripheral societies.[20]

These inter-state relations between periphery and centre are broadly reproduced on a similar scale in societies of immigration due to the low-class status of migrants in such societies. The process also applies to the cultural and artistic creations of migrants and their descendants. Even multi-culturalism and positive discrimination fail to break the spiral of discrimination, a fact which an increasingly self-confident generation of Turkish Germans has begun to notice and point out. B.V. Yaltirakli has, for instance, drawn attention to certain artists of Turkish origin, who do not wish to see their work stigmatised as so-called *Gastkunst*, a label which, by analogy with the term *Gastarbeiter*, reminds the guests that they will soon have to go home again. These artists are tired of hearing German critics indulge and patronise them with the attitude: 'Of course, this kind of *Gastkunst* means we have to be lenient'. Yaltirakli demands that critics should judge by the same strict criteria applied by the artists themselves, and in doing so recognise the claim of Turkish artists to equal and universal treatment, thus putting an end to the 'repressive tolerance' which stigmatises Turkish cultural products as second rate.[21] Turkish artists are struggling to express more than just the life story and perceptions of migrants. Their work shows signs of those 'social processes of intellectual change' that P.R. Gleichmann has identified as one element of potential emancipation from the underclass status of a migrant community. Rather, they articulate social processes of intellectual change which carry the seed of potential emancipation from their underclass status for Germany's migrant communities.[22]

The Emergence of a Literary Avant-Garde

The greatest progress in this direction has been made by writers. In the 1960s and 1970s, literary texts tended to focus on the experience of encountering Germany in all its foreignness. In the late 1980s, the paradigm shifted to finding one's own identity in the foreign land.[23] This paradigm shift affected language, style and contents. Generally speaking, migrants' literature moved from using the language of the country of origin to using the language of the country of immigration.[24] This shift was accompanied by a process of integration into the literary life and organisations of the country of immigration and by a change of balance from the collective to the individual, the writer is becoming: 'less co-operative and more concerned with individual performance and creativity.'[25]

These changes are also applicable in the case of Turkish-German writing. In the 1970s, works of literature by Turkish writers were normally written in Turkish and later translated into German. In the late 1980s and in the 1990s, most works by Turkish-German writers were written in German and most were about German society, or about more general themes without a specific foothold in the migrant community. Representing this genre are writers such as Safer Senocak, Kemal Kurt, Akif Pirinci and Renan Demirkan. Pirinci and Demirkan were the first 'German-language authors of non-German origin' in the forty-year history of migration to post-war Germany to head the literary best-seller lists for several months. Some authors make conscious play with the two languages, their mother tongue and their target language, creating a new mix of German and Turkish in their works. Prime examples of this approach are *Charlie-Kemal* by Özgen Ergin and *Life is a Caravanserai* by Emine Sevgi Özdamar.[26]

Academics and Intellectuals

Alongside writers, academics constitute a group which may exert considerable cultural influences. In the university system, Turkish academics occupy a similarly marginal place to their Turkish writers in the cultural life and traditions of their society of immigration.[27] Universities in Turkey have tended to emulate the university system of the centre, notably the U.S. system, even to the point of teaching partly in English. German universities also possess considerable powers of attraction for their Turkish partner institutions and for Turkish students. The attractions of Germany may have been boosted by a political history in which Prussian military personnel served for nearly a century as military advisors to the army of the Ottoman Empire which they equipped to German technical standards. The prestigious reputation of technical subjects and engineering at German universities may also be a factor in this, as also the fact that academics exiled from Nazi Germany took up posts in Turkish universities.

Turkish migrants and their descendants have as yet barely gained a foothold in the German university system where career paths tend to be more rigid than those in Turkey and less accessible to outsiders. In their rigidity, they constitute a formidable obstacle. There are some signs, however, that members of the second and third generation, and Turkish students who have moved to Germany to take up their studies and opted to remain, are beginning to become an integral part of the student population and enjoy some improved employment prospects.

In the humanities and social sciences, many of these students have changed their focus in a manner comparable to the changes noted for writers. The first generation of migrants and Turkish students tended to write their dissertations and theses about aspects of their homeland, Turkey. The second generation has begun to produce analyses of the migrant situation itself and the impact of migration on minorities and their members.[28] They are a new voice in German academic life, although research into the impact of migration has been a more established field in other Western countries. Given the impact of social sciences on the image of ethnic minorities, the contribution of Turkish academics and intellectuals to understanding migration and its consequences are important. In time, they may succeed in breaking down the ethnocentric monopoly views of German researchers, thus making the debate more pluralistic.

Conclusion

Germany includes a large group of people whose identity, for the foreseeable future at least, will be a German-Turkish identity. Turks from Turkey have long recognised this distinctive identity and coined a new word for it: *almanyali*, somebody from Germany. In sound only a slight variation on the word for 'German', *alman*, it stresses the German, not the Turkish connection. As yet, characteristically, there is no equivalent formulation in German that recognises bi-lingual identity in discourse. Of course, German can link two nationalities by means of a hyphen to signify that a person somehow straddles both. It is possible to speak of *Deutsch-Türken* (German-Turks) but it sounds strange, and the hyphen cannot eradicate the fact that German identity rests on origin and is deemed superior to that based on location. The two nations linked by hyphen in the German *Deutsch-Türken* are therefore not seen as equal. It is for this reason that the German language neither knows nor strives to find a word for bi-culturalism, while other languages have no such difficulties. Terms such as 'Sino-American', 'Pakistani-English' or 'Irish-American' have become normal expressions of cultural mix in immigrant situations.

In Germany, cultural mix, ambivalence and a synthesis of background or traditions remains socially unacceptable in the light of the pressures for cultural homogeneity which emanate from the tradition of the nation state.[29] The host society continues to insist on its right to define the parameters of culture without incorporating minorities' perspectives. To portray the situation of Turks in Germany as a life between two cultures would be to overlook the asymmetry between German and Turkish culture and the dominance of the former over the latter. In culture, as in society, the position of the Turkish minority at the disadvantaged end of the spectrum, has been and remains decisive. The fundamental question is whether the mechanisms of social disadvantage will be consolidated and perpetuated, or whether they will be modified as a gradual equalisation of opportunities and social strata takes effect.

Is there evidence that a Turkish middle class and Turkish elites are emerging in Germany? The answer cannot be straightforward: in a global perspective and compared to their country of origin, first-generation migrants have experienced improvements in their lifestyles and gained a sense of upward mobility. This generation lives in a state of inequality with German society which it broadly accepts and which has been called a 'harmonious' inequality. For the second and third generations, the point of comparison and reference has shifted from Turkey, the society of origin for their parents, to Germany, the society of immigration. This focus cannot but highlight the disadvantaged status of Turkish residents and their unfavourable place as an underclass in German society. At the same time, however, a slender elite is beginning to develop which, unlike comparable groups in other countries, remains almost completely unknown.[30]

Can Turkish intellectuals, can a slim Turkish elite, help break the deadlock by providing professional, social or cultural role models and means of orientation? In modern knowledge-based societies, intellectual elites normally play a key role.[31] The tension between a slim stratum of intellectuals and an increasingly stagnant, immobile social underclass of the same ethnic background creates an uneasy climate of dissatisfaction, conducive to the formation of new elite protest groups. Their ideological aims and socio-psychological make-up may have a decisive influence on the future course of events. Will they for instance succumb to those pressures that would reduce them to mere objects of exotic interest? Will they beat a defensive cultural retreat, themselves becoming fossilised and fundamentalist? Or will they be capable of struggling for recognition and equality of opportunities?

Without a German-Turkish professional culture, without the contribution of a German-Turkish middle class and intellectual elite, German-Turkish everyday culture will tend to look back, retrench, segregate.

The future of German-Turkish everyday culture lies not in a fundamentalist, conservative or nostalgic clinging to the past, but rather in an innovative change through developing and retaining a bi-cultural approach, a German and Turkish cultural identity.[32] The prospects for Turkish everyday culture and its innovative potential in Germany depend on such an emergence of bi-culturalism among the Turkish minority and no less strongly on the acceptance of bi-culturalism in the German society of immigration.

NOTES

1. E.J. Dittrich and F.-O. Radtke, 'Der Beitrag der Wissenschaft zur Konstruktion ethnischer Minderheiten', in *Ethnizität*, ed. E.J. Dittrich and F.-O. Radtke, Opladen, Westdeutscher Verlag, 1990, pp.11–40.

2. E. Kürsat-Ahlers, 'Einwandererfamilien: Ihre Struktur- und Funktionsweise im Migrationsprozeß', in *Neue Lebensformen – Zeit-Krankheiten und Psychotherapie*, ed. P. Buchheim, T. Cierpa and T. Seifert. Berlin/Heidelberg/New York, Springer, 1994, pp.9–105.

3. Zentrum für Türkeistudien, *Türkei Sozialkunde*, Opladen, Leske & Budrich, 1994, p.127.

4. N. Elias and J.L. Scotson, *Etablierte und Außenseiter*, Frankfurt/Main, Suhrkamp, 1990 (translated from the 1965 English edition *The Established and the Outsiders. A Sociological Enquiry into Community Problems*).

5. P. Antes, *Der Islam als politischer Faktor*, Hanover, Landeszentrale für politische Bildung, 1991, p.12.

6. M.S. Abdullah, 'Gibt es eine gemeinsame Basis für den interreligiösen Dialog? Christlich-Islamischer Ökumenismus aus der Sicht des Islams', in *Die multikulturelle Gesellschaft: Der Weg zur Gleichstellung?*, ed. E. Kürsat-Ahlers, Frankfurt/Main, IKO, 1992, pp.184–211.

7. The expert on Islam writing for the *Frankfurter Allgemeine Zeitung*, Wolfgang Günther Lerch argued that the death threat against Salman Rushdie gave fundamentalist tendencies more prominence and intensified negative reactions to Muslims in West Germany. See 'Es begann mit Maulana Sadruddin', *Frankfurter Allgemeine Zeitung* 18 June 1993, p.12.

8. For a detailed discussion see H.-P. Waldhoff, *Fremde und Zivilisierung: über das Verarbeiten von Gefühlen der Fremdheit. Probleme der modernen Peripherie-Zentrum-Migration am türkisch-deutschen Beispiel*, Frankfurt/Main, Suhrkamp, 1995.

9. See A. Schulte and D. Tan, *Zur Lebenssituation älterer Ausländer in Niedersachsen*, Hanover, Niedersächsisches Sozialministerium, Ausländerbeauftragte, 1990, pp.58–60.

10. M. Özata, 'Die türkische Sprache in Berlin' in *Eingewanderte ArbeiterInnen in Berlin 1961–1993*, ed. Berliner Geschichtswerkstatt, Berlin, Eigenverlag (self-funded publication), 1994, p.100.

11. A theory of emotional and cognitive reference points has been developed by L. Ciompi, *Affektlogik. Über die Struktur der Psyche und ihre Entwicklung. Ein Beitrag zur Schizophrenieforschung*, Stuttgart, Klett-Cotta, 1994, esp. pp. 43–93.

12. Özata, 'Die türkische Sprache in Berlin', p.101.

13. Ibid. p.102.

14. In Turkish-German, for instance, bilingualism is called 'double language competence' after the German *doppelsprachig*, although Turkish has a word for bilingualism, 'iki dilli'. Turkish migrants in Germany, however, tend to use 'double language competence' i.e., its Turkish equivalent 'cift dilli' even when speaking Turkish. For a detailed analysis see Ibid., p.103.

15. Ibid., p.101. The Gedächtniskirche is one of the landmarks of (West) Berlin. The burnt-out ruin remains standing next to a new church as a memorial to war-time destruction.

16. *Der Spiegel* no.17, 1995, pp.132–134.

17. I. Wallerstein, 'Culture as the Ideological Battleground of the Modern World System' in *Global Culture: Nationalism, Globalisation and Modernity*, ed. M. Featherstone, London, Routledge, 1990, pp.31–55.

18. H.-H. Nolte, 'On the loneliness of Russia and the Russian Idea' in *Coexistence*, vol.32, 1995, pp.39–48.

19. For detailed discussion see Waldhoff, *Fremde und Zivilisierung*, pp. 276–279.

20. P. Kappert, 'Nachwort' in *Türkische Erzählungen des 20. Jahrhunderts*, ed., P. Kappert and T. Turan, Frankfurt/Main/Leipzig, Insel, 1992, p.283.

21. U. Yaltirakli, 'Gedanken über türkische Kultur in Berlin', in *Die Brücke*, vol.21, 1990, p.8.

22. P.R. Gleichmann, 'Über gesellschaftliche Intellektualisierungsprozesse. Intellektuelle und wissenschaftlich-technische Intelligenz im Vergleich. Vergleichende Beobachtungen zu ihrem langfristigen Aufgabenwechsel', in *Berliner Journal für Soziologie*, vol.3, no.1, 1993, pp.89–101.

23. S. Sölçün, *Von der Begegnung mit der Fremde zur Selbstbegegnung in der Fremde: zur deutschen Literatur nichtdeutscher Autoren*, Vortragsmanuskript, Universität Hannover, 1 March 1995. See also Chapter 1 in this volume.

24. U. Reeg, *Schreiben in der Fremde. Literatur nationaler Minderheiten in der Bundesrepublik*, Essen, Klartext, 1988, p.45.

25. Reeg, *Schreiben in der Fremde*, p.200; see also N. Elias, *Engagement und Distanzierung. Arbeiten zur Wissensoziologie*, Frankfurt/Main, Suhrkamp, 1993.

26. See the detailed discussion of this work in Chapter 3 of this volume.

27. H. H. Nolte, *Die eine Welt. Abriß der Geschichte des internationalen Systems*, Hanover, Fackelträger, 1993, p.38.

28. S. Özkara, 'Folgen der Migration im Spiegel der türkischen Intellektuellen. Einleitung', in *Türkische Migranten in der Bundesrepublik Deutschland: Stellungnahmen der türkischen Wissenschaftler, Intellektuellen, Lehrer, Gewerkschafter*

und Sozialberater zu Ausländerfragen und Ausländerpolitik, ed. S. Özkara. Frankfurt/Main: IKO, 1988, pp.9–18.

29. Z. Baumann, *Moderne und Ambivalenz: das Ende der Eindeutigkeit*, Hamburg, Junius, 1992, pp.33–72.

30. Compare for the United States e.g., A. Edwards and C.K. Polite, *Children of the Dream. The Psychology of Black Success*, New York, Doubleday, 1992.

31. N. Stehr, *Arbeit, Eigentum und Wissen: zur Theorie von Wissensgesellschaften*, Frankfurt/Main, Suhrkamp, 1994, pp.159–161; pp.350–419.

32. A. Hettlage-Varjas, 'Bikulturalität – Privileg oder Belastung? in *Die multikulturelle Gesellschaft: Der Weg zur Gleichberechtigung?* ed. E. Kürsat-Ahlers, pp.142–167.

CHAPTER 8

Turkish Cultural Orientations in Germany and the Role of Islam

Yasemin Karakasoglu

Introduction

Issues of culture seemed irrelevant when representatives of the German and Turkish governments negotiated the recruitment of *Gastarbeiter* in 1961. On both sides, economic interests predominated, while the cultural impact of the labour transfer on the receiving country and in particular on the labour migrants themselves was ignored. Moreover, Turkey was emphatically Western in its orientation at the time and expected Turks in Germany to meet their cultural or religious needs without any support from the Turkish government. The West German government endorsed the official Turkish position that religious and cultural orientations were a matter for the individual in his or her private sphere. As guests, labour migrants were expected to fit into the mainstream culture of the host society, not establish a culture of their own. This pragmatic approach overlooked the fact that cultural identity tends to assume a fresh and crucial importance as migrants attempt to come to terms with their new living conditions.

Among the 'intellectual, spiritual, artistic and practical expressions that constitute the cultural identity of a group of people,'[1] religion has proved of particular importance for Turks in Germany. More than any other manifestation of their cultural values, Islam is regarded as the one feature that most strongly differentiates them in terms of identity from the majority host society. For migrants, a distinctive religious identity may have both positive and negative effects.[2] On the one hand, religious differences tend to encourage segregation and the establishment of separate 'cells' in the host society. On the other hand religion may, as a stabilising influence both psychologically and morally, result in organisational networks which make it easier for migrants to integrate into their new social environment. This ambiguity of religion as a force for segregation and integration can also be seen to characterise the position of the Turkish minority in Germany. Before considering examples of this, it should first be stressed that to equate Turks with Muslims in the religious sense is a vast over-simplification. The term 'Muslim' is primarily a cultural attribution that is by no means synonymous with actual religious practice. The latter, as in most religions, varies enormously. It can find expression in such conscious, public demonstrations of faith as weekly attendance at Friday prayers, fasting during Ramadan or wearing specific garments to cloak parts of the male or female body. Equally, however, it is possible to think of oneself as Muslim without adhering to any such practices. Among Turks in Germany there is also a relatively small group who, under the strong influence of Kemel Atatürk's secularisation policies, have largely turned their backs on Islam or even see themselves as atheists. If nothing else, however, Islam will have played a key role in most people's upbringing.[3]

Whatever the different schools of thought and varieties of religious practice among Turks in Germany, Islam has been the moving force behind the development of organisational networks within the Turkish minority. Examples of this are the independent Turkish religious organisations, by far the most co-ordinated in Europe; the Turkish language press which, despite relatively low circulation figures, is constantly gaining new readers[4] and the emergence of a largely religious-fundamentalist Islamic video market in Germany. By the early 1990s, Turks were more likely than Germans to own a video recorder. Watching religious videos in Turkish had become a major leisure activity.[5] While religion has given the Turkish minority an element of cohesion and even welded it into a community, it has also acted as a barrier between the minority and its German environment. A study on health education among Turks in North Rhine-Westphalia, for instance, showed that Turks were not reached by an intensive publicity campaign on AIDS because received Islamic views on the matter outweighed all health warnings.[6]

In Germany, as in other European countries, Muslims only

began to constitute a visible section of the population in the wake of labour migration from Turkey, North Africa and the Balkans, and after migrants turned into residents. In 1961, 6,500 Muslims lived in Germany; by 1995, their number had risen to 2.5 million, making Islam the third largest denomination in the country after Protestantism and Catholicism. Eighty-nine percent of Muslims in Germany originate from Turkey. Yet despite the extent of Islam in contemporary Germany, knowledge of the religion and its place in the cultural identity of Turks has remained sparse. As shown earlier in this volume, contacts between Turks and Germans remain the exception even for second- and third-generation migrants who have never lived outside Germany.[7] The public image of Islam has also been blurred by the rivalry between Turkish organisations and groups, all claiming to be the authoritative voice of Islam in Germany, whereas in reality they only represent factions and sectional interests.

Islam may be 'an obstacle to integration',[8] but it is by no means the only one. Given the German link between *jus sanguinis* and citizenship, and the emphasis on cultural homogeneity, 'integration' itself has tended to be understood as assimilation or 'adjustment of an individual or a group in conformity with the characteristics of other groups or of a whole people'.[9] To accommodate the distinctive traditions, culture and needs of a minority, a different concept of integration would have to be developed. This would encompass cultural diversity by means of 'a gradual adjustment to [the] living conditions [of German society] and a peaceful co-existence of people of different origin, each respecting the other's national, cultural and religious views of themselves'.[10] Integration all too often seems to aim for assimilation and a renunciation by members of a given minority of all visible differences in their personal, cultural or religious lives. Although the Basic Law guarantees freedom of religion, a consensus has yet to emerge in German society that such freedom includes differences of dress, religious rites, customs, behaviour, values and beliefs. German policy makers still need to develop a code of practice for religious equality that will meet the challenge of a religious pluralism that *de facto* already exists.

Migration and Islam in Germany

Not unlike the development of the Turkish minority, that of Islam in Germany has been characterised by the transformation of a

predominantly male migrant labour force into a resident population with an increasingly 'normal' social structure. As the Turkish
minority settled in Germany, the private sphere saw varying
degrees of Islamic religious practice established, whilst in public
Turkish-Islamic organisations were set up, some of them on a
political basis that can be termed Islamist.

In the days of labour migration, there were scarcely any
mosques in Germany apart from prestige buildings in Hamburg
and Munich, constructed with funds from Middle Eastern countries like Saudi Arabia and Iran, and those founded by the
Ahmadiyya movement in Frankfurt and Hamburg.[11] Turkish
Muslims had to apply for permission to use rooms in their
hostels, factories or other work places in which to perform their
daily prayers. Prayers were led by lay members who took on the
role of *imam*. Based on the somewhat naive popular faith of the
Turkish homeland that contained strong elements of Sufism,
this kind of religious observance was not grounded in orthodox
Islamic theology, especially since few of the migrant workers
were themselves strictly religious.

In the 1970s, as Turkish everyday life shifted from hostels to
houses or flats, and as family reunion recast the social fabric of the
Turkish minority, religion took on a new centrality, thus creating a
need for mosques. Initially, disused factories met this need, and
until the early 1990s most Turkish mosques were still located in the
industrial districts of West German cities or at the rear of tenements. One reason for choosing such unglamorous locations was
the shortage of funds among Turkish Muslims in Germany. A
more important reason was the reluctance of local planning committees to authorise buildings clearly identifiable as Islamic.
Although today Germany boasts isolated 'real' mosques with
cupolas and minarets, none was constructed without a prolonged
argument.[12] German residents claimed that the existence of a
mosque would turn the surrounding district into a Turkish ghetto,
create parking problems, inconvenience non-Muslim residents,
spoil the architectural ambience of a town or neighbourhood, and
encourage the spread of Islamic fundamentalism in Germany.
Nowhere were Turks able to exercise their constitutional rights to
cultural and religious freedom without controversy and objections.

The increased importance of Islam was inextricably linked
to the demographic transformation of the Turkish minority. As
women and children settled in Germany, traditional patterns of
social control re-emerged along established Turkish-Islamic

lines. In the hostels, Turks had lived apart from their families and segregated from German society. In their new residential neighbourhoods, they set out to create their own distinctive way of life within a culturally different German society. In this process of defining their identity as a minority, religion played a key role. In their attempt to preserve their values and norms, first-generation migrants turned back to the cultural and value orientations of their home country, not to those in the surrounding host society. Adjustments to the world of work had already taken place during the period of labour recruitment. They were followed by a re-instatement of values and customs in the private sphere which originated from a Muslim or Turkish cultural context and tradition, and were to underpin the transformation from labour migrant to settled resident. Everyday values were, above all, related to the family and the social behaviour of its members. Values such as 'family honour', 'respect for the head of household', 'regard and obedience' that were of scarcely any relevance to migrant workers without family, came to dominate the private sphere after family reunion got under way in the mid-1970s.

Family Structures

The family occupies a key position in the society and culture of Turks in Germany. In societies where social policy and institutions are underdeveloped the family has tended to provide material security for its members. Moreover, by passing social norms on to the next generation, the family contributes to the stability of established value systems. Turkish families have been based on obedience and an acceptance of the structure of authority. Specifically, the father claims the dominant role as head of the family, while the role of women, in the family-fold as in society at large, is strictly prescribed. The 'honour' of the family itself tends to be linked to the 'honourable' behaviour of its female members and their adherence to their traditional role. For women, such honourable behaviour means virginity before marriage as well as conducting themselves with socially appropriate modesty.[13]

The extent to which families adhere to these values in their daily lives depends on the urban or rural living environment and on the social status, educational qualification or religious orientation of the parents, and the conformist pressures which may emanate from their immediate neighbourhood.[14] In Turkey and also in

Germany, Turkish families develop their own interpretation of traditional values, not all of them adhering with equal intensity to the prescribed role models and social codes.

In both countries and across all shades of Turkish family organisation, however, mutual assistance and responsibility constitute an important function for the family in contemporary society. Turks in Germany use their income to support their extended families in Germany as well as in Turkey. Based on the principle that male members are responsible for the welfare of female members, and older members for the young, the family in Germany has proved to be the most reliable social institution in their new environment for the first generation of Turks in particular. As members of this generation approach retirement, they tend to look to the family, and not to German social institutions or care networks, to support them in old age. Among first-generation Turks, concern has begun to surface as to whether their own children have remained as committed to the social-support function of the family as they themselves are with regard to their own parents and relatives.[15] As mentioned earlier, the new living conditions in Germany are also leaving their mark on the role distribution within Turkish families, as fathers lose some of their predominance and young people use their superior command of the German language and their familiarity with German society to act as intermediaries between Turkish and German social norms, thus assuming non-traditional leadership functions inside and outside the family.[16]

Young Turks in Germany are confronted with two partly contradictory value systems: that of their Turkish home and that of their German social environment. These conflicting pressures affect girls more than boys, since the notion of 'honour' requires them to maintain a demonstrative distance from German influences and adopt a visibly traditional, conformist behaviour. For boys it seems easier to appear compliant with Turkish norms and nevertheless taste some of the freedoms German society has to offer.[17] The discrepancy between Turkish and German values can either result in over-assimilation or withdrawal. Many young people, however, feel that they are not fully accepted in Turkey or in Germany. As one young man complained in an interview: 'On holiday in Turkey, people constantly call me *Almanci*, but in Germany, I can eat like a German, walk like a German and I still remain a Turk'.[18] Yet most Turkish youths feel at home in both cultures and, having grown up in Germany, have developed a

German-Turkish identity. This identity differs from that of their parents which had been shaped by their own Turkish regional and religious background, and it also differs from that which prevails among the German population generally. For the identity of some young Turks in Germany, religion is also important. Unlike their parents, however, these young German-Turks have begun to develop their own approach to Islam. This includes learning Arabic so as to be able to read the Koran in the original, as well as using their command of German to read religious texts in German translation and discuss religious issues with members of their own generation.

Islam and Turkish Everyday Life in Germany

Conflicts between religious observance and the secular organisation of everyday life tend to arise most frequently in two key areas: at work and at school. At work, it is for individual employers to decide whether to accommodate the religious needs of their workforce, for instance by allowing unpaid leave to observe Muslim holy days or setting time (and rooms) aside for prayers. At school, the practice in Germany is more unified, which means that accommodating the religious needs of Muslims is more dependent on political will and educational action, than on decisions taken in the individual school or classroom.

At the time of writing, none of the German Länder has included religious education in Islam for Muslim children in the regular curriculum, as has been standard practice for Christian denominations. There are voices in the Muslim community demanding that religious education should be offered within the regular curriculum, be geared to strengthening the Islamic roots of young Turks in Germany, and be treated either on an equal basis with Christian religious instruction or, where comparative religion is taught, 'given its full due.'[19] The official view of the regional ministries responsible for education policy has been that religious education should assist young Muslims to retain their identity, but within German society, not isolated from it. Instruction of Muslim pupils in Islam within German state schools is supposed to be conducted in such a way that young Muslims understand that theirs is a minority in a society where the majority of people belong to other faiths. In this vein, the Standing Conference of the Regional Ministers of Culture recommended in 1984 that religious education should 'assist pupils to develop a Muslim identity in a non-Muslim world. It should help Muslim children and young people to understand and accept the values and norms of German society and to endure the tension arising from the different value systems of Muslim and non-Muslim.'[20]

In the federal structure of Germany, issues of education are regional matters and decided at regional level. This includes religious education. In developing policies for this part of the curriculum, the German Länder have tended to consult with the churches concerned and entrusted church representatives with the actual teaching. Islam does not have a representative body which can speak for all Muslims and take the lead in discussions. Different regions have therefore developed different approaches.[21]

Two basic models characterise religious education in Islam in Germany. The first model allows for 'religious instruction for female and male Muslim pupils' within the framework of extra lessons given to Turkish children in their mother tongue. This model was pioneered by North Rhine-Westphalia, a region noted for curricular development and innovation. Initially designed for children under the age of ten, it was extended in 1991 to also include forms five and six (children aged eleven and twelve). By 1995/1996, the relevant curricula will have been approved to also offer religious education in Islam, and in the Turkish language, to pupils in forms seven to ten. Learning is supported by materials which have been specially developed by the Regional Institute for Schools and Further Education in Soest. Islamic education teachers are vetted and employed by the regional government, not by the Turkish state. In line with German educational priorities, the programme is designed with the specific problems and experiences of Turkish children in Germany in mind. In contrast to Christian religious education, however, lessons in Islam are voluntary and not part of the core curriculum.[22]

The second model, entitled 'Religious Instruction on the Basis of Islam for Muslim Pupils', also operates in the context of additional and voluntary instruction in the mother tongue, but is offered by Turkey, and to a lesser extent other Islamic states, to children of their own national citizens. Originally, this model had been developed for children of foreign diplomats, but it has been extended to apply to all children of foreign nationals who live in certain German regions. Lessons are conducted by teaching staff from, and in accordance with curricula approved by, the country of origin. The German contribution consists largely in supplying teaching rooms but may involve financial subsidies. Legally classified as private education catering for specific needs, this model of religious instruction in Islam applies in Baden-Württemberg, Berlin, Bremen, Hamburg, the Saarland and Schleswig Holstein, i.e., those Länder where additional lessons in the mother-tongue are the responsibility of the relevant consular representatives. For these lessons, particular subjects are as a rule not strictly timetabled. The amount of time devoted to general language work, area studies or religious instruction is therefore a matter for the discretion of individual teachers. They are all employees of the Turkish state, which means that German education authorities have absolutely no say in this form of religious instruction. Since the language of instruction is also Turkish, Muslim children never acquire the concepts and terminology that would enable them to communicate with their fellow German pupils on religious matters. Moreover, the course materials, having been devised in Turkey, bear little or no relation to the actual day-to-day experiences of Turkish children living in the Federal Republic.

As mentioned earlier, Turkish organisations such as the Central Council for Muslims in Germany and the Islamic Council for the Federal Republic of Germany favour religious instruction parallel to that offered to the Christian denominations and likewise taught in German. One of the main obstacles to putting these demands into practice is the current shortage of Muslim religious-education teachers able to conduct lessons in German.

The half-hearted approach to establishing a place for Muslim religious education in German schools also stems from the lack of consensus in the Turkish minority about the type of religious education they would wish, and the preference of orthodox Muslims for special Koran Schools. Organised outside the German educational system, these schools are not linked to curricular programmes that have been approved by German education authorities. Several organisations and bodies have been involved in setting up Koran Schools according to their own pedagogical and, in particular, religious preferences. Since their courses are taught outside regular school hours, Koran Schools can make significant additional demands on their pupils' time. An investigation carried out in Hamburg found that in the mid-1980s some 24 percent of Turkish schoolchildren, i.e., roughly 2,000 pupils, were attending Koran classes.

Other surveys suggest that considerably more Turkish parents would like their children to receive religious education but are either unable or unwilling to send them to Koran Schools.[23]

The common denominator of Koran Schools has been a focus on Muslim orthodoxy that both in style and content disregards the special situation of young Muslims in Germany. Depending on the organisation running them, this has also involved varying degrees of Islamic ideological influence. As a result, Koran Schools in general have acquired the reputation of being hostile to any policy of integration.

The Emergence of Organised Islam in Germany

Demographic changes in their community structure of the kind already mentioned have not been the only factor behind the increased importance of Islam in the lives of Turkish migrants in Germany. Changes in their social situation have also been significant. Each stage of the economic recession, for instance – first in 1973, then again in the early 1980s, and lastly after unification – saw increased unemployment and greater fear of job-losses among the Turkish work-force. As a result, Islamic organisations acquired a new function as providers of social support and material assistance, for they were well placed to offer their members community networks and a trusted framework in which to reaffirm their traditional Turkish values.

Initially, Islamic associations were, above all, meeting places for members of the first generation of migrants. They created a space where Turks could gather to fulfil their religious needs, without being subject to the rules and prohibitions of the host society. One reason for increased participation in religious associations in the early 1980s was a decline in the popularity of extremist political organisations amongst Turks in Germany. This followed in the wake of the Turkish military putsch of 1980, when the ideologies that had divided Turkish migrants in Germany, just as much as Turks in their home country, gave way to a period of depoliticisation. An 'alternative-ideology' now gained ground, a 'Turkish-Islamic Synthesis' which aimed at and broadly succeeded in creating a new political consensus beyond nationalism and socialism. As the political divisions of yesteryear receded, Islam thus emerged as a common core of

Turkish identity and gained a prominence which it had not possessed when migration into Germany first began.

The shift from political to religious associations and organisations was further intensified by the West German government's attempt to encourage Turks (and other non-German minorities) to leave the country in return for material and financial rewards (returnees' premium). Rather than persuading Turks to return to Turkey, the legislation strengthened their resolve to remain in Germany for good. As the former workforce became a resident minority, many challenges of social integration impinged on their religion. Pre-school education in Germany, for example, is dominated by the Christian churches who run eighty percent of approved institutions. Nursery provision for Muslims has thus posed great problems. Previously inexperienced nursery attendants, teachers or social workers in areas with a high concentration of Muslims have had to acquaint themselves with the cultural heritage of their new clientele, and this has of course also entailed some knowledge of Islam. The lack of acceptable provision has, however, persuaded many Turkish parents to seek assistance closer to home and turn to Turkish-Islamic organisations to obtain the services that German society does not appear to offer. A similar behaviour pattern has emerged among the first-generation *Gastarbeiter* who are now reaching old age. Many are turning even more emphatically to Islam than in their younger years, not only because Turkish-Islamic organisations can be expected to offer support, but also to a large extent, because Islam requires each believer to settle any debts with God during his or her lifetime. Since one way of making amends for sins is to participate in the prescribed Muslim prayers five times per day in the community of others, facilities for this are now needed in larger numbers and in more locations than ever before. Here, Islamic organisations obviously have a key role to play.

For the second generation of Turkish migrants, religious orientation and the function of Islamic organisations in their lives are linked to experiences in the German host society. Given their command of the German language, their German educational background, and their motivation to improve their social status through qualifications and employment, they are much more likely to see their hopes and expectations dashed by the experience of social exclusion and limited opportunities, and in particular by the recent wave of xenophobic violence. Fears of violence have become more prominent among Turks in the 1990s than at any time since their arrival in Germany. Under these conditions, Islam and its affiliated organisations offer security and acceptance even for Turks who were born in Germany and who have developed a dual German-Turkish identity. When xenophobic attacks intensified after German unification, Islamic organisations played a leading role in organising protests or in consultations with local authorities, of the kind that took place after the murder of Turkish residents in Solingen and Mölln. More generally, Islamic organisations are emerging as advocates of equal rights and co-determination for Turks, and as vociferous critics of their continued exclusion as 'foreigners' from the political and social fabric of German society.

In addition, world events have had a considerable impact on the strengthening of Islam in Germany. Since the emergence of Islam as a political force, Muslim organisations and communities in Germany have received financial support, teaching resources and religious personnel from abroad, enabling them to consolidate their infrastructure and offer an increasingly comprehensive range of facilities, from mosques and cemeteries to religiously oriented educational programmes. In the 1990s, the personal religious orientation of Turkish Muslims in Germany also appears to have acquired a broader context and a quasi-political significance. Like other Muslims living in Western Europe, they have acquired a sense of solidarity with Islamic states that, in their eyes, have fallen victim to the aggression of Western powers. Events helping to fuel these sentiments were the European Union's rejection of Turkey's membership application, the Gulf War and, most recently, the civil war in Bosnia-Herzegovina. Members of the younger generations in particular have been made much more strongly conscious of their religious heritage as a result of such developments. Alongside religious practice and education, it is, for instance, significant that funding and delivering aid to Bosnian Muslims has become a major activity of Turkish-Islamic organisations in Germany.

The Structure of Turkish-Islamic Organisations in Germany

In 1995, more than two thousand Turkish-Islamic organisations existed in Germany with an estimated membership of up to one hundred thousand and an actual membership of half a million.[24]

Membership data are notoriously difficult to establish with regard to Turkish-Islamic organisations. Not only is there a grey zone between fully paid-up membership and occasional users of the facilities or services offered, but membership also tends to be calculated on the basis of the head of household, whilst in fact including all other members of the family. Given that the average Turkish family numbers 4.1 people, actual membership may be four times as high as that indicated by paid-up numbers.

Generally speaking, Turkish-Islamic organisations in Germany no longer hark back to Turkey and replicate the political divisions there, but are firmly rooted in the purpose of serving Turks who have settled in Germany. This purpose is also reflected in the organisational leadership. In the past, leaders tended to come from Turkey or retain strong links with Turkey as recent migrants. Today, the majority of organisational leaders have lived in Germany for at least ten years; many are even members of the second generation born and educated in Germany. With the exception of the Turkish-Islamic Association of the Turkish Institute for Religious Affairs (DITIB), which is headed by religious leaders on five-year secondment from Turkey, Turkish-Islamic organisations today tend to be led by Turks who have completed their secondary education or even obtained a university degree in Germany, and who are therefore better equipped than the leaders of the early 1980s to represent German-Turkish interests in German society. Nowadays, too, the organisations have largely distanced themselves from the internal Turkish political confrontations they had been involved in during the 1980s. Putting much more emphasis on the Islamic elements in their programmes, they clearly wish to be regarded first and foremost as religious rather than political groupings. Nevertheless, Turkish politicians make occasional appearances at major gatherings of the Turkish Federation and other organisations, a sign that connections with the Turkish political scene have not been entirely severed.

Turkish-Islamic organisations in Germany are grouped together under eight umbrella organisations of varying size, some defined by their religious orientation, some by their political affiliation. In 1993, the largest umbrella organisation, the Turkish-Islamic Association for Religious Affairs (DITIB),[25] which is closely affiliated to the Turkish government, included 740 member associations. The second largest umbrella organisation, the Association for a New World View in Europe (AMTG),[26] which is not so much secular as Islamist in orientation, included 262 member organisations. Other organisations emphasise different religious and political trends within Islam. These include a militant fundamentalist grouping with some fifty associations; the Turkish extremists sometimes known as Grey Wolves, who have recently incorporated a religious element in their programme (180 associations); an intellectual 'order' with thirty training schools, and eighty-two Alevite communities who, most recently of all, have formed a joint organisation to represent their own specifically Anatolian form of Shiite Islam in Germany.[27]

In the context of this chapter it is not possible to present a detailed account of the organisational diversity of Turkish Islam in Germany. Suffice it to say that the existence of a broad range of competing organisations all display a broadly religious orientation and subscribe to supporting the social, religious and cultural needs of Turks in Germany. Since the mid-1980s, moves have also been afoot to set up a central body, capable of representing the interests of all or most Turkish Muslims in Germany. Founded in Berlin in November 1986, the Islamic Council for the Federal Republic of Germany comprised twenty-three membership organisations and cultural centres by June 1995. Although ostensibly devoted to Islam as a religion and culture, the Islamic Council has been described as a major advocate of Muslim integration into German society, where Islam constitutes one of several religions in an essentially secular state and social environment.[28]

The Central Council of Muslims in Germany (named after and modelled on the Central Council of Jews in Germany) was founded in December 1994 as a successor to the Islamic Association in Germany, which dated back to 1991.[29] By June 1995 it included representatives of most influential Turkish-Islamic organisations and religious communities among its members. Created as a pressure group to ensure that German public authorities would grant legal recognition for Muslim religious practices such as ritual slaughter, the Central Council of Muslims in Germany 'does not want to replace existing mosques, Islamic associations and organisations, or enter into competition with them, but intends to represent their joint interests vis-à-vis German authorities and fight for their right to live as a religious community in Germany'.[30] The Central Council aims to improve the legal and social situation of Muslims in Germany, constitute a forum for discussion among its members, and represent the interests of Muslims in German administrative, social or legal contexts.

Given the variety of Turkish-Islamic organisations, their

detailed aims reflect the multi-faceted structure of the Turkish minority and its religious orientations. On a general level, however, all but the most fundamentalist Turkish-Islamic organisations share the basic aims of supporting the Turkish migrants in Germany and finding an effective voice for Turkish-Islamic demands and expectations in German society. Although some divisions prevail, it seems likely that Turkish-Islamic organisations in Germany will in the medium term establish a working consensus to achieve these objectives.[31] Members of the first generation may have joined originally in the hope of effecting political change in Turkey. Today, members join Turkish-Islamic organisations to improve their lives in Germany.[32]

No longer, therefore, do Turkish-Islamic organisations restrict themselves to offering purely religious facilities such as prayer rooms, instruction in the Koran, burial funds to support the majority of Turks in Germany who prefer to bury their dead in Turkey, and the organisation of pilgrimages to Muslim holy places. In addition, they now provide specialist courses and counselling services modelled on those previously offered only by state welfare organisations or the churches. These include literacy programmes, courses in German and in sewing for Turkish women and girls, courses in computer skills or Arabic, as well as leisure pursuits such as martial arts for young men. Some mosques have set up their own citizens' advice centres to help with claiming benefit and dealing with German bureaucracy. Many also offer translation services to members.

A small number of fundamentalist Muslim organisations in Germany purport to be the 'voice of Turkish Islam'. One of the best known and most extreme organisations focuses on the late 'Khomeini of Cologne', one Cemalattin Kaplan, who went as far as to proclaim an 'Islamic-Turkish state in exile' in Germany. Organisations such as the 'Association of the National View' or the 'Association of Islamic Cultural Centres' speak a somewhat more moderate language, but subscribe to the similarly radical aim of setting up an Islamic state. The diverse range of Turkish-Islamic organisations in Germany shows clearly that the Turkish minority cannot be treated as if it were a homogeneous or even homogeneously Islamic-fundamentalist entity. In practice, none of the Turkish-Islamic groupings can be regarded as the authoritative voice either of Islam or of the Turkish minority; each represents only a sectional, local or regional facet of Turkish cultural diversity in Germany.

Membership in any given organisation is in any case often dictated by circumstance rather than religious or political preference. The majority of Turks choose the prayer house or mosque nearest to their home or their place of work, and join the organisation that happens to be affiliated with it. Only in some big cities are organisations and religious institutions numerous enough to allow a choice, whereas in small towns or rural areas only a rudimentary Islamic infra-structure of one or possibly two organisations exists. Given the centrality of religion in contemporary Turkish culture, the majority of Turks are members of a religious community in their neighbourhood without having taken out a specific membership in an organisation or group with more general religious or Islamic-political goals. The integration of religious, social and support functions blurs the boundaries between religious observance and Turkish-Islamic organisations and their various aims. Although the existence of numerous such organisations testifies to the diversity of Turkish culture in Germany, it would be misleading to infer that they enjoy the support of hundreds of thousands of Turks, all committed to a militant form of Islam.

Recent Developments and Prospects

The second and third generations of Turkish migrants regard Islam, not unlike their parents, as the major unifying element of Turkish identity and culture in Germany, but they have tended to develop their own distinctive approach to religion. More intellectual than the popular Islam of their parents, it includes an emphasis on Arabic as the language of the holy book, on individual study of the Koran and on the discussion of religious issues, often in German, which in many cases has taken over from Turkish as their native language. The dual immersion in the German language and in Turkish Sunni religious traditions could generate more points of contact between the two cultures than were possible for the first generation of Turks in Germany, and create new cultural impulses both in the host country and the country of origin.

It is too early to determine whether Turkish organisations in Germany will influence Islamic thought and practice in Turkey. Until the mid-1980s, all Turkish-Islamic organisations in Germany were affiliated to partner organisations or political groupings in

Turkey and received financial and spiritual support from them. Since then, a reversal has taken place, as more and more organisations and Turkish communities based in Germany take an active role in supporting and funding religious developments in Turkey such as the construction of a new mosque or the establishment of religious schools.[33]

At the time of writing, ideological currents emanating from the Islamic intelligentsia in Turkey are still influencing the most intellectually inclined movements in Germany. Books published in Turkey on the contemporary role of Islam have been eagerly received by second and third-generation Turkish migrants in Germany in their search for a religious focus. Most important in this respect have been the works of the leading Turkish intellectuals Ali Bulac and Abdurrahman Dilipak. From the vantage point of young Turks in Germany, confronted with a majority culture demanding their full integration, and at the same time facing political, economic and social exclusion as that very society continues to treat them as 'foreigners', re-discovering their Islamic identity and belonging to an ethnically and denominationally cohesive community offers a means of asserting themselves and opportunities to assume leadership functions. Organised Turkish-Islamic culture offers young Turks who feel at home in both the German and the Turkish context, a chance to advance swiftly into key positions as self-confident representatives of the interests of their minority vis-à-vis the host society.

In pursuing their aims, adherents of Islamic organisations in Germany have tended to argue their case on the basis of European Enlightenment concepts such as 'human rights', 'religious freedom' and 'human dignity' in an effort to persuade German society to accept the religious strictures and practices prescribed by Islam. In demanding, for example, that Turkish girls in German schools should not be required to take part in physical education classes, they argued that such classes conflicted with an Islamic sense of decency and honour. In August 1993, a Berlin court accepted this position, ruling that the basic right to religious freedom was more important than the duty to take part in mixed physical education classes, even though these were deemed obligatory for all male and female pupils of their school.

The young generation of fervent Muslims who insist on religious practices and on social integration (on their terms) into German society may be called 'post-modern Muslims'. For them,

adherence to traditional dress codes is not at all incompatible with
the leisure-wear fashionable in the youth culture of Germany and
Europe generally. Thus it is by no means unusual to see young
Turkish women wearing the *chador* whilst at the same time sporting
popular brands of jeans and trainers. Behind such mixed cultural
phenomena lies the conviction that certain aspects of modern
society and technological development can be combined with
Muslim traditions and practices. This new interpretation of Islam,
rejecting the political ideologies of the past, which it considers
have failed, presents itself as an alternative in which religious
observance and modern living can go hand in hand.[34]

Turks of a fundamentalist persuasion, by comparison, have
made little headway. In 1995, an estimated one percent of
Muslims in Germany were members of fundamentalist groupings compared to 25 percent in other Turkish-Islamic
organisations.[35] The fundamentalists offer the same broad social
and religious infra-structure as other organisations, but have
appealed in particular to Turks who perceive their social position as marginal and their prospects as poor. Keenly aware of
their inferior opportunities in education and training, resentful
of their limited political and social participation and the ban on
mobility between European countries, these younger generation
Turks are demanding equal status for Islam as one of the major
religions in Western societies, and accuse Western states of
ignoring the social disadvantages of Muslims and Turks. Recent
instances of xenophobia seem to have made fundamentalist
positions more widely acceptable. Yet, although feelings of
discontent, social exclusion and anxiety about xenophobia are
widespread among Turks in Germany, the majority have not
opted for fundamentalist solutions. Instead, they have taken the
course of re-affirming their more moderate Muslim identity and
culture in their non-Muslim country of residence.

In Germany, the emergence of a moderate European version of
Islam is more likely than a shift towards fundamentalism among
the Turkish minority. As mentioned earlier, a consensus among
Islamic organisations is slowly taking shape. Attempts to group the
diversified religious culture into umbrella organisations and join
forces to gain concessions with regard to the observance of religious festivals or practices, are first signs of an emergent coalition
of interests. Friendly contacts and visits between different organisations and their leaders, which were unheard of in the past, are
beginning to take place. In the past, representatives from Turkey

would address key rallies of organisations in Germany; now, representatives of other Islamic-Turkish organisations may also be present. In some localities, religious organisations from different camps (the DITIB and the AMGT for instance) have agreed to share the use of a mosque and its facilities, while elsewhere one organisation funds the mosque, another the *imam*. Pragmatic collaboration has begun to supplant the rigid and isolated ideological positions adopted in the past. Only the zealots of the Kaplan movement refuse to collaborate with anyone.

During the course of their twenty-year history, many Islamic Turkish organisations have developed considerable experience and skill in dealing with German administrative authorities and policy makers. The acquisition of these skills can be regarded as a successful induction into democratic forms of political participation at the local level. This involvement is intensifying as Turkish organisations take an active role in the advisory councils for foreigners that operate in many areas and regions of Germany. In order to maximise their chances of election to these councils, Islamic-Turkish organisations have begun to establish joint 'Islamic lists'. Although consensus between the various organisations remains slim, four religious issues are emerging as focal points for co-ordination and co-operation:

1. winning recognition for Islam as a legally established religion in Germany, comparable to the Christian churches;
2. obtaining special permission to slaughter animals according to Islamic rites;
3. provision of religious instruction in Islam within the regular curriculum of German schools for all Muslim children;
4. securing the support of regional governments and local authorities for the purchase of land and the construction of new mosques in Germany.

In addition, all Turkish-Islamic organisations aspire to extend their members' scope for participation in politics. Regardless of religious differences or political preferences, all organisations are demanding voting rights for non-Germans at local level, and the introduction of dual citizenship in Germany. The active participation of Islamic Lists in elections to foreigners' councils has been greeted with concern by some observers who fear that Muslims will soon dominate at the expense of other non-Germans. Case studies in Hesse in 1994 disprove these fears, suggesting that a less emotional and more pragmatic approach to developments is required.[36] Contributions in Hesse's foreigners' councils, whether by members of Islamic Lists or by representatives of other groups, remained ineffective if they merely stuck to pre-determined sectional interests. What is required is the modification of positions and the arrival at a consensus between members, in order to optimise the limited political scope available to these councils. Rather than exacerbating fundamentalist radicalisation, participation in foreigners' councils can then have the opposite effect of incorporating democratic traditions, such as acceptance of majority decisions and pluralism, into Turkish-Islamic organisational practice. Such participation also forces organisations to declare their aims openly in public, thus making their roles as interest groups more transparent, which can only be a good thing, both for the Turkish minority and society at large. The emergent consensus between Turkish-Islamic organisations in Germany and their nascent participation in local advisory bodies is serving to integrate these organisations more closely into West German democracy and fostering a change from authoritarian to democratic decision-making processes in this key area of Turkish culture in Germany.

NOTES

1. Definition from *Meyer's Großes Handlexikon,* 14th revised edition, Mannheim/Wien/Zurich, Brockhaus, 1985, p.473.

2. P. Gleason, 'Immigration, Religion and Inter-Group Relations: Historical Perspectives on the American Experience', in *Immigrants in Two Democracies: French and American Experiences,* ed. D. L. Horowitz and G. Notriel, New York/London, New York UP, 1992, pp.167–187.

3. See Chapter 7 in this volume.

4. For a detailed analysis, see *Türkei-Sozialkunde,* ed. Zentrum für Türkeistudien, 2nd revised edition, Opladen, Leske & Budrich, 1994; *Zum Integrationspotential der türkischen Tagespresse in der Bundesrepublik Deutschland,* ed. Zentrum für Türkeistudien, Opladen, Leske & Budrich 1991.

5. In 1991, 44 percent of German households and 64 percent of Turkish households owned a video recorder. Turks were also more likely than Germans to have cable television, in order to receive programmes in Turkish. See *Türkische Muslime in Nordrhein-Westfalen. Endbericht zur Studie 'Dialog mit einer neu etablierten religiösen Minderheit in NRW, türkische Muslime und deutsche Christen im Gespräch'*, ed. Ministerium für Arbeit, Gesundheit und Soziales, Nordrhein-Westfalen, Düsseldorf, June 1995, p.76.

6. *Gesundheitsbewußtsein der Migranten aus der Türkei in Nordrhein-Westfalen*, ed. Zentrum für Türkeistudien, unpublished study, Bonn, 1991.

7. See Chapter 6 in this volume.

8. See *Türkische Muslime in Nordrhein-Westfalen*, pp.11–12. Also 'Emma Dossier: "Fundamentalismus"', in *Emma*, no.4, July–August 1993, pp.36–57.

9. Definition of 'assimilation' from the German dictionary *Duden*.

10. This definition was formulated by the Federal Commissioner for Foreigners' Affairs, Liselotte Funke, when working on the German government programme (1981–1990) to assist the integration of non-Germans into German society.

11. D. Khalid, 'Der Islam in der Diaspora: Europa und Amerika', in *Der Islam in der Gegenwart*, ed. U. Steinbach and W. Ende, 3rd edition, Munich, Beck, 1991, p.452.

12. Of the 2,000 mosques that were in operation in 1995, only a handful were constructed in the traditional style with a minaret, and only the mosque in Dortmund had permission for a Muezzin to call for prayers from the minaret once a day.

13. See M. Matter, 'Ehre und Moral', *Hessische Blätter für Volks- und Kulturforschung*, Neue Folge, vol.29, 1992, pp.95–104.

14. *Türkei-Sozialkunde*, p.140f.

15. *Lebenssituation und spezifische Problemlage älterer ausländischer Einwohner in der Bundesrepublik Deutschland*, ed. Bundesministerium für Arbeit und Sozialordnung, Bonn, 1993, p.96f.

16. See Chapter 7 in this volume; also M.-L. Abali, 'Entwicklungsprobleme bei türkischen Kindern und Jugendlichen in Berlin. Psychologische Aspekte der Identitätsbildung', in *Identität. Veränderungen kultureller Eigenarten im Zusammenleben von Türken und Deutschen*, ed. C. Elsas, Hamburg, E.B. Verlag-Rissen, 1993, p.197.

18. H. Straube, *Türkisches Leben in der Bundesrepublik*, Frankfurt/Main, Campus, 1987, p.334.

19. From 'Ein Blatt im Strom', *Der Spiegel*, no.11, 1993.

20. See S. M. Abdullah, 'Der Islam will in Deutschland heimisch werden', in *Der Islam im Abendland*, Special Issue of *Die Brücke*, Saarbrücken, 1992, p.38.

21. Report from the Secretary to the Standing Conference of Regional Ministers of Cultural Affairs, dated 20 March 1984, Bonn 1984.

22. In 1986, for instance, the Regional Institute for Schools and Further Education in North Rhine-Westphalia prepared a draft curriculum entitled 'religious instruction for Muslim pupils'. Developed in consultation with distinguished Islamic theologians, the programme was intended for use at primary-school level, and included twenty-four teaching units in Turkish and German. Since then, a school textbook for religious instruction in Islam has also been published.

22. G. Mahler, 'Möglichkeiten religiöser Unterweisung muslimischer Kinder an öffentlichen Schulen in den Ländern der Bundesrepublik Deutschland entsprechend dem Beschluß der Kultusministerkonferenz', in *Rahmenbedingungen und Materialien zur religiösen Unterweisung für Schüler islamischen Glaubens*, ed. Landesinstitut für Schule und Weiterbildung, Berlin, Express Edition, 1987, p.146.

23. See P. Kappert and R. Niemeyer,'Islamischer Religionsunterricht für muslimische türkische Schüler an Hamburger Schulen', in *Erziehung zur Kulturbegegnung. Pädadogische Beiträge zur Kulturbegegnung*, vol.3, ed. J. Lähnemann, Hamburg, 1986, p.73.

24. Quoted from *Türkische Muslime in Nordrhein-Westfalen*, pp.76–77. Data on mosques also in *Statistisches Jahrbuch der Bundesrepublik Deutschland* for the various years.

25. DITIB, Diyanet Isleri Türk Islam Birligi, which translates in full as Turkish-Islamic Association of the Turkish Institute for Religious Affairs.

26. AMGT, Avrupa Milli Görus Teskilatlari, translates as Association for a New World View in Europe.

27. For a full survey of Turkish-Islamic organisations, their organisational purpose, membership and contact addresses, see *Türkische Muslime in Nordrhein-Westfalen*, pp.83–128.

28. Quoted from Muhammed Salim Abdullah, the former head of the Islamic Council and the Director of the Central Institute of the Islamic Archive in Germany and a major proponent of Muslim integration into German secular society. For details, see *Türkische Muslime in Nordrhein-Westfalen*, p.121.

29. See the Turkish daily paper *Milliyet*, 8 December 1994.

30. *Türkische Muslime in Nordrhein-Westfalen*, p.124.

31. *Islamische Organisationen der türkischen, marokkanischen, tunesischen und bosnischen Minderheiten in Hessen. Studie im Auftrag des Büros für Einwanderer und Flüchtlinge*

im Hessischen Ministerium für Umwelt, Energie, Jugend, Familie und Gesundheit, ed. Zentrum für Türkeistudien, Essen, 1995, p.179.

32. M. S. Abdullah, *Was will der Islam in Deutschland?*, Gütersloh, Verlagshaus Gerd Mohn, 1993, p.37.

33. Via its religious charities, the Association of Islamic Cultural Centres finances several student hostels and boarding schools in Turkey.

34. R. Schulze, *Geschichte der islamischen Welt im 20. Jahrhundert,* Munich, Beck, 1994, p.310.

35. *Islamischer Extremismus und seine Auswirkungen auf die Bundesrepublik Deutschland,* ed. Bundesamt für Verfassungsschutz, 2nd edition, January 1995, p.6.

36. This section is based on information gathered during interviews conducted by the author in preparation for the study *Islamische Organisationen der türkischen, marokkanischen, tunesischen und bosnischen Minderheiten in Hessen,* (see note 31).

Conclusion

Eva Kolinsky

Emine Sevgi Özdamar, the writer whose work features in this volume, refuses to take sides. Her Turkish culture in German society comes in Western dress with prayers in Arabic. She writes in the German language about Turks whose identity includes personal and national memories, family histories and Turkish history. The regional and religious conflicts that appear to be dividing Turkey all concern her as part of her personal experience, but no side is deemed to be better than the other. Their complex juxtaposition matters, not the simplification of taking sides. For Özdamar, taking sides means distortion and thrives on isolation. People who do not know each other adopt rigid positions or resort to stereotypes to define their own space and that of others. Where communication has taken root, ascribed identities, nationalities, background or characteristics fall by the way-side as a common purpose or activity sets the agenda. Not mute forbearance or exaggerated civility– the initial period of love and peace in *Black Eye and His Donkey* – signal understanding, but the rough-and-tumble of disagreement and concurrence which is the hallmark of normal social interaction.

Özdamar's story relates her own positive experiences of working with her multi-national and multi-cultural cast, but its subtext tells the more troubled story of how national stereotypes and prejudice persist and obstruct acceptance between different cultural or national groups. In German society, this subtext of non-communication constitutes normality, while the model of Özdamar's parable remains an exception. Germans and non-Germans live separate lives in separate societies and with separate cultures.

Turkish Culture in German Society Today has set out to explore the cultural orientations and social position of Turks, the largest and the least accepted group of resident non-Germans in Germany. As outsiders in national and cultural terms, 'foreigners', 'strangers', 'migrants' have either been viewed as an exception likely to destabilise society and adulterate its homogeneity, or as an exception likely to need special protection against an unfair and unjust social environment. Although diametrically opposed, both approaches treat the 'others' as an exception whose status and identity is defined by its minority status alone and as an adjunct of the host society. Without ignoring the German context and its influences, *Turkish Culture in German Society Today* has focused on the Turks themselves, their culture and their lives in Germany. It is a book about post-migration adjustment, about everyday normality and, above all, about the meaning of Turkish identity in Germany today.

By way of conclusion, let us briefly take stock of some experiences and structures which have shaped the everyday lives of Turks, and contributed to the emergence of a Turkish identity in German society.

Labour recruitment of *Gastarbeiter* was based on the assumption that contract labour would be non-resident, temporary and outside key institutions of social integration. *Gastarbeiter* were not regarded as rightful members of the society, but tolerated as auxiliaries to assist economic prosperity. The majority of Turks arrived in the late 1960s at the end of the recruitment period. Coming late brought advantages and disadvantages. Until the change of legislation in 1965, non-Germans were forced to leave if they became unemployed or found themselves dependent on benefit, although equal pay and conditions at work had been secured from the outset. While the threat of exclusion and forcible repatriation has never fully subsided, non-Germans with valid residency permits have won social citizenship and entitlement to welfare provisions. Compared with the historical legacy of excluding foreign labour from German society altogether, the inclusion of non-Germans in the social net constituted a major advance in social justice.

Social citizenship enables non-Germans in principle to benefit from educational, occupational and personal opportunities on the basis of ability, not background. In reality, non-Germans have been disadvantaged and have enjoyed less social mobility than Germans. Turks in particular have remained at the most disadvantaged end of society in blue-collar and unskilled employment, without vocational training opportunities, more likely than Germans and other national groups to be unemployed, in poor housing and in the lowest income groups. In the mid-1990s, one in five depended on income support and was threatened by poverty.

Across the Länder, the treatment of non-Germans has not been identical. Until the revised Foreigners' Legislation of 1990 standardised procedures, regional authorities could define their own rules. Thus, Länder with SPD-led governments tended to accept non-Germans, develop social support systems and aim to reduce exclusion. Länder with conservative governments adopted a more restrictive approach to issuing residency permits and other matters. The different approaches to religious education highlight the diversity: generally speaking, German educational policy does not recognise Islam as a religion for which state education should be provided within the regular curriculum. Länder with an established commitment to *Ausländerpolitik*, such as North Rhine-Westphalia, pioneered a programme of religious education in schools which aimed at assisting young Turks to retain their Islamic identity and knowledge of religious traditions as a constituent part of their lives in German society. Most Länder, however, opted for a different model. Islam is taught outside the school setting by teachers and with materials supplied and monitored by Turkey and its religious establishment. Here, religious education does not serve to bring the two identities of young Turks, the German and the Islamic dimension together, but aims to keep them apart.

For the non-acceptance of Turks in German society, the differences of religion and the differences in everyday culture, values and behaviour arising from it, cannot be over-estimated. When the *Anwerbestopp* of 1973 forced Turks to choose between returning to their home country or settling in Germany, most chose to stay. Coming to work in Germany had not been 'migration' with a view to remaining there. It had been no more than an employment move for a limited time in order to improve their economic prospects and material conditions at home. Even after choosing to live in Germany, many Turks lived between countries, often supporting their families in Turkey financially, often having their children raised and educated in Turkey, and keeping in touch through an annual trek back home during the summer vacation. For first-generation *Gastarbeiter*, these contacts were a lifeline to their own past and background; for subsequent generations, contacts with Turkey lost some of the personal significance but became a formative experience of what it meant to live between cultures. In Germany, Turks were Turks, regardless of the fluency of their German language and the Western style of their dress; in Turkey, Turks from Germany were German-Turks, not members of but visitors to the land of their fathers.

The transformation from *Gastarbeiter* to a settled and resident group was set in motion by the *Anwerbestopp*, whose prime and declared purpose had, of course, been to rid Germany of non-Germans after the labour shortage and the era of the economic miracle had come to a halt. The new residents were protected by the rule of law and the extension of social citizenship to non-Germans, but they were not shielded from non-acceptance in society. Exclusion took the form of housing segregation and stigmatisation as an underclass. It also took the form of negative views and open rejection of foreigners which fluctuated over time but never subsided. Since the early 1970s, hostility towards *Gastarbeiter* has constituted a prominent theme in extreme right-wing and neo-Nazi agitation in Germany, alongside anti-Semitism and a glorification of National Socialism and its leadership.

Public policy has been divided. On the one hand, exclusion tended to dominate policy as governments attempted to assuage fears among Germans about economic uncertainties and the pressures on the welfare state. In 1982, a programme of financial rewards was designed to promote re-migration. Few Turks could be enticed to leave. In 1993, after two years of violence against settled non-Germans and incoming asylum seekers, an all-party majority in the German Bundestag voted to amend the Basic Law and restrict the right of political asylum it had included since 1949. Moreover, new legislation increased the powers of police and border guards to refuse entry, and reduced the rights of non-Germans to material support and welfare provision. Although aimed at asylum seekers, the new legislation was billed as an answer to what seven out of ten Germans called an *Ausländerproblem*, a problem with foreigners and their presence among them.

The unification of Germany aggravated the pressures of

exclusion. In the East, society had been German-only, with foreigners segregated by privilege or, more commonly, by their status as contract workers without access to civil liberties or freedom of movement. Here, foreigners had no place and were not accepted as inhabitants of a new Germany. After unification, open hostility broke out in the East before spreading to the West. Even before that, foreigners in East Germany were dismissed from their employment, evicted into homelessness from their hostels, and made to leave the country.

In the West, the national exhilaration of the first hour was, of course, short lived, but the preoccupation with German-German unification (paired with the determination to curtail the influx of asylum seekers) obscured the fact that the old Länder at least had long ceased to be German only and included sizeable non-German groups and their culture. The unification of Germany re-instated mono-culturalism, pushing multi-culturalism into the background. East Germans generally and West Germans to the right of centre even welcomed unification as an affirmation of German national homogeneity and strengths.

Before unification, a debate had begun to take shape in West Germany about the legitimacy of excluding non-Germans and in particular their German-born offspring from German citizenship. The emphatically nationalist zeal of unification suspended this debate and created a climate in which resident non-Germans were equated to asylum seekers and tarred with the same brush of illegitimacy. As xenophobic violence in the old and the new Länder shocked those for whom the inclusion of non-Germans constituted a core-dimension of a democratic society, the debate regained momentum. Not only pleading for acceptance and toleration of non-Germans, it has targeted German citizenship legislation and begun to campaign against *jus sanguinis* and for *jus soli* and dual citizenship. Dual citizenship, it is argued, should be legalised in order to recognise the dual identity of non-Germans between Germany and their original country of emigration. Although supported by the left of the political spectrum, notably the Greens and the SPD, the debate on citizenship is unlikely to change government policy or the German concept of citizenship going hand-in-hand with an immersion in and acceptance of German culture, the German language, German ways of life, traditions and values. This kind of conformism does not appeal to Germany's non-Germans. Relinquishing Turkish citizenship and conforming with German cultural rules, for instance, conflicts with the dual German-Turkish identity which most of the second and third younger generations of Germany's Turkish inhabitants perceive as their own.

Generation has been a powerful agent of change. The first generation to make their home in Germany took refuge in the social orientations and religious values they were familiar with during their transformation from migrants to residents. As *Gastarbeiter* they had little need of religion and did not attempt to establish mosques and related social institutions. For the settled population with families, Islam provided the framework and the rules of social interaction. While education, employment and contacts with public bodies exposed Turks to German influences, practices and values, this public sphere remained largely separated from a private sphere of family life where social roles and behaviour codes tended to emanate from Islamic rather than German traditions. By German standards, families were authoritarian and patriarchal in structure, with restricted rights of participation and decision making for women, children and young people. Established Islamic customs such as arranged marriages, traditional dress for women, and the social restrictions arising for women from the notion of honour held by Muslim men, have been interpreted as evidence that the infrastructure of Turkish everyday life violates human rights and is undemocratic. Islamic traditions, more than any other aspect of Turkish culture, have evoked hostility across the political spectrum. Among the extreme right, Islam confirms the alien status of Turks in a society which should be reserved for Germans, while democrats from the centre to the Green and Feminist left regard Islam as backward, anti-modern and an outrage in the age of equality. The emergence of Islamic fundamentalism and the anti-Kurdish policies of the Turkish government have made it all too easy to suspect the whole Turkish population of Germany of unsavoury social and political leanings.

The clamour of indignation or xenophobia has tended to drown the fainter sounds of social change. In the families, the uneven competence of generations in German culture has begun to erode the traditional role of the male head of household and created new avenues of participation and social freedom for German-Turkish men and women. As the second and third generation of Turks reach adulthood and rise into positions of leadership within their community, the segregation of Islam from German society is set to dwindle. The community leaders of tomorrow embrace Islam as part of their dual German-Turkish identity and consider its teachings, values and social institutions as means to articulate and sustain that dual identity, not to revert to a Turkish-Islamic orthodoxy. The new generation of religious and community leaders possesses the command of language, the cultural competence and the political will to consolidate the place of Turkish residents in Germany, and mould them from a socially and religiously divided population into a minority with agreed interests and cohesive organisational representation at all levels of German society and politics. A beginning has been made with Turkish representatives participating at local level in advisory councils on foreigners. For the new generations of Turks, at least, involvement in democratic consultation processes has replaced the authoritarian structures which the *Gastarbeiter* generation and Islamic orthodoxy from Turkey would take for granted.

Breaking down the segregation between Turks and Germans has been greatly helped by the creation of special agencies to facilitate communication. Organised at local level and designed to assist non-Germans with matters of social or personal orientation, from the filling in of forms or coping with German bureaucracies, to combating discrimination, offices of Foreigners' Representatives have also elevated non-Germans to positions of authority and created new avenues of social mobility. Although each office operates to a local agenda, all have contributed to blunting the pressures of exclusion and boosting the chances of acceptance for non-German residents. At national level, a similar office was created in the early 1980s with the specific brief of disseminating information about non-Germans and their culture, and encouraging a discourse of acceptance.

First-generation Turkish *Gastarbeiter* – even as they approach pensionable age – have lacked the courage and the self-assuredness to argue their case in the public sphere, and have tended to retreat into the private niche of their families, ghettos, prayer halls and Islamic traditions. Their children and grandchildren have learnt to utilise the channels of participation that are open to them, articulate their views in public, and expect a response. As German young people have begun to turn against political parties and public agencies in the belief that none of them meets their expectations and heeds their concerns, young Turks are beginning to show similar signs of disillusionment. Confident in their claim that Turks in Germany constitute a minority with their own culture and rightful identity, a blend of German modern living and Islamic tradition, their expectations conflict with persistent non-acceptance and the barriers of exclusion.

The majority of Turks in German society remain trapped at the lower end of the social scale. A tiny, articulate and educated elite, however, has begun to emerge. This elite is German and Turkish in its identity and insistent that equal rights and the socio-cultural status of a minority should be granted to Turkish residents in Germany. Many of their elders are too fearful or too steeped in their orthodoxy to join in their demands for social acceptance. On the German side, a majority from all political camps also objects. Those on the right resent the manifestations of a German-Turkish identity and expect foreigners to blend into German culture before accepting them; those on the left question the political correctness of Islamic traditions inside German democracy.

Turks of the younger generations have found a voice of their own and begun to articulate their expectations and assert their identity. This very assertiveness, however, may arouse further hostility in a society and culture that has always required its minorities to relinquish their visible differences and subscribe to German behavioural codes prior to social acceptance. The emergence of a German-Turkish identity demonstrates that a plurality of cultures exists. The agenda of exclusion has been modified and may even be hidden at times, but is yet to be rewritten.

Literature has a special role to play in rewriting the agenda of exclusion. The writers, their stories, their imaginary worlds and their language all defy the generalisations and stereotypes that underpin exclusion. The 'migrants' who write and publish today in German come from a variety of national and cultural backgrounds. There is no such things as *Ausländerliteratur,* a literature of non-Germans in Germany, nor is there a German-Turkish, German-Portuguese, German-Greek school of writing. Each writer is an individual with his or her own cultural or cross-cultural identity. Each has a story to tell, characters to introduce, emotions to kindle, reflections to impart. Even in the first hour of *Gastarbeiter* literature, writers had no formula, but a palette of individual experiences, sufferings and hopes. The *Gastarbeiter* reader would find echoes of his or her own experiences and uncertainties in these stories. At the very least, they may have eased the pain of separation from the home country, family and friends, whilst giving expression to the shared disorientation of migration and adjustment. Written in German, however, these early stories were also aimed at German readers, allowing them to obtain an inside view of the experiences and feelings of ordinary labour migrants and their everyday lives. As tales from this other world, *Gastarbeiter* literature created in virtual reality the kind of inter-personal contacts that actual reality precluded. In order to learn about *Gastarbeiter*, Germans could turn to literature, even if they did not choose to go to the length of emulating Günter Wallraff by disguising themselves as *Gastarbeiter*, working among them, and facing the hostilities of their daily lives.[1]

In the 1990s, the literature of *Betroffenheit*, the narrative of personal experience, had had its day, although it was still given to literature to reveal complexities and individual experiences which are not normally accessible. The non-German writers of the second and third generations can be said to address two distinct readerships: both readers from the minority communities themselves, and German readers who gain from this literature a view of individuals they would not normally meet, cultural tendencies they would not normally understand, experiences they may not have had. As with all literature, readers immerse themselves in a new world and understand it by a complex mixture of identification, emotional involvement and following the story line. In a society where few personal contacts exist between Germans and non-Germans and even fewer between Germans and Turks, migrants' literature is a window to the personal world of Turks in Germany and the values of their culture.

Among German readers and readers of other cultures, migrants' literature contributes to an understanding of cultural diversity and identity. Among readers of the same culture, this literature helps to constitute or restore a sense of history and cultural origins which may have been obliterated by German culture or curtailed by partisan rivalries between competing religious or political factions. Of course, Özdamar's tapestry of Turkish history, regions, religious traditions and their animosities, may have been woven to introduce German readers to the beauty and fascination of her Turkish background and challenge monochrome views of 'The Turks' by enmeshing accounts of individuals. Her story may, however, also have been told to remember a forgotten past – that of Turkey and the many pasts of its people – and bring it through language into the present. From her own life, we know that Özdamar learned Arabic to regain a dimension of her cultural heritage that her migration and German life style had blocked out. In a similar mode, the narrator and protagonist in *Karawanserei* uses ritualistic expressions which link her to her grandparents, her family history and to other Muslims, adding an element of cultural continuity to her daily life. *Bismillâh* comes to symbolise this continuity and the centrality of memory and the past to identity.

German-Turkish identity includes, not excludes, religious diversity and practice; it includes, not excludes Turkish history; it includes, not excludes migration and the resulting challenge to create a new sense of belonging and a personal sense of Turkish culture. The writings by Özdamar and other 'migrant' writers in Germany tell many different stories but tackle one common theme: the theme of identity. A theme of modern writers generally, identity within a cultural framework highlights the conflicts between individual perceptions and social norms. Turkish and other non-German writers belong to this intellectual context, and the conflict between individual and society is equally central to them. Their experiences and their writings, however, include the added dimension of cultural diversity. Non-Germans in Germany cannot sever their links with their backgrounds, and plunge for assimilation. Thus, Turkish identity in Germany may include head scarves, prayer books and other preferred signs of visible difference. In its dual commitment without taking sides, German-Turkish identity is a ferment of a culture of diversity which has begun to take shape in German society and may be seen as a forerunner of a multi-cultural future.

NOTE

1. G. Wallraff, *Ganz Unten*, Cologne, Kiepenheuer & Witsch, 1985.

NOTES ON CONTRIBUTORS

SABINE FISCHER is a research student in Germanic Studies at the University of Sheffield. She is currently completing her doctorate on 'Yoko Tawada in the context of migrants' writing in Germany' and is co-author with Moray McGowan of 'Migrantinnenliteratur' in *Sozialgeschichte der deutschen Literatur* (ed. H.A. Glaser, 1996).

DAVID HORROCKS is a lecturer in German at Keele University. Specialising in twentieth-century German literature, especially the novel, he has published a number of essays on Hermann Broch, as well as articles on Hauptmann, Kafka, Hesse and Nietzsche, Andersch, and Böll.

YASEMIN KARAKASOGLU is a researcher at the Centre for Turkish Studies at the University of Essen. Her special fields of interest include the development of Islam and the situation of Turkish women, children and young people in Germany. On behalf of the Centre for Turkish Studies she has conducted surveys on the cultural and religious identity of Turks in North Rhine-Westphalia and Hesse, published as *Türkische Muslime in Nordrhein Westfalen* (1995) and *Islamische Organisationen der türkischen, marokkanischen, tunesischen und bosnischen Minderheiten in Hessen* (1995).

EVA KOLINSKY is Professor of Modern German Studies and Director of the Centre for the Study of German Culture and Society at Keele University. She is editor of the *German Studies* and *Culture and Society in Germany* book series, co-editor of the journal *German Politics* and has published widely on aspects of social change and political culture in Germany. Recent books include *Women in Contemporary Germany* (1993), *Women in 20th Century Germany* (1995), *Between Hope and Fear. Everyday Life in Post-Unification East Germany* (1995).

FRANK KRAUSE is *Lektor* in German at Keele University. Currently completing a doctoral thesis on German Expressionist literature, he is a co-editor with Ingolfur Blühdorn and Thomas Scharf of *The Green Agenda: Environmental Politics and Policy in Germany* (1995).

ELÇIN KÜRSAT-AHLERS is a lecturer in sociology and director of a research programme on migration and immigration at the University of Hanover. From 1989 to 1992 she was head of the Foreigners' Department of Bielefeld City Council. Her research focuses on aspects of migration and her publications include *Gesundheit für Alle* (ed. 1985), *Die multikulturelle Gesellschaft: Der Weg zur Gleichstellung* (ed. 1992) and *Zur frühen Staatenbildung von Steppenvölkern* (1994).

MORAY McGOWAN is Professor of German and Head of Germanic Studies at the University of Sheffield. He has published widely on aspects of modern German literature, including a monograph on Marie-Luise Fleißer (1987). He is currently directing a research programme on minorities'/migrant literature in Germany and is co-author with Sabine Fischer of 'Migrantinnenliteratur' in *Sozialgeschichte der deutschen Literatur* (ed. H.A. Glaser, 1996).

DURSUN TAN is a lecturer in sociology and a member of a research group on migration and identity at the University of Hanover. After graduating in Social Science and Social Work, he contributed to research projects at the universities of Oldenburg and Hanover and also worked in education and as a translator. His publications focus on aspects of migration, criminology and Turkish youth culture.

HANS-PETER WALDHOFF is a lecturer in sociology and co-director of a research group on migration and identity at the University of Hanover. His main research interest concerns the theory of civilisation and aspects of migration and his publications include *Fremde und Zivilisierung; über das Verarbeiten von Gefühlen der Fremdheit. Probleme der modernen Peripherie-Zentrum-Migration am türkisch-deutschen Beispiel* (1995).

SELECT BIBLIOGRAPHY

Abdullah, M.S. 'Der Islam will in Deutschland heimisch werden', in *Der Islam im Abendland*. Special Issue of *Die Brücke*, Saarbrücken, 1992.

——'Gibt es eine gemeinsame Basis für den interreligiösen Dialog? Christlich-Islamischer Ökumenismus aus der Sicht des Islams', in *Die multikulturelle Gesellschaft: Der Weg zur Gleichstellung?* ed. E. Kürsat-Ahlers. Frankfurt/Main, IKO, 1992.

—— *Was will der Islam in Deutschland?* Gütersloh, Verlagshaus Gerd Mohn, 1993.

Ackermann, I. ed., *Als Fremder in Deutschland. Berichte, Erzählungen, Gedichte von Ausländern*. Munich, dtv, 1982.

—— ed., *In zwei Sprachen. Berichte, Erzählungen, Gedichte von Ausländern*. Munich, dtv, 1983.

—— ed., *Türken in deutscher Sprache. Berichte, Erzählungen, Gedichte*. Munich, dtv, 1984.

Ackermann, I. and Weinrich, H., eds, *Eine nicht nur deutsche Literatur. Zur Standortbestimmung der Ausländerliteratur*. Munich, Piper, 1986.

Adelson, L. 'Migrantenliteratur oder deutsche Literatur? Torkans *Tufan: Brief an einen islamischen Bruder*', in *Spätmoderne und Postmoderne. Beiträge zur deutschsprachigen Gegenwartsliteratur*, ed. P.M. Lützeler. Frankfurt/Main, Fischer, 1991, pp.67–72.

Alpheis, H. 'Erschwert die ethnische Konzentration die Eingliederung?', in *Generation und Identität*, ed. H. Esser and J. Friedrichs. Opladen, Westdeutscher Verlag, 1991.

Antes, P. *Der Islam als politischer Faktor*. Hanover, Landeszentrale für politische Bildung, 1991.

Arbeits- und Ausbildungssituation ausländischer Jugendlicher: 'Zukunft ohne Beruf', ed. Deutscher Gewerkschaftsbund Bildungswerk. Düsseldorf, 1990.

Arndt, S.T. et al., *Juden in der DDR. Geschichte. Probleme. Perspektiven.* Duisburg, Brill, 1988.

Bade, K.J. *Vom Auswanderungsland zum Einwanderungsland? Deutschland 1880–1980.* Berlin, Colloquium, 1983.

Bade, K.J. ed., *Population, Labour and Migration in 19th and 20th Century Germany.* Oxford, Berg, 1987.

——, ed., *Deutsche im Ausland – Fremde in Deutschland. Migration in Geschichte und Gegenwart,* Munich, Beck 1992.

Benz, W. ed., *Integration ist machbar. Ausländer in Deutschland.* Munich, Beck, 1993.

Bergmann, W. 'Anti-Semitism and Xenophobia in the East German Länder', *German Politics,* vol.3, no.2, 1994.

Bergmann, W. and Erb, R., eds, *Neonazismus und rechte Subkultur.* Berlin, Metropol, 1994.

Bericht der Beauftragen der Bundesregierung zur Integration der ausländischen Arbeitnehmer und ihrer Familienangehörigen, Bonn, March 1991.

Bilke, J.B. et al., *Die Vertriebenen in Mitteldeutschland.* Deutschlandpolitische Schriften no. 10, Bund der Vertriebenen, Bonn ,1991.

Borris, M. *Ausländische Arbeiter in einer Großstadt.* Frankfurt/Main, Europäische Verlagsanstalt, 1975.

Brubaker, R. *Citizenship and Nationhood in France and Germany.* Cambridge/Mass, Harvard University Press, 1992.

Castles, S. and Miller, M.J. *The Age of Migration. International Population Movements in the Modern World.* London, Macmillan, 1993.

Chiellino, G. *Literatur und Identität in der Fremde. Zur Literatur italienischer Autoren in der Bundesrepublik.* Kiel, Neuer Malik Verlag, 1989.

Cohn Bendit, D. and Schmidt, T. *Heimat Babylon. Das Wagnis der multikulturellen Demokratie.* Hamburg, Hoffmann & Campe, 1993.

Daten und Fakten zur Ausländersituation. Mitteilungen der Beauftragten der Bundesregierung für die Belange der Ausländer, Bonn, October 1994.

Delhaes-Günther, D. von et al., 'Rückwanderung – eine Perspektive für ausländische Arbeitskräfte', in *Aus Politik und Zeitgeschichte* B32, 1984.

Dietzel-Papadyrkakou, M. 'Ältere ausländische Menschen in der Bundesrepublik Deutschland', in *Expertisen zum Ersten Altenbericht der Bundesregierung III: Aspekte der*

Lebensbedingungen ausgewählter Bevölkerungsgruppen, ed. Deutsches Zentrum für Altersfragen. Berlin 1993.

Dittrich, E.J. and Radtke, F.-O., eds, *Ethnizität.* Opladen, Westdeutscher Verlag, 1990.

Dove, R. 'Writing in the margin. Social meaning in *Gastarbeiterliteratur'*, *Quinquereme,* vol.9, 1986, pp.16–31.

Elias, N. *Studien über die Deutschen.* Frankfurt/Main, Suhrkamp, 1990.

—— *Engagement und Distanzierung. Arbeiten zur Wissensoziologie,* Frankfurt/Main, Suhrkamp, 1993.

Elias, N. and Scotson, J.L. *Etablierte und Außenseiter.* Frankfurt/Main, Suhrkamp, 1990 (translated from the 1965 English edition *The Established and the Outsiders. A Sociological Enquiry into Community Problems*).

'Emma-Dossier "Fundamentalismus"', in *Emma,* no.4, July–August 1993.

Erichsen, R. 'Zurückkehren oder bleiben? Zur wirtschaftlichen Situation von Ausländern in der Bundesrepublik' in *Aus Politik und Zeitgeschichte,* B 24, 1988.

Esser, H. 'Ist das Ausländerproblem in der Bundesrepublik ein "Türkenproblem"?' in *"Fremde raus?" Fremdenangst und Ausländerfeindlichkeit,* ed. R. Italiander. Frankfurt, Fischer, 1983.

Fischer, S. and McGowan, M., 'From "Pappkoffer" to Pluralism: migrant writing in the German Federal Republic' in *Writing Across Worlds: Literature and Migration,* ed. R. King et al. London, Routledge, 1995, pp.39–56.

Frey, M. 'Ausländer in der Bundesrepublik. Ein statistischer Überblick' in *Das Parlament,* 26 June 1982.

Frey, M. and Müller, U. *Ausländer bei uns – Fremde oder Mitbürger?* Bonn, Bundeszentrale für politische Bildung, vol.186, 1982.

Friedrich, H. *Chamissos Enkel. Zur Literatur von Ausländern in Deutschland.* Munich, dtv, 1987.

Gleason, P. 'Immigration, Religion and Intergroup Relations: Historical Perspectives on the American Experience' in *Immigrants in Two Democracies: French and American Experiences.* eds, D.L. Horowitz and G. Notriel. New York/London, New York UP, 1992.

Gleichmann, P.R. 'Über gesellschaftliche Intellektualisierungsprozesse. Intellektuelle und wissenschaftlich-technische Intelligenz im Vergleich. Vergleichende Beobachtungen zu ihrem langfristigen Aufgabenwechsel', *Berliner Journal für Soziologie,* vol.3, no.1, 1993.

Gökberk, Ü. 'Fremdheit verstehen. "Ausländerliteratur" zwischen Relativismus und Universalismus', *Sirene,* vol.7, no.13/14, 1994, pp.43–76.

Griese, H. M. ed., *Der gläserene Fremde. Bilanz und Kritik der Gastarbeiterforschung und der Ausländerpädagogik,* Opladen, Leske & Budrich, 1984.

Gugel, G. *Ausländer, Aussiedler, Übersiedler. Fremdenfeindlichkeit in der Bundesrepublik.* Tübingen, Verein für Friedenspädagogik, 1992.

Hamburger, F. 'Migration und Armut' in *Informationsdienst Ausländerarbeit,* no.3/4, 1994, pp.36–42.

Hamm, H. *Fremdgegangen – Freigeschrieben. Eine Einführung in die deutschsprachige Gastarbeiterliteratur.* Würzburg, Königshausen & Neumann, 1988.

Hanesch W. et al. *Armut in Deutschland,* Reinbek, Rowohlt, 1994.

Heinze, H. *Migrantenliteratur in der Bundesrepublik Deutschland.* Berlin, Express Edition, 1986.

Helm, J. A. 'No Laughing Matter: Joking About Turks', *German Politics and Society,* vol.31, 1994, pp.47–62.

Hof, B. 'Möglichkeiten und Grenzen der Eingliederung von Zuwanderern in den deutschen Arbeitsmarkt' in *Aus Politik und Zeitgeschichte* B 48, 1994.

Homze, E.L. *Foreign Labor in Nazi Germany,* Princeton University Press, 1967.

Islamischer Extremismus und seine Auswirkungen auf die Bundesrepublik Deutschland, Bonn, Bundesamt für Verfassungsschutz (2nd edition), 1995.

Jacobmeyer, W. *Vom Zwangsarbeiter zum heimatlosen Ausländer,* Göttingen, Vandenhoeck und Ruprecht, 1985.

Kappert, P. and Niemeyer, R. 'Islamischer Religionsunterricht für muslimische türkische Schüler an Hamburger Schulen' in *Erziehung zur Kulturbegegnung. Pädadogische Beiträge zur Kulturbegegnung,* vol.3, Hamburg, 1986.

Kappert, P. and Turan T. eds, *Türkische Erzählungen des 20. Jahrhunderts.* Frankfurt/Main/Leipzig, Insel, 1992.

Katzenstein, P. *Policy and Politics in West Germany.* Philadelphia, Temple UP, 1987.

Kessler, M. and Wertheimer J. eds, *Multikulturalität. Tendenzen, Probleme, Perspektiven im europäischen und internationalen Horizont.* Tübingen, Stauffenburg 1993.

Khalid, D. 'Der Islam in der Diaspora: Europa und Amerika' in *Der Islam in der Gegenwart,* eds U. Steinbach and W. Ende, 3rd edition, Munich, Beck, 1991.

Klee, E. ed., *Gastarbeiter. Analysen und Berichte.* Frankfurt/Main, Suhrkamp, 1975.

Kleßmann, C. *Die doppelte Staatsgründung. Deutsche Geschichte 1945–1955,* Göttingen, Vandenhoeck & Ruprecht, 1982.

Koch-Arzberger, C. et al. *Einwanderungsland Hessen? Daten, Fakten, Analysen.* Opladen, Westdeutscher Verlag, 1993.

Kolinsky, E. 'A Future for Right-Extremism in Germany?' in *The Extreme Right in Europe and the USA,* ed. P. Hainsworth, London, Pinter, 1992.

——, 'Foreigners in the New Germany. Attitudes, Experiences, Prospects', *Keele German Papers Research Series,* ed. T. Scharf, no.1, 1995.

Koller, B. 'Aussiedler in Deutschland. Aspekte der sozialen und beruflichen Eingliederung' in *Aus Politik und Zeitgeschichte* B 48, 1993.

König, P. *Die Situation der ausländischen Arbeitnehmer und ihrer Familienangehörigen in der Bundesrepublik Deutschland.* Repräsentativuntersuchung 1985. Bonn, 1986.

Korte, H. ed., *Die Wohnsituation ausländischer Mitarbeiter der Ruhrkohle AG.* Schriftenreihe Landes- und Stadtentwicklungsforschung des Landes Nordrhein-Westfalen, Dortmund, 1984.

Korte, H. 'Guestworker Question or Immigration Issue? Social Sciences and Public Debate in the Federal Republic of Germany' in *Population, Labour and Migration in 19th and 20th Century Germany,* ed. K.J. Bade, Oxford, Berg, 1987.

Kreuzer, H. 'Gastarbeiter-Literatur, Ausländer-Literatur, Migranten-Literatur? Zur Einführung', *Zeitschrift für Literatur und Linguistik,* vol.56, 1984, pp.7–11.

Küchler, M. 'Germans and "Others"', *German Politics,* vol.3, no.1, 1994.

Kürsat-Ahlers, E. 'Die Fabrik als Präge- und Zivilisierungsinstanz der Migration' in *Spannungsfeld Personalentwicklung,* eds S. Laske and S. Gorbach, Vienna, Manz, 1993.

Kürsat-Ahlers, E. 'Appelle an das Gewissen der Mächtigen reichen nicht aus: Verspätete staatliche Gleichstellungsrechte für Migranten' in *Utopie Kreativ,* no.39/40. Jan–Feb. 1994, pp.23–40.

Kürsat-Ahlers, E. 'Einwandererfamilien, ihr Struktur- und Funktionswandel im Migrationsprozeß' in *Neue Lebensformen – Zeit-Krankheiten und Psychotherapie,* eds P. Buchheim, Th. Cierpke and T. Seifert Berlin/Heidelberg/New York, Springer, 1994.

Kürsat-Ahlers, E. ed., *Die multikulturelle Gesellschaft: Der Weg zur Gleichstellung?* Frankfurt/Main, IKO, 1992.

Layton-Henry, Z. *The Politics of Immigration.* Oxford, Blackwell, 1992.

—— ed., *The Political Rights of Migrant Workers in Europe.* London, Sage, 1990.

Leggewie, C. and Senocak, Z. eds, *Deutsche Türken. Türk Almanar.* Reinbek, Rowohlt, 1993.

Lehmann, A. *Im Fremden ungewollt zu Hause. Flüchtlinge und Vertriebene in Westdeutschland, 1945–1990.* Munich, Beck, 1991.

Mahler, G. 'Möglichkeiten religiöser Unterweisung muslimischer Kinder an öffentlichen Schulen in den Ländern der Bundesrepublik Deutschland entsprechend dem Beschluß der Kultusministerkonferenz' in *Rahmenbedingungen und Materialien zur religiösen Unterweisung für Schüler islamischen Glaubens*, ed. Landesinstitut für Schule und Weiterbildung, Berlin, Express Edition, 1987.

Malchow, B. et al. *Die fremden Deutschen. Aussiedler in der Bundesrepublik*. Reinbek, Rowohlt, 1990.

Marshall, B. 'German Migration Policies' in *Developments in German Politics*, eds G. Smith et al. Basingstoke, Macmillan, 1992, pp.247–263.

——— 'Germany's New Refugee Policy – a critical assessment'. Paper presented at Chatham House, March 1995.

Matter, M. 'Ehre und Moral', *Hessische Blätter für Volks- und Kulturforschung*, Neue Folge, vol.29, 1992.

McCrudden, O.J. Smith and Brown, C. eds, *Racial Justice at Work*. London, Policy Studies Institute, 1991.

Mehrländer, U. *Die Situation der ausländischen Arbeitnehmer und ihrer Familienangehörigen in der Bundesrepublik Deutschland*. Repräsentativuntersuchung 1980. Forschungsbericht im Auftrag des Bundesministers für Arbeit und Sozialordnung. Bonn, Friedrich Ebert Foundation, 1981.

———, *Türkische Jugendliche: Keine beruflichen Chancen in Deutschland?* Bonn, Friedrich Ebert Foundation, 1983.

———, 'Ausländerpolitk und die sozialen Folgen' in *Der gläserne Fremde. Bilanz und Kritik der Gastarbeiterforschung und der Ausländerpädagogik*. ed, H.M. Griese, Opladen, Leske & Budrich, 1984.

Minai, N. *Schwestern unterm Halbmond. Muslimische Frauen zwischen Tradition und Emanzipation*. Munich, dtv, 1991.

Murray, L. M. 'Einwanderungsland Bundesrepublik Deutschland? Explaining the Evolving Positions of German Political Parties on Citizenship Policy', *German Politics and Society*, Issue 33, Fall 1994.

Neumann, U. *Die Erziehung ausländischer Kinder*. Düsseldorf, Pädagogischer Verlag Schwann, 1981.

Nolte, H.H. *Die eine Welt: Abriß der Geschichte des Internationalen Systems*. Hanover, Fackelträger, 1993.

Oschlies, W. *Die Sorben – Slawisches Volk im Osten Deutschlands*. Forum Deutsche Einheit no. 4, Bonn, Friedrich Ebert Foundation, 1990.

Öskara, S. *Türkische Migranten in der Bundesrepublik Deutschland: Stellungnahmen der türkischen Wissenschaftler, Intellektuellen, Lehrer, Gewerkschafter und Sozialberater zu Ausländerfragen und Ausländerpolitik*.Frankfurt/Main, IKO, 1988.

Ostow, R. *Jews in Contemporary East Germany. The children of Moses in the land of Marx.* Basingstoke, Macmillan, 1989.

Özata, M. 'Die türkische Sprache in Berlin' in *Eingewanderte ArbeiterInnen in Berlin 1961–1993*, ed. Berliner Geschichtswerkstatt, Berlin, Eigenverlag, 1994.

Reeg, U. *Schreiben in der Fremde. Literatur nationaler Minderheiten in der Bundesrepublik Deutschland.* Essen, Klartext, 1988.

Riemann, W. *Das Deutschlandbild in der modernen türkischen Literatur.* Wiesbaden, Harrasowitz, 1983.

Rittstieg, H. 'Einführung in das Ausländerrecht' in *Deutsches Ausländerrecht*, 7th edition. Munich, Beck Texte, dtv, 1990.

Rösch, H. ed., *Literatur im interkulturellen Konflikt.* Berlin, TUB Dokumentation, 1989.

Scheuer, H. 'Das Eigene ist das Fremde', *Der Deutschunterricht*, vol.41, no.1, 1989, pp.96–104.

Schierloh, H. *Das alles für ein Stück Brot. Migrantenliteratur als Objektivierung des 'Gastarbeiterdaseins'.* Frankfurt/Main, Lang, 1984.

Schulte A.T. and Tan, D. *Zur Lebenssituation älterer Ausländer in Niedersachsen.* Hanover, Niedersächsisches Sozialministerium, 1990.

Schulze, R. *Geschichte der islamischen Welt im 20. Jahrhundert.* Munich, Beck, 1994.

Schwab, S. *Deutsche unter Deutschen. Aus- und Übersiedler in der Bundesrepublik.* Paffenweiler, Centaurus, 1989.

Schwencke, O. and Winkler-Pohler, B. eds, *Kulturelles Wirken in einem anderen Land.* Loccum, Evangelische Akademie, 1987.

Seifert, W. 'Am Rande der Gesellschaft?' in *Informationsdienst zur Ausländerarbeit*, no.3/4, 1994.

Sölçün, S. *Sein und Nichtsein. Zur Literatur in der multikulturellen Gesellschaft*, Bielefeld, Aisthesis, 1992.

Steinbach, U. and Ende, W. eds, *Der Islam in der Gegenwart.* 3rd edition, Munich, Beck, 1991.

Stenzaly, G. 'Ausländertheater in der Bundesrepublik Deutschland und West-Berlin am Beispiel der türkischen Theatergruppen', *Zeitschrift für Literatur und Linguistik*, vol.56, 1984, pp.125–141.

Straube, H. *Türkisches Leben in der Bundesrepublik.* Frankfurt/Main, Campus, 1987.

Suhr, H. '"Ausländerliteratur": Minority Literature in the FRG', *New German Critique*, vol.46, 1989, pp.71–103.

Teraoka, A. '"Gastarbeiterliteratur". The Other speaks back', *Cultural Critique*, vol.7, Fall 1987, pp.77–101.

Theisen, A. 'Die Vertreibung der Deutschen – ein unbewältigtes Kapitel europäischer Zeitgeschichte', in *Aus Politik und Zeitgeschichte* B7–8, 1995.

Thränhard, D. 'Die Bundesrepublik Deutschland – ein unerklärtes Einwanderungsland' in *Aus Politik und Zeitgeschichte* B 24, 1988.

Türkische Muslime in Nordrhein-Westfalen. Endbericht zur Studie 'Dialog mit einer neu etablierten religiösen Minderheit in NRW, türkische Muslime und deutsche Christen im Gespräch', ed., Ministerium für Arbeit, Gesundheit und Soziales, Nordrhein-Westfalen, Düsseldorf, June 1995.

Waldhoff, H. P. *Fremde und Zivilisierung: über das Verarbeiten von Gefühlen der Fremdheit. Probleme der modernen Peripherie-Zentrum-Migration am türkisch-deutschen Beispiel*. Frankfurt/Main, Suhrkamp, 1995.

Wallerstein, I. 'Culture as the Ideological Battleground of the Modern World System' in *Global Culture: Nationalism, Globalisation and Modernity*, ed. M. Featherstone, London, Routledge, 1990.

Wallraff, G. *Ganz Unten*. Cologne, Kiepenheuer & Witsch, 1995.

Weigel, S. 'Eine andere Migrantenliteratur oder eine andere Frauenliteratur' in *Gegenwartsliteratur seit 1968*, eds K. Briegleb and S. Weigel, Hansers Sozialgeschichte der deutschen Literatur, vol. 12, Munich, Hanser, 1992, pp.222–226.

Weinrich, H. 'Um eine deutsche Literatur von außen bittend', *Merkur* vol. 37, 1983, pp.911–920.

—— 'Gastarbeiterliteratur in der Bundesrepublik Deutschland', *Zeitschrift für Literaturwissenschaft und Linguistik* vol.56, 1984, pp.12–22.

Wetzel, J. '"Displaced Persons" Ein vergessenes Kapitel der deutschen Nachkriegsgeschichte' in *Aus Politik und Zeitgeschichte* B 7–8, 1995.

White, P. 'On the use of creative literature in migration study', *Area*, vol. 17, no.4, 1985, pp.277–283.

Willems, H. *Fremdenfeindliche Gewalt. Einstellungen, Täter, Konflikte*. Opladen, Leske & Budrich, 1993.

Zayas, A-M. de *The German Expellees. Victims in War and Peace*. Basingstoke, Macmillan, 1993.

Zentrum für Lehrerbildung der Universität Bielefeld ed., *Untersuchungen zur Bildungsbeteiligung ausländischer Kinder in Bielefeld. Zwischenbericht*. Bielefeld, 1992.

Zentrum für Türkeistudien ed. *Selbständige Ausländer in Deutschland.* Opladen, Leske & Budrich, 1991.

———, *Gesundheitsbewußtsein der Migranten aus der Türkei in Nordrhein-Westfalen.* Unpublished Survey, Bonn, 1991.

———, *Zum Integrationspotential der türkischen Tagespresse in der Bundesrepublik Deutschland.* Opladen, Leske & Budrich, 1991.

———, *Türkei Sozialkunde.* Opladen, Leske & Budrich, 1994.

———, *Islamische Organisationen der türkischen, marokkanischen, tunesischen und bosnischen Minderheiten in Hessen.* Studie im Auftrag des Büros für Einwanderer und Flüchtlinge im Hessischen Ministerium für Umwelt, Energie, Jugend, Familie und Gesundheit, 1995.

INDEX

GERMANY'S NEW POLITICS
Parties and Issues in the 1990s

Edited by David Conradt, Gerald R. Kleinfeld, George K. Romoser, Christian Søe

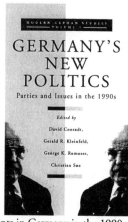

Four years after unification, Germany has just completed what has been called the "super election year": no less than nineteen elections, culminating in the Bundestag vote on October 16, 1994. Four years after unification, the elections of 1994 reveal the state of German unity and the interplay of new forces in post-Cold War Europe. This book analyses the elections for specialists as well as for students, placing them in the wider context of political and economic developments in Germany in the 1990s. An appendix with full data on previous Bundestag elections and relevant charts on party developments enhances the value of this volume which students, scholars and the general reader interested in German affairs will find indispensable.

March, 336 pages tabl., statistics; ISBN 1-57181-032-3 hardback **$35.00/£25.00**
ISBN 1-57181-033-1 paperback **$15.00/£11.50**

POLITICS AND GOVERNMENT IN GERMANY, 1944 - 1994
Basic Documents

2nd, revised edition
Edited by **C.C. Schweitzer, Detlev Karsten, Robert Spencer, R. Taylor Cole†, Donald P. Kommers** and **Anthony J. Nicholls**

This revised and enlarged edition brings the successful original volume of 1984 right up to date, taking into account the most recent developments. Each section begins with an introduction that provides the context for the following documents. There is no comparable volume of its kind available in English, and most documents have not previously been translated.

C.C. Schweitzer is Professor Emeritus, Department of Political Science, University of Bonn; **Detlev Karsten** is Professor of Economics and the Didactics of Economics at the University of Bonn; **Robert Spencer** is Professor Emeritus of History and Director of the Graduate Center for International Studies in the University of Toronto; **R. Taylor Cole** was James B. Duke Research Professor at Duke University; **Donald P. Kommers** is Professor of Government and International Studies at the University of Notre Dame and editor of *The Review of Politics;* **Anthony J. Nicholls** is Official Fellow and University Lecturer, St. Antony's College, Oxford.

496 pages 20 tables, 6 fig., gloss., bibliog., index, ISBN 1-57181-854-5 hardback
$75.00/£51.00
ISBN 1-57181-855-3 paperback **$24.50/£17.50**

165 Taber Avenue • Providence, Rhode Island 02906
Phone: 401-861-9330 • Fax: 401-521-0056 • E-mail: BerghahnBk@aol.com

THE AMERICAN IMPACT ON POSTWAR GERMANY

Edited by **Reiner Pommerin**

It is only with the benefit of hindsight that the Germans have become acutely aware of how profound and comprehensive was the impact of the United States on their society after 1945. This volume reflects the ubiquitousness of this impact and examines German responses to it. Contributions by well-known scholars cover politics, industry, social life and mass culture.

Reiner Pommerin is Professor of Modern and Contemporary History at the Technische Universität Dresden

208 pages, ISBN 1-57181-004-8 hardback $32.00/£25.00

TABOOS IN GERMAN LITERATURE

Edited by **David Jackson**, *Senior Lecturer, School of European Studies, University of Wales College of Cardiff*

Students of German literature will have asked themselves at one stage or another why certain topics have received saturation treatment over the last two centuries while others have either been ignored entirely or, at best, grossly neglected. This book tackles this fascinating issue and illuminates why, at various junctures, specific topics and attitudes were regarded by influential sections of society as being either inadmissable or presentable only in particular, prescribed ways. While the presentation of sexual matters such as homosexuality and lesbianism is inevitably at the heart of the book, political, social and ideological issues also loom large. The editor has recruited a team of prominent scholars to provide a penetrating, comprehensive focus that ranges from individual writers and their works, i.e., Goethe, Hölderlin, Kafka, and Thomas Mann, to specific issues, movements and periods.

May, ca. 224 pgs., bibliog., index
ISBN 1-57181-881-2 hardback, c.a. $45.00/£30.00

POSTWAR WOMEN'S WRITING IN GERMAN

Edited by **Chris Weedon**, *Centre for Critical and Cultural Theory, University of Wales College of Cardiff*

Women in the Federal Republic, the former German Democratic Republic, Switzerland and Austria have initiated a remarkable literary movement, particularly since 1968, that is also attracting growing attention elsewhere. Informed by critical feminist and literary theory, this broad-ranging collection, the first of its kind, examines the history of these writings in the context of the social and political developments in the respective countries. It combines survey chapters with detailed studies of prominent German authors whose work is often available in English.

July, ca. 288 pgs., bibliog., index
ISBN 1-57181-902-9 hardback $49.95/£35.00
ISBN 1-57181-048-X paperback $17.50/£14.95

165 Taber Avenue • Providence, Rhode Island 02906
Phone: 401-861-9330 • Fax: 401-521-0056 • E-mail: BerghahnBk@aol.com